Peter Schledermann

VOICES
IN
STONE

A Personal Journey
into the Arctic Past

To William Wike
With best wishes

Komatik Series, Number 5
The Arctic Institute of North America
of The University of Calgary

Published by The Arctic Institute of North America
of The University of Calgary
2500 University Drive N.W.
Calgary, Alberta, Canada T2N 1N4

Canadian Cataloguing in Publication Data

Schledermann, Peter.
    Voices in stone

    (Komatik series, ISSN 0840-4488 ; 5)
    Includes bibliographical references and index.
    ISBN 0-919034-87-X

    1. Schledermann, Peter. 2. Excavations (Archaeology)—
Northwest Territories—Ellesmere Island. 3. Ellesmere Island
(N.W.T.)—Antiquities. 4. Inuit—Northwest Territories—
Ellesmere Island—Antiquities. I. Arctic Institute of North
America. II. Title. III. Series.
E99.E7S325 1996   971.9'5   C96-910660-2

Credits:
Bird illustrations by Brenda Carter
Copyediting by Luisa Alexander Izzo
Cartography by Marilyn Croot, Sun Mountain Graphics, Calgary, Alberta
Cover design by George Allen and Christine Spindler, Carbon Media Inc., Calgary, Alberta
Production by Jeremy Drought, Last Impression Publishing Service, Calgary, Alberta
Printed and bound by Printcrafters Inc., Winnipeg, Manitoba

Cover photos:
• The late Dorset longhouse on Knud Peninsula — Peter Schledermann
• Dorset carving found in a Thule culture house ruin — Sisse Brimberg
• Author on the summit of Washington Irving Island — Karen McCullough

For Jimmy Nowra

Contents

Illustrations

Colour Plates

- Using a bipod to photograph hearth row features.
- The 1990 joint Greenlandic and Canadian team excavating a late Dorset communal structure on Knud Peninsula.

Preface

*A culture is never independent. It is not built up like a geological
sediment series, in which each stratum has no inner connection with
the foregoing one and the following one.*

(Kaj Birket-Smith, 1929:12)

Voices in Stone grew out of years of impressions, reflections, and maturing convictions about the world we live in. It is a journey of discovery, a portrait, and a history of the human presence in the far northern regions of Canada as we currently understand it. The setting is the High Arctic Islands, where the human capacity to adapt and prevail has been tested in the extreme: a physical and cultural landscape seen through eyes that reflect not only my background in geography and anthropology, but, perhaps more importantly, my introduction to the concept of human ecology at the University of Alaska in the late 1960s. The study of human culture, past and present, as an interactive part of the total environment in which it exists provided me with a framework and an approach to my work as an archaeologist. Years of field research and data analysis strengthened my fascination with prehistoric demography in the Far North, the appearance and disappearance of human populations, and the many possible causes underlying these events. This curiosity about human adaptability and cultural survival skills is not by any means confined to the past; the challenges facing our troubled species are, if anything, more overwhelming today than they were thousands of years ago.

My more conscious introduction to a distant past took place on the barren, windswept shores of St. Lawrence Island in mid-October 1965. A well-used DC-3 took us on a bumpy flight over the silty, brown waters of the Bering Sea, from Nome on the west coast of Alaska to Savoonga, a tiny cluster of weather-blasted wooden houses huddled on the north shore of the island. I was part of a small team of professors and students from the University of Alaska who had been asked to investigate reported remains of a newly uncovered prehistoric site just west of Savoonga. Although that site turned out to be a natural accumulation of driftwood in a small lagoon, my subsequent visit to the nearby prehistoric Kukulik village mound, east of Savoonga, was unforgettable. For centuries, hunters and their families had constructed winter houses in this place using sections of whale bone, pieces of driftwood, stones, and sod. Layer upon layer of house ruins, like a Middle East tell, the Kukulik mound rose impressively over the boggy surrounding landscape. Hunters from Savoonga sat comfortably sheltered from the blasting winds behind walls of old whale bone and driftwood. Not many gulls passed the hunting blinds and lived to do it again. Walking around on the mound that day, I had no idea that I would be spending a good deal of my life trying to provide answers to the many questions we have about Arctic prehistory and the cultural strands that connect the ancient peoples of the Bering Sea region, the Canadian Arctic, and Greenland.

The years between 1965 and 1975 were filled with what seemed like endless studies and exams, happily separated by exciting field seasons in Alaska, Canada, and Greenland. It was an exhilarating geographical and anthropological venture into life in the Arctic, today, yesterday, and centuries ago; unforgettable summers in Cumberland Sound on the east coast of Baffin Island; stumbling attempts on my part to communicate in Inuktitut; meals of raw or cooked seal meat and bannock, hungrily devoured inside cozy old canvas tents; warming cold hands around scalding hot cups of tea on windswept ice floes, while trying to stomp some warmth into deadened feet after hours of pushing freight canoes through floes of shifting pack ice; sledging across vast stretches of frozen sea, and recording ancient habitation sites on low stretches of barren land. It was pure magic.

In the summer of 1976, I arrived in West Greenland to participate in a project aimed at investigating old Norse and Inuit settlements in the region around present-day Nuuk, the old Norse settlement of Vesterbygd. Having just finished six seasons of fieldwork in the Canadian Arctic, I was struck by the environmental and ecological differences between the two sides of Davis Strait. The land and the seas from the shores of western Alaska to the southwest coast of Greenland had presented a great variety of environmental and ecological challenges to each wave of newcomers migrating across the vast North American Arctic.

The introductory chapters of this book provide the reader with a general impression of what archaeology is about, both as a methodology and as a science. As in all scientific studies involving human behaviour, subjective impressions and educated guesswork play a part. In many ways, the exactness of the interpretations depends on the level of inquiry. We can determine with certainty that people settled in a particular place. However, questions like *when*, *from where*, and *why* must be approached with considerably more caution. They can be answered, but usually only as a matter of probability rather than with certainty; writing the history of prehistoric events requires close attention to empirical evidence combined with a good deal of intuition.

Voices in Stone describes our search for prehistoric sites on the east coast of Ellesmere Island in the High Arctic. Twelve seasons of travelling, camping, and working in isolated, remote, occasionally dangerous, and always unpredictable areas provided their own excitement. The story of the prehistoric past is extracted from ancient artifacts and what they reveal about the life of their makers: people who, for certain periods, mastered the art of surviving in a natural world of the most forbidding kind. It is about human life on the thin edge of survival, where one miscalculation, one shift in the seasonal prey cycle, often resulted in disaster and death from starvation. The High Arctic was a dangerously alluring land to enter: a hunter's paradise one season, a people's nightmare the next. And for some it was indeed a wonderful place, a land and an ocean, frozen or open, rich in game and materials for building and making tools. The many large prehistoric sites attest to the good fortune of the inhabitants during such times. The High Arctic was a place where children played and imitated the ways of their parents—a study of life skills that ensured the continued survival of the group.

Each chapter represents a stage in this human drama, from the pioneering efforts more than 4000 years ago of the people we refer to as Palaeoeskimos to the impressive arrival of the Arctic whale hunters, the Thule culture Inuit or Neoeskimos. The arrival of Western explorers, adventurers, and scientists in the nineteenth century marked the beginning of an overwhelming transition for the Thule culture Inuit. Their own assimilation of the Dorset people was but a foreshadowing of the turbulent changes they themselves would face in the twentieth century, beginning with the Canadian government's establishment of Royal Canadian Mounted Police (RCMP) posts in the High Arctic as a display of Canadian sovereignty. Like the land, cultures are never static; the history of the human species records a continuing series of changing dynamics. It is not a question of right or wrong, acceptable or unacceptable; it is simply a matter of human cultural evolution.

The final chapter deals with the illusive relationship between the past and the present. *Homo sapiens sapiens* have lived on this planet for tens of thousands of years. Yet, despite recent, enormous advances in technology, we live as much on the edge of survival as before. Are we incapable of eradicating the behavioural traits that are destroying us?

In most scientific disciplines, it is usually not difficult to think of interesting and worthwhile research projects. For some, a project may require little more than a laboratory, computer access, and plenty of time. For others, data gathering requires a more elaborate schedule involving time spent in the field. The field can be many things; but for Arctic researchers, including prehistorians, it usually translates into a journey to distant and remote regions. Getting there and extracting the kind of information needed to answer particular questions becomes a sizeable task in itself.

Our many years of field research on Ellesmere Island could not have been accomplished without the generous logistic support of the Polar Continental Shelf Project (PCSP). The equally necessary financial support was obtained principally from the Social Sciences and Humanities Research Council of Canada, the Arctic Institute of North America of the University of Calgary, the Royal Canadian Geographical Society, the National Geographic Society, and the Government of the Northwest Territories.

The brief, but all-important initial site visit to the Bache Peninsula region in 1977 was made possible through the support of the Polar Gas project, for which I had directed an extensive archaeological impact survey in the Arctic that summer. At the Alexandra Fiord RCMP station, we had the good fortune to join a helicopter reconnaissance flight by Tom Frisch and Bill Morgan of the Geological Survey of Canada, which greatly extended the territory we were able to cover during the short stay.

So many people assisted with the research over the years, both in and out of the field. I am most indebted to my co-investigator and co-director Karen M. McCullough, who for nearly 20 years has provided invaluable assistance, direction, and organization to the myriad details involved in a long-term, occasionally large-scale, research project. On the pioneering survey in 1977, I was delighted to be accompanied by my friend and colleague the Norwegian archaeologist Tore Bjørgo. It is one thing to develop the concept of a particular project and get the funding and logistic support; however, without enthusiastic and hardworking field assistants and co-directors, little is accomplished. Sincere thanks to Rochelle Allison, Charles Arnold, Erik Blake, Arne Carlson, Eric Damkjar, Frank Day, Laura Ettagiak, Peter Francis, Sheila Greaves, Jeffrey Gruttz, Carol Hanchette, Elisa Hart, Dennis Kenny, Hans Lange, Diane Lyons, Laila Mikaelsen, Jimmy Nowra, Betsey Nicholls, Ian Pengelly, Ian Robertson, Doug Ross, Rose Scott, Gerry Thompson, Edson Way, and Cathy Yasui.

Particular gratitude is extended to the helicopter and Twin Otter pilots who did everything possible to transport us safely and expediently to the many remote places we wanted to investigate. For many years, the Royal Canadian Mounted Police kindly granted us the use of their facilities at Alexandra Fiord.

A special thanks to Weston Blake, Jr. of the Geological Survey of Canada for providing many of the radiocarbon dates, and to Mike Wayman of the Department of Mining, Metallurgical and Petroleum Engineering, University of Alberta, and the Canadian Conservation Institute for the analysis of metal artifacts. A particular note of appreciation is extended to my colleagues Jette Arneborg, John Dunn, Don Gardner, Bjarne Grønnow, Karen McCullough, Scott Raymond, Steve Smith, and an anonymous reviewer for their critical comments on the manuscript.

I am indebted to Marilyn Croot for her drafting of maps and artifact drawings, to Jim Peacock for the artifact photography, and to George Allen and Christine Spindler for the cover design. Steve Johnson of LGL Limited explained the migratory patterns of Arctic birds, while Canadian artist Brenda Carter kindly provided the bird sketches. National Geographic photographer Sisse Brimberg generously agreed to the use of the shaman's face for the cover.

Some aspects of this story of the human presence in the Canadian High Arctic were presented in a series of public lectures at Trent University, Peterborough, Ontario, during my tenure as Northern Chair for 1988–89. I am grateful to the Northern Chair Committee for providing me with the opportunity to present the lectures.

A special note of appreciation to Mike Robinson, executive director of the Arctic Institute of North America, for providing the funding for publication of this book; to Luisa Alexander Izzo for her excellent copyediting of the manuscript; and to Jeremy Drought for production. In the end, one person meticulously assembles all of the elements that finally turn into a book. For that extraordinary and often thankless task, I owe Karen McCullough, editor of the Arctic Institute's journal *Arctic*, a very special measure of appreciation.

Prologue

It was my turn to watch for polar bears. From a vantage point high in the cliffs behind camp, I could look eastward to the ice-covered Northumberland Island off the coast of Greenland. To the south, vast unbroken fields of ice and frozen bergs stretched to the horizon. Below me, surrounded by a more or less useless bear warning fence, our little cluster of tents: home away from home. Silent remains of ancient settlements were scattered along the raised beach terraces: stone caches for meat, supports for skin-covered boats, fox traps, and tent rings, all relics of everyday life and laughter ringing through the crystal air eons ago. I found it easy to imagine the persistent howling of hungry dogs, children at play, and parents going about their daily tasks: butchering seals near shore, staking out a polar bear skin on the ground, repairing a kayak. The image vanished with a sudden, cool gust of wind brushing through clumps of sparse grass.

The lookout had been used by others. At my feet were hundreds of tiny waste flakes of stone, evidence that points and knives had been sharpened by hunters patiently scanning the ice for seals or the seals' other predator, the polar bear. Even when the last stone flake fell to the ground thousands of years ago, the scenery probably looked much the same—an eternal world where only the location of each year's crop of trapped icebergs changed. Such timelessness releases the mind from earthly constraints, bringing the peace of recognizing one's insignificance in the universal scheme.

Yet the land is far from static. In mid-February, the first rays of the sun explode over the horizon, gradually pushing aside the winter darkness until the time of spring equinox, when Ellesmere Island joins the rest of the planet in a brief celestial union marked by 12 hours of day and night. Reluctantly winter relaxes its tight grip on the frozen landscape, the first trickle of running water mixes with the chirping of snow buntings, cheerfully announcing the arrival of spring. Under a blazing, 24-hour sun, spring turns into the fleeting weeks of summer. The jarring sounds of rock slides and fracturing icebergs rip through the air, reminding us that even eternity is rooted in change: an uncomplicated truth worth remembering, a fact of life on the edge, a deceptive feeling of regularity of process that might easily be misconstrued by the uninitiated. The hunters of ancient times knew that open water and abundant game one summer were no guarantee of similarly generous future conditions. Only through a careful study of the landscape and the behaviour of their prey could they hope to be successful providers. Small groups of extended families migrated seasonally from place to place, capitalizing as best they could on the vaguest notion of predictability. They had learned to respect the magic of life and the world of spirits: survival also depended on being on good terms with the guardians of creation.

Such imagining is not hard to come by on a solitary vigil in the Arctic summer night. It also strengthens my sense of alienation. How could it be otherwise? I was raised in a cultural milieu that has done everything possible to remove itself from the natural order of things—a world increasingly cluttered with outlandish, insignificant cleverness. With only feeble voices of protest, we are speeding up our journey into this cultural black hole, convinced that the destruction in our wake is somehow an expression of our own significance. Yet, at the same time, we seek from within this heap of mesmerizing technology something that occasionally resembles simplicity and reality, something that is perhaps not an illusion. Most archaeologists experience a peculiar intimacy with the land and the humans who occupied it. Perhaps it is the nearness to ghosts that provides an illusion of closeness to unknown builders, ancient beings who cast aside their refuse in nearby middens unaware that in a future time, biochemical transformation of their refuse bones would help develop the soil and the basic elements needed for an annual explosion of brilliantly purple saxifrage flowers.

As human ecologists exploring the fascinating complexities of ancient times, we take the occasional flight into the world of fiction, essentially because our ultimate goal of fully comprehending prehistoric cultures is unattainable. Even with the most powerful computers and the fanciest model building, the search for one central, unified, comprehensive truth about past human life is beyond reach and probably always will be. To attain even a small measure of that illusive truth, it is necessary to keep speculations and discussions to more restrictive parameters of understanding and predictability. Only then are we reasonably safe in making assumptions about past cultures. Beyond those margins, we move steadily into the realm of fantasy.

1

Challenge of the Unknown

Yet without the old the new is meaningless.
(George B. Schaller, 1994:59)

The aluminum wings slice through thin, frigid air. Below us lie the Arctic landscapes of yesterday, today, and tomorrow, seemingly untouched by human hands. Would it have looked different a thousand years ago? A little, perhaps. At that time a climatic warming trend, the Neo-Atlantic, stimulated a northward expansion of stunted, black spruce trees into the tundra; glaciers retreated from their self-constructed end moraines, and the annual ice-free period of the Arctic Ocean lasted a little longer.[1] It may not have amounted to much in terms of annual temperature increases; but in Arctic regions, even small changes can be significant. The picture would be much more dramatic if the geological clock were pushed back another 10,000 years, to a time when the same landscape was covered by massive ice sheets, much like the present-day interior of Greenland. In time the climatic pendulum swung again: the huge Laurentide Ice Sheet began its gradual retreat from most of its former domain, leaving only the remnant ice caps we observe today, scattered over high mountain ranges on Ellesmere, Devon, and Baffin Islands. That's the world below us, spellbinding with its huge glaciers and snowcapped mountains, icebergs majestically proceeding like a regatta of sailing ships heading for a southern finish line. The land is preparing itself for the briefest of summers.

So many times I've stood on the Arctic tundra looking up at grey vapour trails drawn by an invisible bullet, silently streaking through the sky. I know what it's like up there far above the earth. I also know something of what it's like down on the land, not just today, but hundreds, even thousands of years ago, long before machines drew fluffy, white lines across the sky. We are once again on our way to Resolute Bay, a tiny centre of human activity in the vastness of the High Arctic—a small party of researchers on our own return migration to the North. I'm beginning to understand what entices migratory birds to abandon southern climes and follow the brightness of the midnight sun.

As always, we're anxious to get back: eager to set up camp in now familiar surroundings and get reacquainted with good friends like Lonesome George, an elderly bull muskox who has never failed to visit within days of our arrival on Knud Peninsula. Defeated in the annual mating ritual and routed by younger bulls, George lives a life of dignified loneliness. Perhaps our annual visits provided a pleasant break in his routine; at least he seemed pleased to have company, even if we were human.

Under the vigilant gaze of the now not-so-lonesome George, we are passionately excited about making new discoveries, finding answers to the multitude of questions we have about the past. Knowledge is our objective: to learn, and to try to understand fully what it is we learn. Yet, there is more to it, something else that draws us northward: a much less tangible, less easily defined set of reasons. In fact it has very little to do with reason, much more to do with instinct and, for some of us, a deep human need to seek places of solitude, even if only for a brief time. It has to do with reaching back through time to touch our common human heritage, the small band of hunters who lived as an integral part of the world around them. Regardless of who we are or where we are today, we all share that heritage; we are all descendants from that way of life. We need to remember that.

In any society there are people who are drawn to the challenge of exploring new frontiers, people for whom the ordinary is not sufficient. They may be thought of as nonconformists, heretics, cultural transformers or, on a less lofty plain, just inquisitive souls intrigued by the unknown. For better or worse, it is a behavioural trait that has pushed humanity irrevocably along the evolutionary path. The accumulation and dissemination of knowledge have enabled us not only to survive, but to seek improvement in our daily lives. Cultural development is a balancing act, a struggle between maintaining the status quo and being responsive to the changes that are bound to occur as long as there is life. Culture is the essential human survival tool, a corpus of transmitted knowledge that shields us and protects us from the world we live in.

Most people have at least some interest in the past, from discoveries in the attic or an awareness of family genealogies to the outcome of epic battles and conquests. Whether known through written or oral traditions, myths, or legends, the past defines who we are. Familiarity provides us with a sense of security, whether through kinship and friends, knowledge of the land and its resources, or an understanding of the traditions and expectations of our community. Immigrants, removed from familiar surroundings, draw on the past to maintain their identity. Observe the way newcomers often choose to live in regions geographically similar to the ones they came from and transplant place-names from the homeland to their new surroundings, however absurdly misplaced.

For some people the past unfortunately has a different value. The search for treasures and antiquities through looting and grave robbing goes back a very long time in human history; it was an ignoble beginning to what has become an increasingly sophisticated discipline with well-developed methodological approaches to attaining complex objectives. It was the nineteenth-century emphasis on the evolutionary process that gave birth to archaeology as a scientific discipline. Aware that stratigraphic excavations reflected geological concepts of depth and relative age, archaeologists began the first systematic descriptions of artifact categories and styles. Since the days of Thomas Jefferson's systematic excavation of burial mounds in Virginia, archaeological investigations have undergone great changes and considerable improvements.[2] As with other disciplines that must to a large extent depend on subjective observations and reasoning, the very nature of archaeological research involves activities and methodologies not easily contained within basic scientific principles. New World archaeology was from the outset linked to the emerging discipline of anthropology, the study of living people and their cultures in all places. In contrast to the Old World, archaeologists easily recognized continuity between the so-called prehistoric past and the present in the Americas. New World archaeology became a subfield of anthropology, providing that discipline with the dimension of time by studying extinct cultural systems. Ethnographic studies of Native cultures and physical anthropological studies of people's biological characteristics were soon related to archaeological findings. In true ethnocentric fashion, Western scholars organized and classified cultures according to somewhat misguided principles of evolutionary progress, a condition generally equated with greater technological skills and more levels of administrative complexity and control.

Until the early 1950s, archaeologists were mostly content to invest their time discovering and excavating sites, analyzing and describing artifacts, and constructing relative chronologies. These activities were essential steps towards the higher level archaeological objective of reconstructing past lifeways.

The development of tree-ring dating (dendrochronology) and radiocarbon dating techniques gave the archaeologist the means to establish the temporal sequence of prehistoric cultural events with some degree of accuracy.[3] The initial enthusiasm and unquestioning adherence to radiocarbon dates has given way to more cautious interpretations. A comparison of radiocarbon dates and tree-ring chronologies that span thousands of years has shown that there can be a considerable difference between calendar years and radiocarbon dates. About the time when the first people migrated into the High Arctic, the discrepancy is considerable: a radiocarbon age of 4000 years B.P. (Before the Present, usually measured from 1950), corresponds to about 4700 calendar years. We have also learned that sea mammal bones tend to produce dates that are too old by anywhere from 100 to 400 years, depending on the waters the animal lived in.[4] Briefly, this so-called "reservoir effect" involves upwelling and mixing of marine organisms that have assimilated carbon from deeper ocean levels, resulting in a skewed radioactive decay picture. Very deep ocean waters can produce a radiocarbon age of several thousand years.[5] No single correction factor of this marine effect will work for all regions, since local conditions are usually quite variable. For example, in the Knud Peninsula region, we have determined that the results from dating walrus bones are not greatly at odds with willow or terrestrial bone dates.

In old fire hearths we often find a mixture of charred land mammal and sea mammal bones, willow, driftwood, and heather. Not only will each sample provide different dates; but it is also important to remember that the dates reflect the death of the organic element, not necessarily the time it was used. For that reason, charred samples of driftwood are highly suspect: we don't know how long the tree had been floating around in the Arctic Ocean before it beached and was eventually used as fuel. Even dates on willow charcoal can be misleading. The High Arctic willow is a very slow-growing plant that can be as much as a hundred years old before it dies or is torn out of the ground for use as fuel. When people arrived in an area where no one had camped for a long time, they most likely found a fair number of old, dead, dry willow branches lying around. It would have been natural for the hunter's wife to select these for the cooking fire as long as they were available. Obviously the date of one of those charred pieces would be much older than the time of the use of the hearth. We have observed such discrepancies when comparing heather and willow dates from the same hearth; the willow dates are usually much older.

Aside from these problems, radiocarbon dates remain a valuable tool, as long as the results are used with caution and in conjunction with other data. A refinement of the radiocarbon dating technique now makes it possible to date much smaller samples.[6] By using this "accelerator" technology, we can, in theory,

Driftwood on a High Arctic beach.

date a variety of samples from the same hearth. This would not only give us a better idea of the variance between materials, but provide a better statistical basis for calculating the approximate period the hearth was in use. The best way to use radiocarbon dates is to refer to statistical ranges within which the event is most likely to have occurred. The greater the range, or deviation, the more accurate the result. Dogmatic dependence on the result of one or two radiocarbon dates rarely advances the understanding of prehistoric events.

The ability to time prehistoric events and their duration more precisely opened the door to studying the rate of cultural change in widely separated areas, and to comparing rates of change in different environments. Many archaeologists began to move away from traditional treatments of data to investigate more complex processes involved in culture change: cause-and-effect relationships, and the how and why of scientific inquiries that had been lacking to a great extent. It was the normal maturation of an emerging discipline. The refinement of approaches, hypotheses, and theoretical developments is at the centre of the continuing evolution of the scientific approach.

An expected outcome of these developments was the realization that other sciences had much to offer the prehistorian. Ancient diets could be studied through the analysis of refuse bone; environments of the past could be determined through pollen analyses and soil studies. Close collaboration with botanists, biologists, and geologists provided important new insights into prehistoric life. The last three decades have seen a proliferation of new approaches to the study of archaeological data, including the use of computer models and remote sensing through satellite photography. It has been a refreshing shift from the perceived and real constrictions of the culture historic approach, an exciting journey into the mysteries surrounding the process of culture change. No longer is it satisfactory to know that people lived in a certain place for a certain period of time. Increasingly we want to know why and how. Our ultimate objective is to find timeless and spaceless cultural processes that can turn our gaze from the past to the future.

Archaeologists have been hard-pressed to develop theoretical concepts that explain cultural processes. Along with more sophisticated research designs for surveys and excavations, there has been considerable borrowing of theoretical models from other disciplines such as biology and sociology. Even with the use of sophisticated computer model reconstructions, archaeology has always lacked one of the fundamental elements of a true scientific approach: objective replication. Data analyses and interpretation remain by and large a very subjective business. Once a site has been excavated, it cannot be replicated with the rigour required of a "true" scientific experiment. And so the arguments leap back and forth. Is archaeology a true science, or should it be seen more as a historical discipline with special limitations and explanatory methods? Despite that debate, archaeology continues to mature as a discipline, with old ideas, theories, and assumptions being tested, adjusted, and corrected, as they should be.

During my own studies at the University of Alaska, it was the concepts of systems theory and cultural ecology that fired my imagination. The systems approach attempted to formulate cause-and-effect relationships between the physical, biological, and cultural worlds and, with the aid of computer technology, to quantify these relationships.[7] As a conceptual model, systems theory had much to offer as long as its limitations were acknowledged. And there were many limitations; quantifying human behaviour is a formidable challenge. For me, the systems approach heightened my awareness of the tremendous interrelatedness of the physical, biological, and cultural spheres and the need to consider human activities within an overall ecological framework. For many of us, Julian Steward's cultural ecological concept of changing adaptations to the natural environment has remained a cornerstone in speculations about causal relationships and human evolution.[8] The cultural ecological approach has served us well in defining the variety of relationships between humans and their environments in both historic and prehistoric contexts.

One important tool used in the interpretation of prehistoric data is ethnographic analogy, which is essentially a way of explaining the past in terms of known cultural practices observed in historic times.[9] The use of ethnographic analogy has been popular in studies of North American prehistory, where observations of Native cultures were made soon after the first European and Native contacts took place. Many of the pioneering anthropological scholars tended to view "pristine" Native cultures in North America as examples of a hunting-and-gathering way of life that had evolved very little for thousands of years.

Whereas ethnographic analogy can be used to compare lifeways between very distant cultures in the world, the direct historical approach is much more confined in space and time. In the Arctic, this approach involves applying what is known of the historic Inuit groups to the unknown, not-so-distant past. In the 1920s and 1930s, when archaeologists first began to unearth data from prehistoric sites in the Arctic, it seemed reasonable to base the functional labels they assigned to the tools and weapons they found on descriptions and identifications of similar tools and weapons used by contemporary Inuit groups in the North. After all, it was assumed that since these people had been barely influenced by contact with Western culture, their way of life should be a mirror of life as it existed in the past. Arctic archaeologists, as an example, will assume that the prehistoric use of harpoon heads was much the same as that observed in recent times; that skin-scraping tools were used in the same manner as they are today, and so on. In many cases these assumptions are undoubtedly correct. The problem is that we can't be certain. All cultures change through time— some quickly, others at a much slower pace.

Many of the broader interpretations of our work in the High Arctic do, however, rest on ethnographic analogy. These interpretations are based on direct observations of human life in Arctic and Subarctic regions as recorded by a variety of people, including trained anthropologists, Arctic explorers, whalers, traders, and missionaries. These observations can be very useful, as long as potential inaccuracies such as biased interpretations or language difficulties are kept in mind. The fact that someone didn't observe particular material items during a brief visit to a Native camp does not necessarily mean that they didn't exist. As long as we treat ethnographic analogy in the same relativistic sense as radiocarbon dates, then we can proceed much more comfortably in our attempt to understand prehistoric life. The greater the level of expected accuracy, the lesser is the chance of its trustworthiness. To suggest that the prehistoric hunters in the Arctic hunted seals is undoubtedly quite accurate; to make statements concerning how, when, and where they hunted seals, moves us to a lower level of certainty.

More recently, archaeologists have moved into what is sometimes referred to as "middle-range theory," essentially aimed at gaining a better understanding of how the archaeological data come about. These studies involve what we call ethnoarchaeological research, where archaeologists may choose to live in an Inuit hunting camp, observing activities and searching for patterns and elements that may explain similar observations made on an archaeological site.[10] Other studies involve the replication of tools and studies of lithic debitage under controlled conditions. Several years ago my friend Don Gardner and I built a replica of a 4000-year-old Arctic dwelling in his backyard. We were particularly interested in finding out how well the central hearth heated the tent structure when the temperature really entered the deep-freeze zone. The box hearth was constructed from stone slabs and filled with sand and fist-sized rocks precisely the way the original hearth had appeared on Ellesmere Island. The experiment provided us with a keen sense of the comfort level (or lack of it) experienced by the early Arctic hunters and their families. In a similar fashion, Don Gardner has studied ancient Arctic bows and a variety of tools and weapons in order to gain valuable insights into the actual function of these implements. On several occasions it has been possible to determine that certain implements, identified as a particular tool type by prehistorians, could not have functioned as originally designated. Aside from that, modern attempts to shape stone tools from raw pieces of flint or chert emphasize the tremendous abilities of the ancient toolmakers. Experimental archaeology has become an important part of data analysis, a complementary tool in the search for a better understanding of the past.

Above all, it is important to appreciate that when archaeologists write what is essentially a cultural history of a particular region, they approach the subject from many different angles. Most archaeologists are cognizant of the difficulties they face and try to reach conclusions based on different types of explanations,

Don Gardner tending fire in a reconstructed Palaeoeskimo dwelling in Calgary, Alberta.

giving appropriate emphasis to the degree of validity inherent in each approach. No two archaeologists agree completely about all aspects of prehistory in a given region. The Arctic is no exception. Each researcher is bound to interpret his or her data somewhat differently; it would be strange if it were otherwise. What is essential is to publish and disseminate research data so that other investigators may benefit from what has been learned.

The most important aspect of scientific archaeological research is the discovery of patterns and associations among the many elements that make up an archaeological site. To uncover and extract these elements from their original context (in situ) is of paramount importance to the overall study. The nonscientific removal of an artifact from an archaeological site, prehistoric or historic, is not only illegal; it also destroys the interpretive value of that item. The past belongs to all of us. It is part of our global heritage, and not the exclusive property of any one group of people. The evidence of that past is truly a nonrenewable resource that must be protected from senseless and thoughtless destruction.

2

Window to the Past

The 1818 encounter between John Ross and the Polar Eskimos (Inughuit).

They exist in a corner of the world among the most secluded which has yet been discovered, and have no knowledge of any thing beyond the boundary of their own country: nor have they any tradition whence they came; appearing, until the moment of our arrival, to have believed themselves to be the only inhabitants of the universe, and to have considered all the rest of the world as a mass of ice.

(John Ross, 1819:168–169)

When we contemplate what it would be like to encounter extraterrestrial beings from a distant solar system or galaxy, our images may not be too different from the fantastic apparition of huge, floating houses with wings approaching the small group of Inuit hunters on the fast ice. Fascinated and undoubtedly anxious, they watched several tall, strangely clad men in outlandish hats looking at them through long tubes, while others were busily adjusting the many wings. It was early August in 1818; John Ross had maneuvered his two vessels the *Alexander* and the *Isabella* safely through the treacherous ice in a huge bay he later named after the first lord of the Admiralty, Lord Melville. A prominent headland to the northwest was named after the Duke of York. As Ross brought the ships closer, he realized that the people on the ice were not shipwrecked sailors but Natives. He was about to become the first Westerner to record an encounter with the Inuit of the Far North, the people he called the Arctic Highlanders.[1]

Seeing the two ships perform a tacking maneuver, the Inuit shouted loudly and fled with their sledges and dogs across the ice towards land. More than a kilometre away, they stopped and looked back to see if they were being followed. In West Greenland, John Ross had hired a Native to serve as translator for just such an encounter. A small boat was lowered to take John Sacheuse to the ice edge, where he placed gifts of knives and clothing. Since that gesture was ignored, a second boat was sent to leave behind a dog with strings of blue beads around its neck. As the Natives still maintained a considerable distance, Ross decided to continue his explorations along the coast. He returned about ten hours later only to find the dog and the presents still untouched. In the distance they saw a sledge disappearing rapidly. Once again a boat was sent to the ice and this time a flagpole was erected near the bag of presents.

That night, there must have been a most extraordinary discussion at the Inuit settlement. The following day, eight sledges approached, stopping far short of the presents. Some of the Inuit ascended a small iceberg, while others came closer to the flagpole. Sacheuse, who as a child had been nursed by an old woman who taught him a northern dialect, approached the hunters with a white flag and presents. He stuck the flag in the snow, walked over to the edge of a small lead that separated him from the others, removed his hat, and made friendly gestures for the hunters to come closer. Cautiously the Inuit moved forward, making loud simultaneous greetings, which were imitated by Sacheuse. One man ventured even closer, dog whip in hand, to make sure that the lead was impassable. Another began shouting at Sacheuse, who held up the presents and called for all of them to come forward. At that point he realized that they were shouting "No, no, go away," obviously believing they were in danger. One of the men moved closer, drew a knife from his boot, and threatened to kill Sacheuse, who did his best to assure them that he was a friend. He then threw strings of beads and a checkered shirt across the lead, but the Natives kept yelling at him to go away and not kill them. Sacheuse then threw them a knife and watched as they cautiously picked it up. They touched the shirt and asked him what animal it was made from. Then they pointed to the ships and asked whether they came from the sun or the moon, and would they provide light by day or by night? Sacheuse answered as best he could, persuading them that he was a man just like them. He pointed south and told them that he came from a distant country in that direction. The hunters remained skeptical and repeated their questions about the ships. When Sacheuse told them they were houses made of wood, they refused to believe him; they had seen the wings move; the ships were obviously alive. When he asked them who they were, they answered that they were men who lived to the north where there was much water and that they had come south to hunt narwhal. The women and children had been sent into the mountains before the men came down to implore the strangers to go away.

At this point they encouraged Sacheuse to cross to their side of the lead. He returned to the ship to report on the meeting and to bring back a plank. John Ross, who had been watching all this through his telescope, urged Sacheuse to persuade the Natives to come to the ship. He had noted that throughout the conversation the Natives had kept one hand down by the knee, apparently ready to pull a knife from their boots. Sacheuse finally persuaded one man to touch his outstretched hand, and they exchanged presents. At this point Ross decided it was time to join the party, as did the remaining Inuit who had been keeping a safe distance. The little gathering counted eight Natives with their sleds, fifty dogs, two sailors, William Parry, John Ross, and Sacheuse. When the Inuit seemed frightened by the approach of Ross and Parry, Sacheuse apparently told the two commanders to pull their noses as a friendly gesture, and the trading resumed. According to my friend Wally Herbert, this nose-pulling story may have been based on a complete misunderstanding on the part of Sacheuse, the gesture conveying nothing more than cleaning out one's nose. Be that as it may, each of the Inuit was given a looking glass and a knife. In return, the Inuit offered their own knives and narwhal tusks.

Courageously, I think, five of the hunters agreed to come aboard. Not surprisingly, they were overwhelmed by the amount of wood on the ship, showed nothing but contempt for a little terrier dog, and were terrified at the sight of a pig. One man stole a hammer, but abandoned it in the snow when they left. Three men stayed to have their portraits made while their knives were examined by the ship's armorer, who thought they were made from iron hoops or flattened nails. Some of the iron was undoubtedly of meteoritic origin obtained in the Cape York area, whereas the flattened nails had apparently been taken from a plank that had drifted onshore. Loaded with presents the men left the ship and made off with the plank brought by Sacheuse to bridge the lead.

Ross remained in the area long enough to obtain a fairly good ethnographic sketch of the people and their culture. He reported that they made no use of vegetable food and used dried moss soaked in seal oil as lamp wicks. As far as he observed, the people didn't have any kayaks, leister spears for fishing, or bows and arrows for hunting caribou. Their sledges were small and quite primitive, made mostly from bones and skins. The Inuit had described their winter houses as built of stone and sod, sunk several feet into the ground, and protruding about as much above it. The houses were entered through an underground passage and the sleeping platforms were covered with skins. Several families occupied each house, each possessing a hollowed-out stone lamp suspended from the roof. Fire was produced by friction or by striking iron and stone, and while seal and narwhal were the preferred foods, dog was also said to be excellent. Ross described their dress as composed of three pieces. The upper one, of sealskin with the hair turned out, had a hood trimmed with fox skin and was lined with eider duck or auk skins. Its bottom, shirt-like in form, ended with tongues at the front and back. Their pants were made of bear or dog skin, the boots of sealskin with the hair turned inward and the soles covered with narwhal hide. He described how the women used ivory needles and seal sinew threads and would not part with any items of clothing. There was a curious reference to a "king" Tulloowak, a very strong, good and beloved man who lived farther north in a large stone house. Many of the Inuit were supposed to live in this house and hand over portions of their catch to him. One man told Sacheuse that nearly every family had an *angekok* (shaman) and that they were often afraid of these people, who could raise the wind and drive away game.

In the annals of exploration this meeting is extraordinary, because it gives us a brief glimpse of a small group of people who had lived quite isolated in the High Arctic for some period of time. It was to be the first of many encounters with people from the outside: whalers, western explorers, or other groups of Inuit. Unlike William Baffin's 1616 voyage,[2] Ross's expedition had not gone unnoticed by the commercial whalers, who followed closely behind the naval ships as they entered the rich whaling grounds of Baffin Bay. Naturally the whalers established their own contact with the Inuit, both in northern Greenland and on Baffin Island. With some notable exceptions, such as William Scoresby Jr., the whalers paid little attention to the culture of the Native people they met and rarely left any written descriptions of such encounters.[3]

John Ross's account provided us with a last-minute glimpse of a prehistoric way of life—a connection to the past we wanted to know much more about. The Arctic Highlanders, the Inughuit of North Greenland, were obviously the descendants of generations of Inuit in the High Arctic. But where had they come from, and when? How often had prehistoric peoples been enticed into these far northern regions, and why? How often had they vanished?

The Norse Greenlanders referred to both Indians and Inuit as *Skraelings*. The Indians were encountered during early Norse exploration of Labrador and the outer regions of the Gulf of St. Lawrence, not long after Eirik the Red and other Icelandic chieftains had established their first settlements in Greenland in A.D. 986. As early as the turn of the first millennium A.D., legendary figures like Leif Eiriksson and Thorfinn Karlsefni probed the shores, inlets, and rivers of the New World.[4] Unlike southern Greenland, where their arrival was unopposed, the new lands to the west, Vinland and Markland, were the domain of a sizable Indian population who cared little for intruders. For a couple of centuries the Norsemen had Greenland to themselves. Then, from the Far North, hunters returned to the southern settlements with stories of encounters with *Skraelings*. In spite of the obvious differences in dress, material culture, and language, the Norsemen probably gave little thought to what constituted an Indian or an Inuit *Skraeling*. The significant historical difference between Indians and Inuit mattered little to them; what they did eventually pay attention to was the danger these new *Skraelings* from the North presented to the Norse way of life in Greenland.[5]

Over the years there has been no shortage of theories and speculations about where and when the first people arrived in the New World. The most widely supported theory involves a gradual migration of people from Northeast Asia across the Bering Land Bridge into present-day Alaska.[6] From there they moved southward through the interior and along the west coast, eventually reaching the southern tip of South America. Such immense distances were obviously not covered in a generation or two, but over hundreds and thousands of years.

The pioneering population movements took place at a time when two major ice sheets, the Cordilleran in the west and the Laurentide in the east, smothered most of northern North America. For tens of thousands of years the ice sheets had locked up enough of the oceans' moisture to expose a northern land bridge between the Old and New Worlds. A 50-metre drop in sea level was needed to expose the land bridge, which was at its maximum extent between 20,000 and

18,000 B.P. and remained exposed until about 10,000 B.P. The term "Beringia" is used by some investigators to describe the land bridge and adjacent coasts of Alaska and Asia. Others prefer a broader definition of Beringia to include the land extending from the Lena River in the west to the Mackenzie River in the east. Large parts of Beringia and perhaps the extreme northern regions of Ellesmere Island and Greenland remained unglaciated during the last glacial maximum of the late Pleistocene epoch. Periodically, a narrow corridor along the eastern foothills of the Rocky Mountains opened up between the Cordilleran and the Laurentide Ice Sheets, enabling people and animals to migrate between Alaska and more southerly regions of the New World. Such a migration route may have been available as early as 14,000 B.P.

The Laurentide Ice Sheet covering most of the Canadian Arctic began to shrink and waste away about 10,000 years ago. The first groups of Palaeoindians moved into the Barren Grounds about 8000 years ago,[8] several thousand years after the Bering Land Bridge had been submerged by rising ocean levels. The disappearance of the land bridge did not mark the end of human population movements between Asia and Alaska.[9] By that time, people were quite capable of crossing the Bering Sea by boat.

All these events took place a great distance from Smith Sound and the land of the Polar Eskimos, or Inughuit, as they are now called. Our search for evidence of their direct ancestors and the peoples occupying the High Arctic before them required a much narrower geographical focus. We were looking for a gateway through which all or most Arctic prehistoric populations had passed on the their way to or from Greenland: a natural crossroads bounded by its environment and physical landscape. After years of research in many different parts of the Arctic, it was my good fortune to find such a location on the east coast of Ellesmere Island.

3

The Search

Just as a landscape is more than an accidental collection of hills,
valleys and rivers, so are the elements of a culture connected together
into what may be called an organic matter.

(Kaj Birket-Smith, 1929:11)

Archaeological sites come to our attention in many different ways. Construction activities, whether in remote or populated areas, may accidentally uncover evidence of ancient habitations. They are usually monitored for just that eventuality. If the area to be investigated is near settlements or within range of local hunters and trappers, it is obviously important to seek their knowledge of site locations. In some cases the area may be situated far from present-day settlements and well beyond the normal range of hunters. In those instances the site survey approach is naturally different, relying very much on pre-field studies of maps, aerial photos, and reports by early explorers and anyone else familiar with the area, including researchers from other disciplines. Any mention of historic or prehistoric site locations is useful; by definition they are all archaeological sites. In fact the term "prehistoric" is somewhat of a misnomer, since all sites pertaining to past human activity reflect human history.

When we approach an area or a region that has been only minimally or perhaps never investigated archaeologically, we must be keenly aware of the overall goals and objectives of the work. Field research in remote regions usually involves a significant commitment in both time and money. In the Arctic, researchers face the additional problem of short field seasons if their project, like an archaeological site excavation, requires snow-free conditions and temperatures above freezing. The progress of any field project needs to be evaluated regularly: Are the goals being met? How does each segment fit into a larger picture? Is our knowledge of the people who once lived in the area being advanced? And how does this knowledge tie in with what we know from other regions? It may be a worn phrase, but it is no less true, that archaeological studies are like giant puzzles whose available pieces are few and hard to come by. We will never know what the entire picture looks like; at best, we can only approximate some distant truth. We study the findings made by other

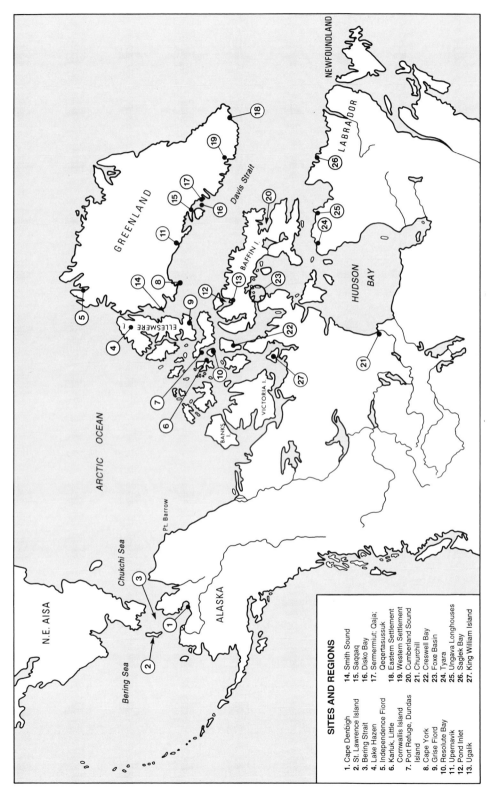

Archaeological sites and regions discussed in the text.

SITES AND REGIONS

1. Cape Denbigh
2. St. Lawrence Island
3. Bering Strait
4. Lake Hazen
5. Independence Fiord
6. Karluk, Little Cornwallis Island
7. Port Refuge, Dundas Island
8. Cape York
9. Grise Fiord
10. Resolute Bay
11. Upernavik
12. Pond Inlet
13. Ugalik
14. Smith Sound
15. Saqqaq
16. Disko Bay
17. Sermermiut; Qaja; Qeqertasussuk
18. Eastern Settlement
19. Western Settlement
20. Cumberland Sound
21. Churchill
22. Creswell Bay
23. Foxe Basin
24. Tyara
25. Ungava Longhouses
26. Saglek Bay
27. King William Island

archaeologists in other regions and compare them to our own data in an attempt to expand our common understanding of the past.

Knowledge about the human presence in the High Arctic has been gathered slowly during the past 70 years; each field season has added new pieces to the emerging picture.[1] Prehistoric occupants of a given area had very specific reasons for locating their camps where they did. Each settlement may have served a different purpose depending on the time of the year and the resources people were seeking. It is our challenge to see the landscape and its resources as they did, to learn which animals they pursued and where and when the hunt took place. We try to understand not only how the local ecosystem works today, but, more importantly, how it might have operated in the past. To arm oneself with as much knowledge of an area as possible before entering the field is an essential part of the planning process; the rest entails mostly a lot of hard work.

There is a general perception, greatly enhanced by the Indiana Jones movies, that the archaeologist's life is filled with constant excitement and danger. Scenes evoking images more akin to treasure hunting show the discovery of priceless artifacts, the key to extraordinary powers and insights, if not to riches. Archaeological fieldwork is far less romantic than these images convey, and filled with considerably more discomfort than most people would like to endure. The slow, methodical, systematic excavation and recording of data involves a significantly greater amount of dedication than it is usually given credit for, notably among indigenous peoples, who often view the excavation of ancient sites as a desecration of their cultural heritage. The bridging of divergent views regarding the value of archaeological research is a major challenge for all of us. The goal of every researcher is to obtain new knowledge in a chosen field of inquiry—a journey that usually involves many steps along the way. Our archaeological field project on the central east coast of Ellesmere Island, a mere 1200 kilometres from the North Pole, is no exception. After that first exhilarating visit to St. Lawrence Island in 1965 and throughout my undergraduate days at the University of Alaska Fairbanks, I never lost my curiosity about human ecology in Arctic regions. I had the privilege of being exposed to the ideas and thoughts of excellent and enthusiastic professors. A two-month investigation of prehistoric sites along the shores of the spectacular Kachemak Bay south of Anchorage and a summer of screening loess from the ancient Campus site on the University of Alaska campus in Fairbanks gave me a taste for the incredible diversity of the Arctic habitat. These experiences broadened my understanding of what was then known about prehistory in the vast, far Northern Hemisphere. The large gaps in our knowledge reflected the enormous distances and regions never investigated. Material from one or two sites in western Alaska was compared to finds from a few sites in central Canada and northern Greenland. Naturally enough, such scarcity of data made for quick comparisons and the formulation of fairly elementary theories. Since those heady days, Arctic prehistory has become a more complex study, reflecting the old saying: "the more we know, the less we know."

In 1969, I headed as far east as it is possible to travel and still remain in North America. Graduate studies in human ecology and anthropology at Memorial University of Newfoundland led to my first introduction to Canada's eastern Subarctic. Setting foot on the rugged coast of Labrador turned out to be one of those crossroads in life one reflects on from time to time: the "what if" conundrum we luckily never know the answer to. Although I journeyed from Alaska to Newfoundland to continue human ecological studies, fate had another agenda in mind. Early in July of 1970, I stood in sleet and rain on a soggy tundra, pondering the daunting task of excavating a huge Thule culture communal dwelling on a small island in Saglek Bay, on the central east coast of Labrador. Before me were the remains of a winter dwelling left behind by an ancient people distantly related to those responsible for the great Kukulik mound on St. Lawrence Island.

The Labrador field season turned out to be a memorable experience, a summer filled with new impressions and contemplations, and an introduction to the physical and cultural environment of the eastern Arctic, a region as severe and unforgiving as any. It was a field season with a sharp learning curve, full of experiences that are better internalized early in one's career, when youth and enthusiasm can overcome the most arduous circumstances. The challenges began almost right away. My first task involved travelling to Nain, Labrador, where I was to hire a boat and crew to sail about 150 kilometres north to Saglek Bay in time to meet up with the research team headed by James Tuck of Memorial University.

This plan sounded reasonable enough until I arrived in Goose Bay, Labrador to discover that there was no public transportation to Nain at that time of year. After I had searched for days for a way to head north, the local RCMP came to the rescue: I thumbed a ride on one of their flights to Nain. It was my introduction to one of the greatest airplanes ever built, the DeHavilland Twin

Otter. As we descended over the small settlement of Nain, only the skill of a seasoned pilot made a landing possible on the shifting ice floes. This was my first serious encounter with pack ice, but we were soon to meet again.

I spent well over a week in Nain making final arrangements for the boat and crew. Two Norwegian anthropologists, Terje and Ann Brantenberg, were kind enough to let me stay in their one-room frame house in what was called "the Eskimo part of town." Nain was laid out in a linear fashion that seemed unhealthy, at least from a social point of view. Inuit lived in the eastern part, Settlers (people of mixed racial origin) in the centre, and Whites to the west. One evening, while we were all eating out of the Brantenbergs' one frying pan, I was introduced to Aba Koyak, one of the best hunters in the community, who expressed a quiet interest in my arrangements to go north. On the eve of my departure several days later, he again came for a visit, and eventually brought up the subject of who was going on the boat with me. When I mentioned the names of the crew, picked out by the boat's owner, Aba looked at me long and hard, shook his head, and said, "Not good." No further explanation was forthcoming.

Next morning, I stood in the stern of the *North Star* as we headed out of Nain harbour. Standing motionless near the waving Brantenbergs was Aba. His brief pronouncement on the choice of crew was still fresh in my mind. The diesel engine on the *North Star* sounded trustworthy enough, and the 45-foot wooden vessel made good headway through the nearly ice-free waters, protected from the open ocean by numerous rocky islands. The sky was clear. A brisk wind stretched the large Canadian flag posted in the stern. From the chart I could see that our route took us along an inside passage protected by the large South Aulatsivik Island. Beyond that, we would have to face the open ocean. A giant, heaving swell met us as we rounded the impressive cliffs of the Kiglapait Mountains. The thunderous roar of waves crashing against vertical cliffs stayed with us for quite some time until we once again reached more protected waters among the islands in Okak Bay, an area selected as a mission site by the Moravians in 1776, just five years after the establishment of their first mission in Nain.[2] So far, the drift ice had not presented a problem, but our luck was about to change. A thin, gleaming-white line of ice rimmed the seaward horizon. Johnny Ikkusik, who was responsible for the vessel, opted to try for an inside route through what was charted as Mugford Tickle. It was no use. The narrow passage was jammed with huge, grinding ice floes. We anchored close to the shore of Cod

Island, waiting to see what the shifting tide might accomplish. I took the opportunity to row to shore in our small dinghy and scout around. Within minutes I was looking at my first eastern Arctic prehistoric site: an oval, boulder-lined structure with a central slab-lined hearth. In future years I was to become very familiar with these early Palaeoeskimo dwelling features.

The rise and fall of the tide had no effect on the ice. We had only one alternative: to retrace our route, round Cod Island, and try our luck on the outside. A heated argument between Ikkusik and Jerry Tuglavina over the two choices available brought a long-standing discord between Jerry and Johnny out in the open; I could now understand Aba's reaction back in Nain. For a while we found enough room between shifting floes to make decent headway, but the going was slow. Just west of a bald, rocky pinnacle called White Bear Island, the ice closed completely around the wooden vessel, adding panic to an already tense situation. Small wooden ships are easily crushed in the grinding pack. With difficulty, we managed to extricate ourselves from the icy grip, steering the vessel from one pocket of open water to the next until we reached the east side of the island. Now there was nothing between us and the south coast of Greenland but the Labrador Sea. Once again the ice jammed around the vessel, forcing us into a small, narrow bight, where we managed to get the boat just far enough behind a rocky ledge to protect us from the ice squeezing into the bight. We could go no farther. I climbed to the top of the island and stared at a sea of ice stretching to the horizon. It was a predicament, all right. That same afternoon I heard a DC-3 lumbering northward just west of our position—Jim Tuck and the rest of the crew, no doubt, expecting to meet us in Saglek Bay. At that moment I wondered if we would ever see the place. But pack ice is a living thing. On the next high tide, I watched as the ice gradually loosened up, exposing dark blue patches of open water that enticed us to attempt an escape. Neither Johnny nor Jerry saw the need to hurry, turning me into a prototype of the irritating, impatient, pushy Southerner they undoubtedly often encountered. Such a clash of objectives is impossible to explain rationally. Ever so slowly, we forced the sturdy vessel through the ice, ramming and pushing floes out of the way, jubilant when the going was easy, cursing when it was not. Pack ice does that to you; it raises hope one minute and dashes it the next. Hour after hour we fought the ice, until suddenly we were completely free. The sea was like a mirror broken by a few solitary ice floes as we approached the prominent mountain marking the entrance to Saglek Bay. Johnny and Jerry seemed to have forgotten their angry confrontation, and we arrived only one day late. It was a portentous beginning to a difficult field season, when many lessons were learned the hard way. Two months in a plastic-wrapped, 35-dollar tent and a see-through sleeping bag leave much room for improvement.

The field project had two primary goals: investigation of the earliest traces of human activity related to both Palaeoindian and Palaeoeskimo cultures, and research into the later appearance of the Thule culture Inuit. Most ably assisted by a hardworking crew of four Newfoundlanders, I turned to the latter project with some trepidation. Before us were two massive sod mounds containing numerous overlapping house ruins. Early houses were covered by later giant communal structures, some over 12 metres in length. We worked in rain and snow and sleet, day in and day out, slowly exposing the interior features of the houses. It was the first excavation of Thule culture winter houses on the north coast of Labrador. Appropriately enough, our team was dubbed "the sod busters" and on especially cold and rainy mornings, hiking across the wet tundra, everyone broke out in a most discordant version of "Please, mister D.A., I don't wanna go." It was a spirited group.

The 1970 sod buster crew in Saglek Bay. From left to right: the author, King Jim, Jim Thistle, Ches Skinner, and Murray Wells.

Camping on the sea ice in Cumberland Sound more than 25 kilometres from shore. Several crew members expressed concern about their safety in the tents, particularly when they noticed that the Inuit slept in their canoes, strapped on top of the sleds.

The Thule culture sites in Saglek Bay produced many cultural elements similar to ones found on prehistoric sites in Greenland; yet geographical impediments, like Davis Strait, Baffin Bay, and the distance between the two regions, seemed to rule out any direct contact. By the end of that long summer on Rose Island, I was determined to investigate regions farther north along the eastern Arctic coast. That decision brought me both west and east: west to enter a Ph.D. program at the University of Calgary, and east to the world's fifth largest island, Baffin Island. For the next three field seasons, I carried out the first systematic archaeological site survey in Cumberland Sound. In my work I was greatly aided by Franz Boas's comprehensive, nineteenth-century ethnography of the Native inhabitants of the region.[3] Every excursion into the field began in Pangnirtung, in my mind one of the most attractive settlements in the eastern Arctic. Not only is the setting spectacular, but the people went out of their way to be helpful and friendly. A request by Don Coles, manager of the Hudson's Bay store, for anyone willing to transport two *kadlunas* (White people) to various destinations in the sound brought me face to face with Kanea Eetooangat, one of the most remarkable people it has been my pleasure to meet. That first summer, my old homestead partner Frank Day and I travelled throughout the northeastern part of Cumberland Sound with Kanea and his family. While they hunted, we mapped and tested archaeological sites. Gradually, we managed some semblance of a conversation aided by much gesturing. The word *imaha* (meaning "maybe" in Inuktitut) was undoubtedly uttered more often by Kanea than he would care to recall, in answer to our endless questions about weather and ice and all the things that really have no answer other than "*imaha*."

In true Inuit fashion, Kanea never told us what to do; we learned by observation and imitation. One incident will suffice as a demonstration of that general principle. Late one dreary, dull, overcast afternoon we were stopped by pack ice along part of the coast that offered little in the way of a decent camp location. While Kanea and his family began pitching their old canvas tent on what looked like a particularly uncomfortable, boulder-strewn spot near shore, Frank and I set off in search of a more attractive location. Not far from shore we spotted what looked like an ideal spot, a narrow, grass-covered ledge just big enough to accommodate our two lightweight nylon tents. Pleased with our discovery of a camp spot so much more comfortable than anything the rocky shore had to offer, we put up our tents. After a meal of cold beans and bannock, we called it a night. A light drizzle descended from the grey clouds, a comforting sound when you are warm, dry, and sleepy. Within an hour the light drizzle had turned to a steady rain. Shortly thereafter, I woke up, not only to the sound of rushing water, but with the distinct feeling of being wet. The tent was flooded. Standing outside in the driving rain, Frank and I stared in amazement at the newly created waterfall gushing over the top of the rock wall behind us, landing only a few feet from our tents. Muttering a few choice phrases, we scrambled to the top of the rock wall and began a futile attempt to divert the flow of water. In the driving rain we could barely see Kanea's tent sitting dry and secure on the well-drained beach. It was a long night. Next morning we packed our soaked belongings under a clearing sky and joined Kanea and his family for some hot tea and bannock. Not a comment was made about our choice of campsite. A good lesson.

The three summers on Baffin Island provided much new information on the Thule culture period in Cumberland Sound.[4] Yet many of the same questions asked in Labrador about the seemingly strong prehistoric cultural connection between the eastern Canadian Arctic and Greenland remained unanswered. My eye roamed even higher on a large composite map of the Arctic, all the way to a place called Smith Sound, where Ellesmere Island and northern Greenland are separated by only 45 kilometres of ice-filled waters in the summer and bridged by solid ice in the winter. Geographically, the area appeared to offer a most convenient crossroads for humans migrating between the High Arctic and

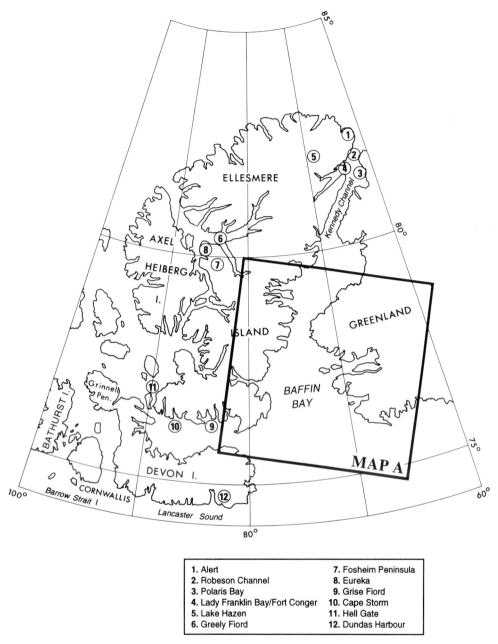

The northern Baffin Bay region.

1. Alert	7. Fosheim Peninsula
2. Robeson Channel	8. Eureka
3. Polaris Bay	9. Grise Fiord
4. Lady Franklin Bay/Fort Conger	10. Cape Storm
5. Lake Hazen	11. Hell Gate
6. Greely Fiord	12. Dundas Harbour

Greenland. That was in 1973. Four more years of fieldwork in other parts of the Canadian Arctic and Greenland intervened before I finally had a chance to head for eastern Ellesmere Island. During the summer of 1977, I directed an archaeological site survey for the Polar Gas Project along a 1500-kilometre projected pipeline route from Melville Island to Churchill, Manitoba.[5] As part

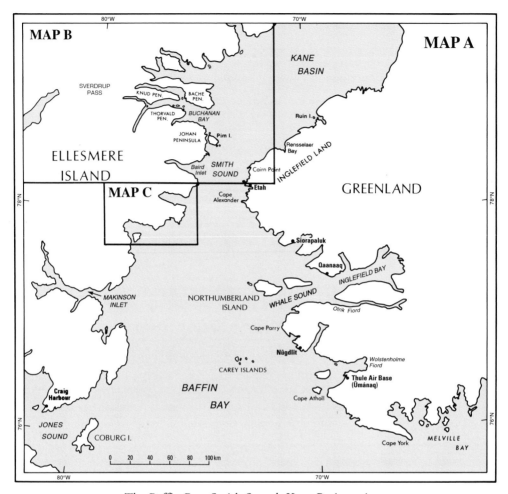

The Baffin Bay–Smith Sound–Kane Basin region.

of the research contract, I was given an opportunity to fly northward from Resolute Bay to the abandoned RCMP station at Alexandra Fiord on the central east coast of Ellesmere Island. My friend and colleague Tore Bjørgo and I would have about a week to explore the area before being picked up and returned south.

Every piece of information I had gathered over the years suggested that the Bache Peninsula region was a good choice for prehistoric studies. First, it represented one of the largest nonglaciated areas along the east coast of Ellesmere Island, with extensive fiords and lowlands that provided potentially rich habitats for marine and terrestrial mammals. Second, the area was accessible both along the southeast coast of Ellesmere Island and through Sverdrup Pass, one of the few ice-free routes between the west and the east coast of the island. More important, perhaps, was the fact that the southern Kane Basin–Smith Sound

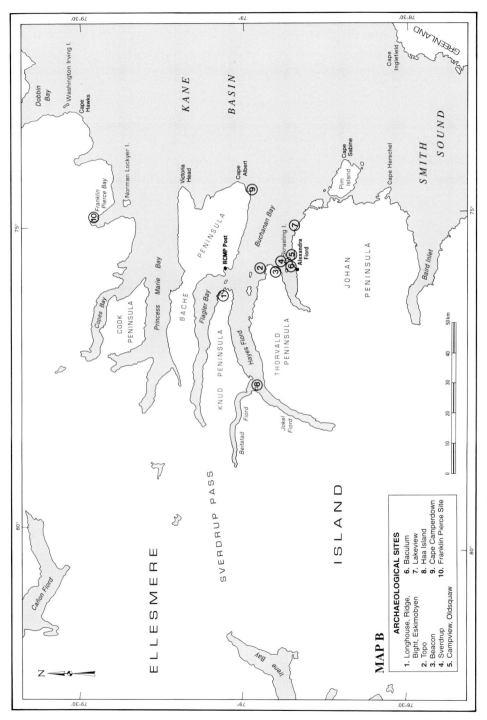

The Bache Peninsula region, including Sverdrup Pass.

area formed the northern boundary of the large North Water polynya. An Arctic polynya is generally described as a regularly occurring open water area encircled by solid fast ice.[6] Some polynyas (like the North Water) never freeze over, although the extent of open water shrinks during the winter. Pim Island and Bache Peninsula would have been natural points of departure and arrival for winter sledge parties crossing the ice bridge between Ellesmere Island and Greenland.

The geographical reasoning seemed sound enough. It was time to dive into all available records of explorers, researchers, and others who had been in the area. Between 1853 and 1861, the American explorers Elisha Kent Kane[7] and Isaac Israel Hayes[8] spent considerable time in the Kane Basin area. Apart from naming a few headlands, neither explorer surveyed Ellesmere Island extensively or made any references to old sites. Both men were driven by the North Pole obsession and made few scientific observations about their surroundings. In August 1875, spurred on by similar ambitions, Captain George Nares of the British navy had a closer look at the bays and fiords of the Bache Peninsula region. He anchored his two ships, the *Discovery* and the *Alert*, in a small, rocky harbour west of the present-day RCMP station at Alexandra Fiord and south of a nearby island he called "Three Sisters Island." Farther north he noticed old tent rings and, in one instance, a site with several ancient sod house ruins containing whale bone. A few days later he discovered two old stone cairns on top of Washington Irving Island, northeast of Bache Peninsula.[9]

We read different accounts of the horrifying 1883–84 wintering on Pim Island by Adolphus Washington Greely and his party, a tragic story of starvation, cannibalism, and the death of all but six members of the 26-man expedition.[10] Escape had been their only concern, not the recording of ancient dwellings.

As for mentioning old site locations, Otto Sverdrup took the prize in his account of the four-year, Second Norwegian Fram Expedition between 1898 and 1902.[11] The Norwegians' first wintering place was a small bight named Fram Havn (Fram Harbour), just west of Pim Island. From there members of the well-planned scientific expedition headed out on extensive sledging trips, mapping, observing, and investigating not only their immediate neighbourhood, but regions far to the west. It was our luck that their keen eyes didn't ignore the location of old campsites. A quick look at Sverdrup's maps and accompanying descriptions made it obvious that my guess about the importance of the Bache region had been a good one; the map showed a number of site locations with names like Eskimopolis and Eskimobyen ("Eskimo town"), that denoted considerable size. One name was particularly intriguing: Skraeling Island. As mentioned earlier, the word *Skraeling* was the rather derogatory term used by Norse Greenlanders when referring to Natives, either Indians or Inuit. The location of the island corresponded to Nares's Three Sisters Island, a name Sverdrup had either chosen to ignore or didn't know about. Although he provided no further details, we surmised that he had seen remains of old Inuit (Skraeling) camps on the island. Sverdrup's renaming of the island turned out to be far more prophetic than he could have imagined.

Nearly three hours after leaving Resolute Bay, the Twin Otter began a slow descent down a broad, glaciated valley leading to the head of Alexandra Fiord. The early August sun was nearing its midnight position, low on the northern horizon. Clear skies had given us a magnificent view of the vast ice sheets still covering much of Ellesmere Island. Few regions in the world offer more breathtaking scenery. On the final approach, flying between steep mountain slopes flanking the deep fiord, we were relieved to see that the pack ice was loose enough to provide open water for our small, inflatable Zodiac rubber boat, which we had brought along to carry out our work along the coast. Just as welcome and fortuitous was the presence of a small party of field geologists from the Geological Survey of Canada. Parked near the RCMP station was the Hughes 500 helicopter they were using for their surveys.

As we pumped up the rubber boat early next morning, we discovered that bears encountered in our previous camp had clawed at the front of the boat, leaving two knife-like slashes that needed attention. The holes were patched, and we quickly embarked on our first survey trip, taking full advantage of the open water. We knew from experience how rapidly ice conditions could change. With 24 hours of daylight and excellent weather, we surveyed about 35 kilometres of coastline east of the station before the ice blocked further passage. Everywhere we stopped, we located prehistoric sites. We camped near a large delta in an area littered with ancient food caches, kayak stands, and tent rings. Next morning, pursued by dense fog and closing pack ice, we retraced our route and headed for Skraeling Island. Moments after setting foot on the island, we spotted what Sverdrup's men had undoubtedly seen: large numbers of ancient, sod-covered house mounds. The scatter of stone chips and tool fragments at higher elevations pointed to much earlier occupations of the island. Day after day we filled our field books with site descriptions. On the final evening of our brief

Stiles Island and Skraeling Island at the entrance to Alexandra Fiord (Photo credit: Tore Bjørgo).

Site of the large Thule culture winter settlement on the east side of Skraeling Island. The tops of the wall stones of an unexcavated winter house ruin are visible in the foreground.

stay, the geologists, Bill Morgan and Tom Frisch, invited us on a midnight helicopter flight to some of the more distant areas we had been unable to reach by boat. On that occasion, we visited the shores of a body of open water—a polynya, as it turned out—between Bache and Knud Peninsulas, where we discovered a large number of prehistoric sites. Next morning, we packed our gear and brought it up to the short, sandy landing strip behind the station. On the flight south to Resolute Bay, plans for the following season's work were already being hatched.

With so much to look forward to, the winter seemed long, but maps and air photos are wonderful ways to pass the time and keep dreams alive. My belief that the Smith Sound region was used extensively in prehistoric times had been confirmed.[12] It was time to develop a more extensive, long-term plan for the work we wanted to carry out. The one organization that would make it all possible was the Canadian government's Polar Continental Shelf Project (PCSP), established in 1958 as a means of strengthening Canada's sovereignty in the Far North through extensive hydrographic surveys and scientific research. The Project's role as a provider of logistic support has grown significantly over the years enabling a great variety of research projects to be carried out in the North.[13]

One wall in the lab at the Arctic Institute in Calgary was used to assemble a mosaic of Ellesmere Island maps covering the area between 78° 30′ and 80°00′N. We later included the Goding Bay area south to 77°30′N. For logistic reasons and greater mobility, we planned to use relatively small research teams. We also decided to split the field season into two parts. During the first half, we would work from a base camp on the northeast shore of Knud Peninsula; then, about the middle of July, we would move base camp to Skraeling Island and work there until the end of the season. The second move was planned to coincide, as far as possible, with the breakup of the fast ice, allowing us to transport ourselves, gear, and supplies by boat between the island and the RCMP station at Alexandra Fiord. We followed this agenda successfully during the first five field seasons. From the two base camps, we conducted a series of short-term exploration trips to different parts of the study area, recording and testing new sites important to the overall study. Over the years, the base camps became as familiar and dear to us as our own homes back south.

The core of the study area is located in a fascinating and varied landscape dominated by glaciated Precambrian mountains north, west, and south of the prominent sedimentary formations of Bache Peninsula. The shorelines are

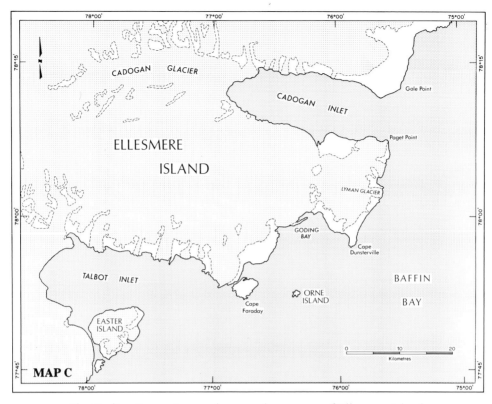

The Goding Bay region on the central east coast of Ellesmere Island.

generally rocky, occasionally interrupted by short stretches of elevated beach terraces. In many places, mountains drop sharply into deep fiords, leaving almost no accessible shoreline. Ancient ice caps send serrated glacial tongues all the way into the ocean or leave them suspended partway down older pathways. During the long winter, the fast ice expands farther and farther eastward out towards Kane Basin, creating a perfect habitat for ringed seals. These were the nutritional mainstay of prehistoric Arctic peoples, who hunted them at their breathing holes in the winter and on top of the melting sea ice in spring and early summer. The edge of the fast ice, the *sina*, was frequented by polar bears and human hunters seeking prey in the open water. The land supported additional food resources such as hares and foxes, as well as the more substantial muskoxen and caribou, which were found mostly in Sverdrup Pass and on the west side of Ellesmere Island.

Knud Peninsula is the second-largest nonglaciated peninsula in the region. Bounded by Flagler Bay and Hayes and Beitstad Fiords, the peninsula shows off a great variety of landscapes, from steep, rugged cliffs to broad valleys, river deltas, and recently emerged lowlands. A number of dissected plateaus culminate in Mount Kola, with an elevation of over a thousand metres. The geology of the peninsula consists of a combination of Precambrian and Ordovician formations, according to Bob Christie, who conducted geological studies in the region in the 1960s, following in the steps of Per Schei, geologist with the Sverdrup expedition.[14]

During the brief summer, the flora in the Bache region is relatively luxuriant, especially in sheltered valleys traversed by glacial meltwater streams. Brilliant purple saxifrage and bright yellow arctic poppies compete for the eye's attention. Twin Glacier Valley, south of the Alexandra Fiord RCMP station, is especially lush; a vast outwash plain carpeted by thick grass, moss, sedges, and heather. Several years after we began our work in the Bache region, the valley became the focus of intensive botanical studies.[15]

Every summer we learned more about the area's dynamic ecological relationships. Each season was different, sometimes only through subtle nuances, but occasionally with major departures from whatever could be considered normal; one year, the fast ice broke up and was blown out of the bays and fiords in mid-June; the next year, it remained in place practically until we left in early August. As the Danish cartoonist Storm Petersen once said, "There is nothing more difficult to predict than the future."

We began to grasp the dynamic interaction between the large North Water polynya and fast ice distribution in the Bache Peninsula region. When the polynya expanded far into Kane Basin early in the summer and strong winds from the west prevailed for a period of time, the fast ice in Buchanan Bay and Princess Marie Bay was free to drift into Kane Basin, where it was caught by the southward flow of the Polar current down through Smith Sound and into Baffin Bay. We could see how that process determined the extent to which white whales, narwhals and, in the past, giant bowhead whales, gained access to bays and fiords, providing a plentiful, seasonal supply of food for local hunters. Conversely, if the North Water did not penetrate into Kane Basin, the fast ice remained locked in the bays and fiords, preventing the larger sea mammals from entering.

We understood why the Flagler Bay polynya played such an important role prehistorically; by its very nature, it was one of the few predictable elements in a most uncertain world—an Arctic oasis. As a geographical feature, the polynya is fascinating. Satellite photos show the appearance of this little body of regularly occurring open water as early as April. Brian Sawyer, former chief of police in

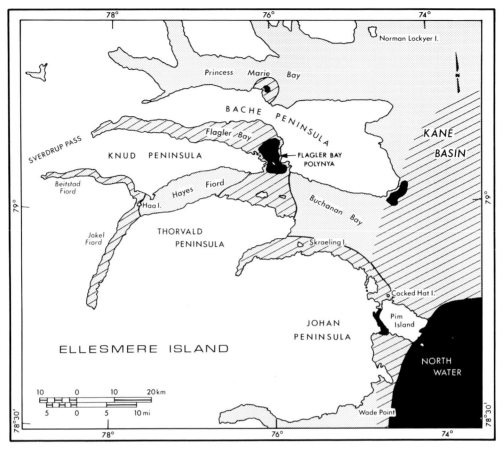

Distribution of primary and secondary polynyas in the Bache Peninsula region. Primary polynyas are indicated by solid black and secondary polynyas by crosshatching.

Calgary, was stationed at Alexandra Fiord between 1954 and 1956. He told us that the ice at the entrance to Flagler Bay was often broken and remained very thin throughout the entire winter.

The biological importance of polynyas in the Canadian Arctic for migratory waterfowl and marine mammals has been well documented.[16] If the Flagler Bay polynya had existed for hundreds, even thousands of years, it was no wonder we were finding so many prehistoric sites along its shores, especially along the low-lying northeastern coastal section of Knud Peninsula. But how long had it been there? We know that during the Ice Age, when thick ice sheets covered most of the Canadian Arctic, the land was pushed down by the sheer weight of the ice. As the ice gradually melted, the land began to rise again, a phenomenon known as isostatic rebound. In the Arctic, this rebound effect can be seen as a series of raised beach terraces extending far inland from the present coastline.

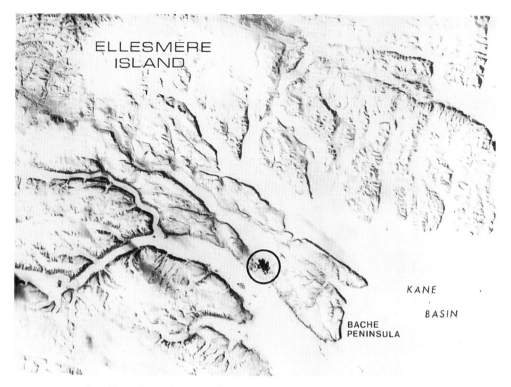

Satellite photo showing the Flagler Bay polynya in early spring.

The rate of rebound was rarely the same from one area to another, reflecting among other things the varying thickness of the original ice cover. Along the central east coast of Ellesmere Island, we estimate that the land has risen at least 15 metres during the past 4000 to 5000 years. Would that change have affected the Flagler Bay polynya?

To answer that question, we have to look at how a recurring polynya forms in the first place. The mechanisms are simple enough: a strong current, possibly tidal in nature; a geographical constriction of the flow of water; and relative shallowness. In Flagler Bay the daily tidal movement provides the current. The constant motion, enhanced by upwelling of bottom waters, not only keeps the water from freezing, but provides a nutrient-rich environment for sea mammals. A quick study of the exposed land around the present polynya clearly shows that raising the sea level about 15 metres, as we believe was the case about 4000 years ago, would have submerged most of the habitable, reasonably level land. Robert Lake of the Frozen Sea Research Group in Sidney, British Columbia, became interested in the problem and ran a computer simulation model of the Flagler Bay area.[17] By studying the tidal flow rate and extent of upwelling at different sea level stages through time, he concluded that the polynya most likely would not have been present earlier than 4000 years ago. So even in a world which appears so formidable in its timelessness, nothing remains static; changes just take place at a different rate.

As we became familiar with the landscape and plotted more and more sites on our maps, a distinct pattern emerged. Not only was there a concentration of sites in the vicinity of the Flagler Bay polynya, but most other prehistoric sites were situated where the winter ice broke up quite early, providing stretches of open water for bearded seals and walrus. We designated these areas as secondary polynyas, less predictable in their appearance, but important nevertheless.

So who were the real Arctic pioneers, the first people to set foot in the High Arctic? When did they first stand on the western shores of Smith Sound looking across at yet another stretch of unknown coast to the east?

4

The True Pioneers

"RED KNOT"
Brenda Carter

The red knot was exhausted after the long flight—buffeted by storms and contrary winds over oceans and barren lands. It was perched on a huge boulder, deposited on top of the island by a glacier now resting far away in the inner part of the deep fiord it had helped to carve.

In Egypt, where the knot's migration had started, people were cultivating fields and herding animals, when they weren't busy killing each other in defence of the Eleventh Dynasty. The knot had seen slaves struggling to transport massive stones to pyramids as tall as mountains. The Sumerian law code of Ur was in effect and the Indus Valley was about to be overrun by northern Aryans. The knot had flown thousands of kilometres across lands and oceans to reach the northern lands where the sun never disappeared. It had never seen people there before, but now, down on the beach below the perch a group of people sat around a smoky fire eating seal meat, disrupting the silent evening with talk and laughter.

Our search for evidence of the earliest habitation sites had taken us to an old beach far above the present sea level. Walking along the gravel terrace we became aware of a regular pattern; a concentration of vegetation separated by short stretches of mostly sterile gravel and sand, which turned out to be a marvelous illustration of the fact that death is merely a transition from one form of life to another. In each instance the vegetation was consolidated in two adjacent areas, one at a higher elevation than the other. The smaller and more elevated growth was surrounded by an irregular outline of boulders, which marked the outer periphery where skin tents had been held to the ground long ago. In the centre were the remains of fire hearths. Downslope was a larger concentration of saxifrage. On hands and knees we searched the ground, quickly discovering bleached bone remains and tiny waste flakes of chert among the brilliant flowers. This was the midden where refuse from the house had landed thousands of years ago. It was easy to envision seal carcasses being hauled into camp, cut up, and distributed among the families. The seal provided meat and blubber for food and fuel and skin for clothing and boat covers. Some of the larger bones had been used to fuel the cooking fires, while

Eric Damkjar and Barry Lopez investigating the scattered remains of an early Palaeoeskimo camp on Stiles Island. Skraeling Island is in the background.

the remaining refuse gradually provided the nutrients needed to sustain soil and the growth now decorating the stony world with splashes of brightly coloured flowers.

The discovery of ancient campsites never ceases to be a thrill. To kneel down next to a small, isolated stone-lined hearth, slightly embedded in sand and gravel, 30 metres above present sea level, provides a physical connection with human activities thousands of years ago. The sites are not always that easy to spot. Even when you know that the earliest sites should be looked for at higher elevations, a good deal of careful searching and imagination is often needed to find them. You must be able to recognize a site when you're looking at it and get used to skeptical glances from neophytes on their first Arctic dig. Lighting is crucial; the best time to search for these ancient camps is usually on a sunlit night when the shadows are long. On more than one occasion we've questioned the validity of such late-night discoveries when viewed later in the harder glare of the daytime sun. Not surprisingly, the success rate for locating old sites increases as the terrain becomes more familiar. Not only is this a compelling reason for long-term studies; it also gives you a strong sense of closing the gap between present and past.

These are the camp remains of the first Palaeoeskimos, the true High Arctic pioneers. The word *pioneer* is often used as loosely as the word *discoverer*; both terms reflect a strong, ethnocentric tendency to ignore all that went before the arrival of, in many cases, Europeans. In this account, the true pioneers were the very first human beings to enter the High Arctic and Greenland. They were part of an extraordinary eastward expansion of peoples who traced their ancestry back to the river valleys and shores of Northeast Asia before arriving and settling along the coasts and interior regions of Alaska nearly 5000 years ago. Interest in these extraordinary hunters of the tundra and the frozen seas goes back a fair while if we include the observation of archaeological sites and collection of artifacts in northern Ellesmere Island by members of the ill-fated Lady Franklin Bay Expedition between 1881 and 1883.[1] Farther east, in northern Greenland, members of the Danmarks Expedition recorded ancient tent ring sites containing faunal remains, including muskox bones, between 1906 and 1908.[2] Not long afterwards, the Danish geographer and anthropologist, Hans Peter Steensby, used this data to support his migration theory of the "Muskox Eskimos," people he also referred to as "Palaeoeskimos," who supposedly advanced into the High Arctic primarily in search of muskoxen.[3] On one of his maps, Steensby indicated

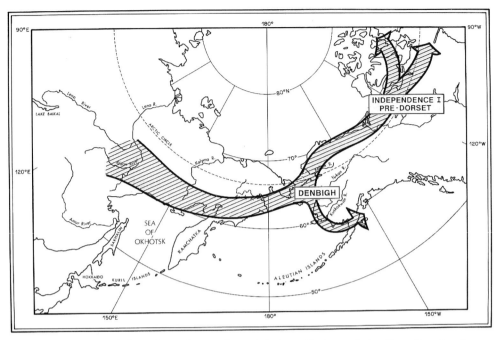

The expansion of the Palaeoeskimos from Asia into Alaska and the Canadian Arctic.

two possible migration routes to Greenland: one through Lake Hazen Valley in northern Ellesmere Island, and the other through Sverdrup Pass and the Bache Peninsula region. Steensby expressed a clear preference for the northern Ellesmere Island route. In 1947, the Danish explorer, artist, and archaeologist, Count Eigil Knuth, launched the first of many Danish Pearyland Expeditions providing further support for Steensby's migration theory. Eigil Knuth referred frequently to the "Muskox Way," and named the pioneering High Arctic culture *Independence I* from find locations in the vicinity of Independence Fiord in northeast Greenland.[4] Far to the west, during the summer of 1948, on a bluff overlooking Norton Sound and the Bering Strait, the American archaeologist Louis Giddings located an assemblage of finely flaked stone tools he categorized as the *Denbigh Flint complex*.[5] Other finds of a similar nature were made in the interior and coastal sites in western and northernmost Alaska. Although the complex could be related to finds made in Northeast Asia, there was an even closer relationship to Eigil Knuth's Independence I finds from North Greenland. Subsequent radiocarbon dates also pointed to a reasonably similar age for the two complexes, slightly more than 4000 years old. A close cultural link between the earliest human inhabitants of the Canadian Arctic, Greenland, and more northerly regions of Alaska had been established. What was needed was a designation that would incorporate these geographically separated tool complexes into a broader cultural entity. In the mid-1950s, William Irving coined the term *Arctic Small Tool tradition* (ASTt) to indicate the strong cultural connection between these distant Arctic sites and to reflect the refined minuteness of the stone tools used by these people, whose brilliantly shaped flint implements can be considered works of art.[6] By the time they settled in Alaska, the people of the ASTt were well adapted to life both on the tundra and along the Arctic coast. There was one major problem: in the interior they faced strong, often violent, competition from hunters of a different cultural background, the ancestors of the present-day Athabascan Indians.

Following Steensby's work, it has become common practice to refer to the people of the ASTt as Palaeoeskimos—a way of suggesting that these early Arctic hunters are related, at least in lifestyle, to the present-day Eskimo or Inuit populations in northern Alaska, Canada, and Greenland. It is not by any means an indisputable relationship. Whereas the present-day Inuit in Canada and Greenland can trace their ancestry back directly to the Thule culture and the Bering Sea maritime cultures of a thousand years ago, their link with the ASTt and the Palaeoeskimos is more ambiguous. Notwithstanding the theoretical and philosophical discussions surrounding this argument, the term *Palaeoeskimos* will be used to refer to the people of the ASTt who inhabited the Canadian Arctic and Greenland for over 3000 years. The term *Neoeskimos* will be used occasionally with reference to people of the Thule culture.

There can be little doubt that the Palaeoeskimos entered the Canadian Arctic in several waves of small groups of extended families pushing into virgin territory. The world they faced was familiar only in its geography. There were no traces of earlier occupations to guide them to the best hunting spots, no former occupants to hinder or aid their progress, no one to tell them what they would find over the horizon. Their survival depended on the degree to which they could use and adapt their knowledge of the Arctic as they went along. Most likely they entered a land fairly rich in game that had never before confronted the cunning human hunter. The early migrations took place towards the end of the Climatic Optimum, a relatively long period of climatic warming (8000 to 5000 B.P.) that had opened the polar oceans considerably more than is the case today. The huge ice sheets that had once covered land and seas were mostly gone. For thousands of years, driftwood from Siberia had been deposited on the Arctic shores, a ready source of fuel for people who, at least initially, didn't use seal-oil lamps for light, heat, or cooking. Their open fires, fueled by driftwood and cracked mammal bones, were not well suited to life in the High Arctic.

As the Palaeoeskimos moved into increasingly remote and isolated regions, their material culture was adjusted to fit the new conditions they were facing. The availability of lithic sources for tools varied from region to region; conservative ways of making tools were passed down to sons and daughters, reflecting styles favoured by the elders. In that way the early ASTt tool kit from West Greenland was bound to be somewhat different from that carried around by Palaeoeskimos in central Canada or northern Labrador or the High Arctic. This material diversity, however minor, provided the reasoning behind distinguishing three different complexes of the early ASTt tradition; the *Pre-Dorset complex*, primarily referring to Palaeoeskimo occupations in the central and eastern Canadian Arctic including the east coast of Labrador;[7] the *Independence I complex*, associated with the earliest Palaeoeskimo occupation of the Canadian High Arctic and northern Greenland; and the *Saqqaq complex*, assigned to the vibrant and long-lived Palaeoeskimo occupation of the more southerly coastal regions of Greenland. The names *Independence I* and *Saqqaq* both refer to find locations in Greenland. The origin of the term *Pre-Dorset* is a little more circuitous. In 1924, a collection of stone tools was sent to the National Museum in Ottawa from Cape Dorset on the south coast of Baffin Island. The collection was studied by the outstanding anthropologist Diamond Jenness, who pronounced that a prehistoric culture, older than the known Thule culture, had existed in the Canadian Arctic.[8] Eventually archaeologists acknowledged that even the Dorset culture had an antecedent: the Pre-Dorset culture, or complex.

The differences, however small, between these complexes provide us with a framework within which we can study more illusive cultural elements. They enable us to ask questions about human migration patterns, trade networks, environmental and social adaptability, and the challenge and response of genetically and culturally related people to changing conditions in different parts of the Arctic world.

A quick look at the Arctic map shows how closely the three early ASTt complexes are related to geographical regions. One of our primary research objectives on Ellesmere Island was to study the degree of interaction and trait flow between these geographically separated Palaeoeskimo populations. Of the three complexes, the most short-lived was the one associated with the

Independence I people in the far northern regions of the Arctic. This is perhaps not surprising, considering the environmental extremes these people had to endure and the relatively few prey species available to their hunters. In contrast, the Pre-Dorset and the Saqqaq complexes survived quite well, especially in the more game-rich areas of the Arctic. During favourable times, some of these extended families were attracted to new hunting areas in more peripheral regions, such as the High Arctic.

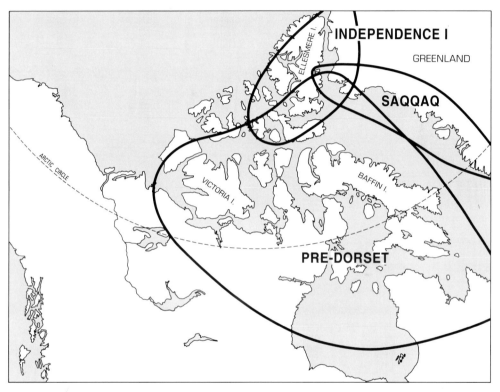

The approximate geographical distribution of the three early complexes of the Arctic Small Tool tradition (ASTt): Independence I, Saqqaq and Pre-Dorset. The Greenland locations extend beyond the boundary indicated.

Using this cultural framework, we spent summer after summer testing and excavating selected dwelling features and middens while continuing the search for new sites. We saw that the choice of camp locations was never a random affair, but a decision reflecting the season of occupation, the degree of shelter required, access to game, and special social events. Height above sea level proved not to be as good a time indicator as we had first expected; some early sites were found as much as 30 metres above sea level, while others from a similar time

A stone-lined axial feature with a well-defined central box hearth from an early Palaeoeskimo dwelling on Johan Peninsula.

period were located at only half that elevation. We quickly learned to distinguish between different types of early camps, from the barely discernible concentrations of lithic waste flakes, flecks of charcoal, and a few boulders, to more impressive dwelling features with distinct hearths and boulder outlines. The size of the settlements remained fairly constant; in each instance, it was clear that the Palaeoeskimos travelled and lived in small groups of one or two extended families, rarely occupying more than one or two dwellings, at least for most of the year.

We noted that the most amorphous camp remains, or "scatter sites," were located consistently at higher elevations, on exposed beach terraces with a good view of the ocean. With reasonable assurance we designated these as summer camps. Occasionally we came across single-hearth features consisting of a box-like structure built of stone slabs. These hearths were usually filled with fist-sized stones, probably heated in the hearth, then dropped into skin bags to boil or at least heat whatever meal was being prepared. Like the scatter camps, the single hearths were undoubtedly used in the summer and early fall. The Palaeoeskimos also constructed a more substantial dwelling, the so-called axial structure, sometimes referred to as a central passage dwelling. The distinguishing feature of this structure is the presence of two parallel lines of upright stone slabs that divide the dwelling into halves. The space between the parallel slabs is further divided by a centrally located, slab-lined, box hearth. In other words, the axial feature is not a passage, but a convenient spatial arrangement enclosing the central hearth, with a forward compartment for fuel and a raised platform in the rear for food and other items, all within easy reach of the people on both sides of the structure. This particular interior arrangement and utilization of space appears to be universal and quite ancient. One suspects that it represents the optimal and most convenient use of space within a round or oval dwelling structure. A fascinating illustrated account of the life of the Laplanders, published in 1767, details the utilization of such structures.[9] The drawings clearly portray the division of the central axial construction. The central hearth is flanked by two compartments, one for fuel and one for utensils. Of great interest are the different spaces allocated to various members of the extended family occupying each dwelling, with children in one area and different categories of elders in others. To what extent the Palaeoeskimos paid attention to such socially prescribed arrangements we may never know.

Two early Palaeoeskimo camps in the Bache Peninsula region, the Lakeview and the Campview sites, each represent a different season of occupation by people associated with the Independence I complex. The reason we stopped at the Lakeview site during the first boat survey in 1977 was probably the same one that had enticed people to the place hundreds and thousands of years ago.

An eighteenth-century drawing of a Laplander dwelling (From Leems, 1767).

While the waters along the Johan Peninsula coast are generally shallow, the Lakeview site is situated on a prominent, rocky headland that provides easy access to the sea even at low tide, when other parts of the coast turn into extensive tidal flats. Forty-five hundred years ago, when sea level was considerably higher, the landscape would have been quite different. The massive, rocky ridge that now forms the core of the site would have remained attached to the mainland by only a narrow tang of land; not long before that, it would have been an island. Most of the old dwelling features are located on the landward side of the ridge, which now overlooks an extensive lowland and gently sloping plateau, dissected by glacial meltwater streams discharging from tongues of receding valley glaciers to the south. Not only does that location ensure protection from the north winds, but by facing south, occupants could have enjoyed the last rays of the rapidly disappearing fall sun.

We visited the site at least once each field season, mapping and testing new camp features. Like so many of the large Palaeoeskimo sites in the area, Lakeview site had been used during different time periods over the past 4000 years. We refer to such sites as "multicomponent" sites, since they contain evidence from many different occupations. The location remained popular through time,

MacMillan Glacier descending into the North Water polynya in Smith Sound.

A trapped iceberg.

Tore Bjørgo checking our boat during the 1977 survey along the Johan Peninsula coast.

Patches of saxifrage mark the site of an ancient camp feature and associated midden.

A 4300-year-old box hearth feature on Skraeling Island.

Detached microblades as they were found on the Baculum site.

A chert core used for microblade production.

Karen McCullough excavating a dwelling feature on the Beacon site. Buchanan Bay and Kane Basin are in the background.

despite the gradually changing landscape, because the feature that had made it attractive, such as easy access to the sea, did not change. To reach one of the earliest Palaeoeskimo camps on the site, we hiked to the top of the glacially scoured, rocky headland overlooking Buchanan Bay and Bache Peninsula to the north. The feature, recorded as number 30 on our site map, was situated on a sloping gravel terrace between 26 and 27 metres above sea level. We managed to walk across it a couple of times before paying attention to it—this was one of those early camp features where imagination came in handy. But it was real enough: a slightly raised, barely discernible, oval, gravel wall outlined the structure, which measured about 4.5 by 3.5 metres. A few of the original tent support boulders were still present in the south-facing part of the structure, where we assumed the entrance had been.

The circular outline of an early Palaeoeskimo summer camp structure, Feature 30, located about 27 metres above sea level on the Lakeview site. The concentration of larger stones is located near the entrance to the round, gravel-walled dwelling. Buchanan Bay and Bache Peninsula are to the north.

In a lightly vegetated centre we made out the hearth, which had been placed directly on top of exposed bedrock and lined with small, flat and round stones, some of which may have been used as boiling stones. The diameter of the hearth

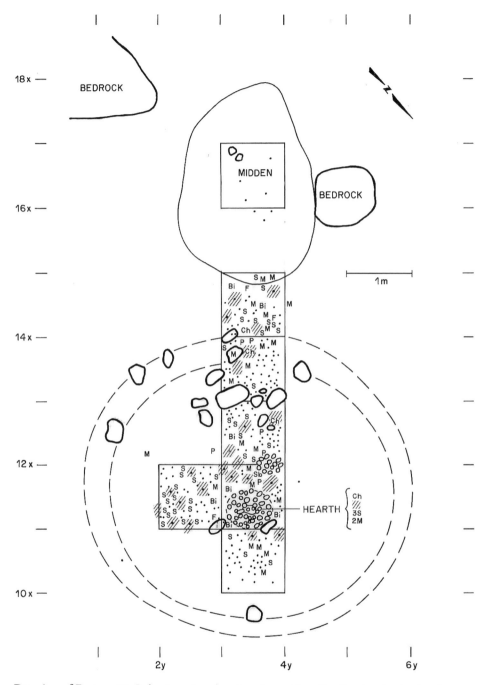

Drawing of Feature 30, Lakeview site, showing the artifact distribution in the 1 × 1 metre excavation units. Ch = charcoal, M = microblades, Bi = bifacially retouched tools, Sb = sideblades, F = flakeknives, S = burin spalls, and P = stone projectile points. The excavation produced 40 burin spalls, which accounts for about 50% of all tools and fragments found. The large number of spalls indicates a considerable amount of work being done using the cutting and incising tool, the burin.

was about 60 centimetres and, after carefully removing the stones, we had to use tweezers to pick up tiny pieces of charred willow. An hour of eye-straining work produced a 196-milligram sample that later gave us an accelerator radiocarbon date of about 3940 B.P. For about 4000 years this camp feature had remained basically untouched. Later users of the site had undoubtedly availed themselves of some of the boulders, but other than that they had shown no interest in the remains. They would have been startled to see us on hands and knees peering at the ground, carefully removing small stones, brushing the gravel, and occasionally picking up tiny flakes of chert and pieces of bone. But they weren't there to witness our strange behaviour; our only connection to their lives came through the scarce remains in the sand and gravel. Their story had to be told by the stone artifacts and bone refuse they left behind.

A light cover of vegetation downslope from the dwelling identified the refuse area. Unfortunately, with the exception of a few chips of walrus ivory and some bird bones, the preservation was poor. The interior excavation consisted mostly of hand picking hundreds of small pebbles, then carefully trowelling through fine sand and gravel to an average depth of 6 to 8 centimetres. We didn't find much, but enough to show us that the occupation was early, as the radiocarbon date confirmed. It is not necessarily the quantity but rather the diagnostic value of the finds that is important. We always hope to find at least one or two whole or fragmentary artifacts that are particularly diagnostic as time markers. Like a coin on a historic site, some items can give you a good idea of when the site was occupied. While the Palaeoeskimos didn't use coins, they did make a variety of tools which, taken together as an assemblage, tell us much about the time period when they were in use. One of the most diagnostic tools is the harpoon head, whose stylistic attributes changed enough through the centuries to be very useful as a time marker. Although we searched Feature 30 in vain for even a fragment of a harpoon head, we did locate a small, serrated, bipointed projectile point. The point was similar to specimens from other Independence I sites in the High Arctic and northern Greenland. We also found several small cutting blades made of chert—microblades struck from the sides of stone cores prepared specifically for that purpose. Each blade was prismatic in cross-section, with two sharp cutting edges, and was either hand-held or hafted in a bone or wood handle. Having studied microblades from many different collections, covering the 3000-year span of the ASTt tradition, we have noticed a minor, but apparently real change in the width of the blades through time. This is the kind of information that in and of itself would be of little use; yet it becomes important when combined with other observations. We have also seen that the popularity of microblades changed through time, as did the method of hafting them. Taken together, all these factors provide an important estimate of the time period when the items were used.

Feature 30 is an excellent example of a Palaeoeskimo summer camp, placed as it is in a location much too exposed to have been used during the stormy winter months. During our lunch breaks, we usually sat on one of the large

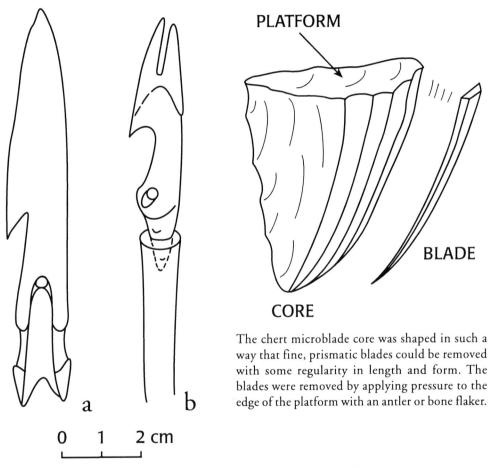

PLATFORM

BLADE

CORE

The chert microblade core was shaped in such a way that fine, prismatic blades could be removed with some regularity in length and form. The blades were removed by applying pressure to the edge of the platform with an antler or bone flaker.

a   b

0   1   2 cm

The Palaeoeskimo hunter entered the High Arctic with two types of harpoon heads in his tool kit: The open-socketed, toggling variety (a) and the nontoggling variety (b). The toggling harpoon head had a foreshaft lashed into the open socket, which ended in two spurs. The nontoggling head ended in a conical spur inset into the end of the throwing shaft. In the Central and High Arctic, the nontoggling harpoon head was quickly replaced by the toggling harpoon head, although in Greenland, Saqqaq hunters used both types. The Pre-Dorset hunters relied almost exclusively on the toggling type of harpoon head.

boulders on top of the hill overlooking Buchanan Bay. Broken pack ice drifted slowly back and forth with the tide and the wind. The ground along the edge of our boulder perch was littered with tiny stone flakes, the result of fine retouch flaking by hunters, who sat on the same rock watching for sea mammals thousands of years ago. To the west, only seven kilometres away, we could see Skraeling Island, where so much of our work took place. One of the many Palaeoeskimo camps we investigated on that island was the Campview site, also used by the Independence I pioneers.

View of two early Palaeoeskimo settlements on Skraeling Island; the Tusk site, a summer camp located about 30 metres above sea level, and the Campview site, a fall/early winter camp located about 15 metres above sea level.

The Campview site was easily named, as it provided a great view of our own base camp across a small bight to the south. This fairly small site, like the Lakeview site, was multicomponent: in this case, it had probably been used on three different occasions throughout the Palaeoeskimo period. A total of six dwellings were distributed between 9 and 20 metres above sea level. The two features we were particularly interested in were located just about 15 metres above sea level. Their close proximity suggested contemporaneous occupation, as did their artifact assemblages, which we treated as a single component.

The central axial construction of Feature 2 on Campview site, showing the 1 × 1 metre excavation units on the left side of the oval dwelling structure.

The raised, flagged meat platform in the rear of Feature 2, Campview site.

We had worked on Skraeling Island for a couple of seasons before we turned our attention to these features. They were impressive enough, each with a slab-lined axial construction, containing a central hearth filled with ashes, blubber-hardened sand, and boiling stones. When we first noticed them, we were under the mistaken impression that the earliest Palaeoeskimo sites would be located about 30 metres above sea level. We had already found and dated the nearby Independence I Tusk site at that elevation, so it seemed reasonable to assume that the two Campview features at half that elevation represented a much later occupation. As the excavation progressed, however, and more and more artifacts were added to the assemblage, it became obvious that the occupants could have called themselves true pioneers. The artifacts included triangular skin scraping tools, ivory needles for sewing, and microblades for cutting up skins. There were not many blades, but their mean width did fit the average measurements from other Independence I sites in the area. A finely serrated projectile point, a thin, lightly ground harpoon endblade, and several burins were easily placed in an early ASTt time frame. The burin, made of chert, was an extremely important manufacturing tool used by the Palaeoeskimos to make other tools. With the burin, toolmakers incised and grooved sections of bone, antler, or ivory into whatever shape they wanted. Unlike the fine cutting edge of the microblades, the working tip of the burin is quite angular and stubby, almost impossible to break. When the tip and scraping edge became dull, a spall was struck off, leaving a sharp, jagged hinge fracture. These hinges tell us how many times the burin was rejuvenated. Naturally enough, most of the burins we find on a site have been almost completely spent. Although by no means as useful as harpoon heads, the style of burins tends to be fairly diagnostic through time.

Our suspicion of great antiquity for the two Campview features was supported when a sample of charred willow from one of the hearths gave us a date of about 4000 B.P. The results of the excavation also established an important isostatic rebound rate for the region. We were now aware that sites as low as 15 metres above sea level could have been occupied 4000 years ago. Clearly there were at least two different types of early Palaeoeskimo camps in the area: the vaguely outlined and briefly occupied features found on exposed beach terraces

A burin spall is removed from the burin to restore the sharpness of the incising edge. The many hinge fractures along the removal edge indicate how many times the burin has been rejuvenated.

An assortment of Independence I artifacts from the Campview site. From left to right, top row: leaf-shaped point, base fragment of a point, three burins; bottom row: two concave sidescrapers, triangular endscraper, endscraper.

overlooking bays and sounds, and the more substantial dwellings constructed in locations offering better protection from wind and weather.

At first we categorized the Campview features as winter dwellings, but as we excavated similar features on other sites in the Bache region, we began to question that interpretation. The dwellings had undoubtedly been used during a dark and cold period, but perhaps not through the entire winter. Despite good preservation of organic materials, we were not finding much refuse inside or outside the dwellings, at least not as much as one would expect had they been used for a whole winter. The location of these axial dwellings also suggested that the people who had built them were responding to similar sets of circumstances. They always selected a sheltered location, usually one facing south, perhaps indicating a desire to take advantage of rapidly declining sunlight in

PALAEOESKIMO BURIN TYPES

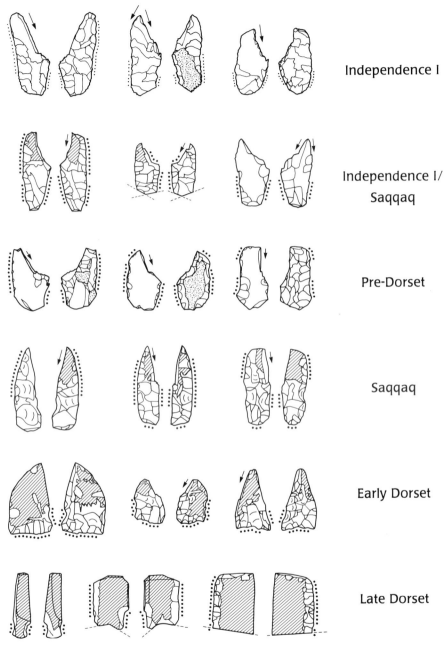

Independence I

Independence I/
Saqqaq

Pre-Dorset

Saqqaq

Early Dorset

Late Dorset

The importance of the burin as a diagnostic element is illustrated in this chart. Three sets of burins from six different Palaeoeskimo time periods are shown. Both sides of the burins are shown as well as the direction of burin spall removal. The dotted lines indicate areas where the burin edge shows strong evidence of retouch from use or as a result of hafting. The cross-hatching indicates areas of the burins that have been ground, and the stippling indicates cortex (the original surface of the stone).

late fall. The concentration of bone, ivory, and stone waste flakes, needles, and other artifacts very close to the hearth pointed to an occupation period when light and heat were necessary; but did that necessarily mean the whole winter? There was another factor to consider: the lack of substantial food caches in the vicinity of these axial features. If people had remained in one dwelling throughout the winter, a reasonably convenient access to stored foods should be in evidence. People occupying the Campview site would have seen the last of the sun about the middle of October; it would not have appeared again until the middle of February. It is not a totally dark world during those four months. For a few weeks on either side of the darkness, the noon twilight brightens the snow-covered landscape. During the darkest period, the moon may provide sufficient light for travel and hunting a couple of weeks each month, if the skies are clear. Even so, it must have been an extremely challenging time to get through. Is it possible that people simply lived a lethargic, indoor existence, eating little and sleeping most of the time, huddled together under layers of skin in a state of near-hibernation? There is the amazing account of the wintering of the Norwegian explorer Fridtjof Nansen and his companion Hjalmar Johansen on Franz Josef Land between 1895 and 1896. Having scooped out a most primitive shelter and stacked a pile of dead bears near its entrance, they did their best to sleep away as much of the long winter as possible, eventually managing to sleep for 20 hours a day.[10]

The Palaeoeskimos may have used these axial dwellings as briefly as the lithic and faunal remains suggest. Perhaps they were occupied only in late fall and early winter as snow blanketed the land, the days became shorter and colder, the sun refused to peek over the southern mountains at noon, and the sea ice grew strong enough to bear the weight of hunters. As winter deepened the Palaeoeskimo families may have moved into snow houses. With the right snow conditions they are easily built, reasonably warm, even without a fire, and ideal for a small group of people who need to move from one hunting area to another during the winter. Of course it is difficult to prove the existence of a dwelling that melts and vanishes when summer arrives.

The fact that we have no evidence to indicate that the Independence I people used stone lamps or vessels might argue against their use of snow houses. The argument would be that such items are necessary to provide heat, light, and the ability to have a hot meal. Would it have been possible for people to cope for any length of time without these items, or have we just not been fortunate

Two Copper Inuit skin tents joined together with a central ridge pole and entered through a centrally located opening. A similar dwelling style may have been used by the early Palaeoeskimos. (photo credit: The Canadian Museum of Civilization).

enough to find them? Stone lamp fragments have been located on early Saqqaq sites in Greenland. They have also been located on northern Baffin Island, in an axial dwelling thought to relate to an early Pre-Dorset occupation. So, with soapstone lamps present in early ASTt complexes in Greenland and northern Baffin Island, it may be only a matter of time before similar fragments are found in the High Arctic. There is also the possibility that lamps and vessels were not necessary for survival in the Arctic winter. Birket-Smith's studies of the Caribou Eskimos during the Fifth Thule Expedition showed that Inuit families in the interior of the Barren Grounds spent the winter in snow houses provided with a small kitchen annex, where cooking took place over an open heather fire. In fact, fire was used almost exclusively for cooking and not as a general means of keeping warm. According to Birket-Smith, most of the Caribou Eskimos passed even the coldest winters without any artificial heat.[11] In such instances, snow houses would undoubtedly have been warmer than snow-banked tents. The evidence and the assumptions we have drawn about early Palaeoeskimo winter dwellings remain a subject of debate.

The Campview site is a good example of the need to understand the implications of a changing landscape. Today, the house ruins face a small, usually ice-choked bay, blocked to the east by a wide gravel bar flooded only during extremely high tides. Four thousand years ago, with a sea level substantially higher, the site location would have made a lot more sense. What is now a shallow bight would have been a deep, swiftly running tide channel, a polynya, in fact, that created a separate island out of the southern portion of Skraeling Island.

We have learned much about the pioneering Palaeoeskimos who ventured eastward from Alaska more than 4000 years ago. We know that some groups moved into the central and eastern Arctic while others headed into the High Arctic and Greenland. It was a time of higher sea levels and a somewhat different landscape; it was during the tail end of the Climatic Optimum, when annual temperatures were beginning to drop to levels more closely resembling those we experience today.

In the High Arctic and northern Greenland, the pioneering Palaeoeskimos, the Independence I people, ran into difficulties within a few hundred years or less, while their central and eastern Canadian cousins, the Pre-Dorset people, fared much better, at least in more economically viable regions. The pioneering Palaeoeskimos who migrated into more southerly regions of Greenland appear to have thrived for over a thousand years. Although the early Independence I and Saqqaq tool kits are distinctive enough to separate at a glance, they must, in large part, reflect the different lithic resources available to the two groups. As far as we can tell, the people used very similar hearth and dwelling structures, hunted much the same animals, and used a very similar tool kit. Saqqaq-related groups also decided to cross over to Ellesmere Island at a very early stage of the High Arctic occupation. Discovery of their sites in the Bache region and at Cape Faraday came as a surprise and led to considerable rethinking about prehistoric developments in the High Arctic.

5

Visitors from the Sunny Side

" NORTHERN WHEATEAR "   Brenda Carter

The northern wheatear must have been relieved to reach the open
water of the polynya. There had been little of that on the last part of
the long flight. For years the wheatear had migrated northward from
the land of the Druids to the land of ice and rocks. A thin thread of
smoke rose from a campfire near shore. Two people were beaching a
small skin boat full of dead birds. The wheatear had seen humans
in the land of eternal sun before, but never at this place. Across the
vast ocean, Druids were preparing to celebrate the summer solstice
at Stonehenge. In India, the Rig-Veda was being composed. At what
some people believed to be the centre of the world, the Cretan
civilization was flourishing; and western Siberia was on the verge
of entering the Bronze Age.

As early as 1907, the Norwegian researcher Ole Solberg published a description of stone tools from Greenland, concluding that at some time in the distant past there had existed an old Stone Age culture in West Greenland.[1] Because the Danish archaeologist Therkel Mathiassen considered all prehistoric finds in Greenland to be part of the Thule culture, Solberg's earlier observations lingered in obscurity until 1948. That year, a collection of stone tools from the small settlement of Saqqaq (*the sunny side* in Inuktitut) in the northern part of Disko Bay arrived at the Danish National Museum in Copenhagen. The tool assemblage was recognized as distinct and classified as the Saqqaq culture.[2] Initially, archaeologists believed the Saqqaq complex to be younger than Eigil Knuth's Independence I from North Greenland. More recent research, however, notably at Itivnera,[3] Qaja,[4] and Qeqertasussuk[5] in West Greenland, strongly suggests that the two expressions of the ASTt are of the same approximate vintage. The two last-mentioned sites have yielded skeletal remains of both dogs and humans, presently the oldest such evidence we have from the Arctic.[6]

The Disko Bay area of West Greenland is a good 1200 kilometres southeast of Ellesmere Island as the raven flies, and while the Independence I finds didn't surprise us, the discovery of Saqqaq material on the central east coast of Ellesmere Island did. The first evidence came our way more by chance than through planning. During the first field season, we were so overwhelmed by the number of archaeological sites in the area that we decided to extend the next season as much as possible, and so early June of 1979 found us once again on the plane to Resolute. Some years the snow disappears early from the Arctic shores and lowlands; other years, it doesn't. It's always a gamble. Unfortunately, it didn't work out as we hoped. If anything, the snowmelt occurred later than usual. We knew that there was a problem even as the jet approached Resolute Bay. Below us the sea ice was solid, and snow covered most of the land. The PCSP station manager, Fred Alt, reported that, if anything, conditions along the east coast of Ellesmere Island were even worse. Descending into Alexandra Fiord, we were greeted by a very white and still landscape. There was no problem finding a landing spot on the snow-covered sea ice below the RCMP station. With their usual foresight, PCSP personnel had provided us with a snowmobile and sled so we could get all our gear across the jumbled, broken shore ice and up to the station. Aware of the problems facing us, I had asked the pilot to fly along the fiords and bays before we landed to see if any coastal areas were free of snow.

On the north shore of Thorvald Peninsula, we spotted a tiny, snow-free gravel beach, which would be, of necessity, our first survey destination. The lateness of the season not only presented us with a site of considerable significance; it also taught us something about the nearby polynya. Being the only open water in the area, it was crowded with thousands of migratory birds and ducks. Obviously its importance was greatly strengthened during colder periods, whether they were seasonal or long-lasting episodes.

The June weather was fantastic: deep blue, cloudless skies swept by a brilliant sun that never touched the horizon. Everywhere on the ice, bunches of ringed seals crowded around breathing holes, ready to slide into the ocean at the first sign of danger. Polar bear tracks, strung out like a trap line, connected all the breathing holes, with occasional detours to the edge of open leads. My experience from three years of travelling on and through the ice in Cumberland Sound with Kanea Eetooangat now came in handy. We had available the same "Baffinland" combination of a small boat, a sled or *komatik*, and a snowmobile. During the first part of the season, the ice appeared so solid that the old RCMP boat was left behind. With field gear, food, and extra fuel securely loaded on the sled, we raced across the crusty, snow-covered ice. As long as we kept a steady speed, the seals paid little attention to our approach; then, with sudden alarm, they lunged for the breathing hole, a compact mass of sausages squeezing into a single breathing hole in the ice. Somehow they all managed to slip away by the time we passed. Having watched Kanea's careful study of ice conditions, I was aware of the danger of leads covered only by a thin and deceptively secure-looking layer of fresh snow. Leads, channels of water through a field of ice, have a habit of forming outward from headlands. As we approached the northeastern tip of Thorvald Peninsula, I slowed down, scanning the ice for any sign of open water. A slightly darker line in the snow gave the lead away. Slowly we approached, poking the snow ahead of us with a long pole brought for that purpose. Suddenly the pole met no resistance, slipping easily into dark waters. Luckily for us, the channel was narrow enough to jump with the snowmobile at full throttle.

In those days we lugged around a fairly cumbersome survey instrument called a Topometer, supposedly a state-of-the-art mechanism for mapping sites and pinpointing surface finds. It might have been handy in another situation; here, it was a heavy pain in the neck, although it did provide a name for the location: the *Topo site*. During the first visits only a small portion of the site was clear of snow, but it was enough to yield several distinctive burins and points, clearly associated with the Saqqaq complex. Willow charcoal from one of several hearths on the site produced a radiocarbon date of 1470 B.C.

The Topo site contained numerous single, isolated hearth features filled with boiling stones, a trait not often found on Independence I or Pre-Dorset sites, but closely associated with Saqqaq settlements in Greenland.

The Topo site finds made us aware of the complexity of cultural developments and population movements in the Smith Sound region. The artifacts were nearly all surface finds and the few well-defined structures on the site turned out to be the remains of old food caches or hearths. We had to find a location with good preservation and one or more well-preserved dwelling features. About a month later, on the northeastern tip of Knud Peninsula, we mapped and named the Bight site. Like most sites in the region, the Bight site was multicomponent, containing camp features at various levels above the present shoreline. The dwelling structures we were particularly interested in were located more than 20 metres above the present sea level, overlooking a small bight on the south side of the Flagler Bay polynya. Today, the height and the precipitous cliffs leading up to the site look forbidding to anyone wanting to get down to shore in a hurry. However, at the time the site was occupied, sea level would have been substantially higher, providing a less troublesome access.

The exposed location of the Bight Site, overlooking the Flagler Bay polynya, provided for many cold days of excavating. Along with the Topo site, the Bight site provided new insights into the complex cultural dynamics of population movements on both sides of the Smith Sound region.

The most well-defined of the two dwellings was Feature 1, an oval, gravel-walled structure measuring about 4 by 3 metres, situated about 22 metres above sea level. The main entrance appeared to be located on the north side facing the polynya, although, for some reason, the most productive midden area was found in the opposite direction, just behind the southwest wall. The gravel wall was 15 to 25 centimetres higher than the interior floor area, which was covered with sand and gravel. Over several seasons we excavated about 85 percent of the dwelling and a good deal of the midden, which had excellent preservation; close to 2000 bones were obtained from the structure and the midden. The interior of the dwelling was remarkable for its lack of distinct structures. There was no clearly defined fire hearth; only small concentrations of charred bone and wood near the centre indicated where cooking had taken place. Artifacts and waste flakes were scattered evenly through the interior; refuse bones were a little more concentrated in the southwestern half. The large midden area along the southwest wall, exposed to the afternoon sun and sheltered from cold prevailing northeasterly winds, suggested that many of the meals had been eaten outside.

Seasonality immediately comes to mind—a time when one could eat outside and perhaps enjoy the last rays of the fall sun. The refuse bones told their own story. Relatively few bird bones suggested a late fall occupation, which would go along with the use of an interior hearth for cooking, light, and heat. Much to our surprise, we didn't find any walrus bones in the refuse; yet, at present, hundreds of walrus arrive in the polynya in early July and remain there until late in the fall. Several reasons come to mind to explain the dearth of walrus remains. First, even if the polynya was present at the time of occupation, the higher sea level may have created a less favourable habitat for walrus. They are bottom feeders and seek their bivalve meals at certain depths. Second, it is also possible that the occupants of Feature 1 arrived in the area after the annual departure of the walrus. Finally, we have to consider the rather unlikely possibility that Saqqaq hunters did not possess the technological skills necessary to regularly hunt the large walrus.

Feature 1 failed to produce even a fragment of a harpoon head. Even so, the stone tools tell quite a story. The projectile points were made from a variety of materials, including argillite and green, light grey, and white cherts. That in itself was very different from what we had observed on Independence I sites, where light and dark grey cherts were selected very conservatively. The Bight site points were leaf-shaped (bipointed) and shouldered, common traits in both Independence I and Saqqaq assemblages. Two small, single side-notched arrowheads from the Bight site are quite rare in assemblages from this period. Unlike the Topo site burins, which were all ground on one or both sides, only one of the Feature 1 burins showed evidence of light grinding, and none of the spalls struck from the burins had been ground. Lack of grinding is an important attribute, because the process of grinding and polishing tools, particularly burins and gravers, is a Saqqaq element rarely associated with Independence I. Scraping tools (endscrapers) for cleaning hides were basically triangular in form. A study of all the local scraper assemblages indicated that the triangular form was more common during the early stages of the ASTt. Microblades constituted 11.5 percent of the Feature 1 artifacts and half of the blades showed evidence of use. The mean width of the blade sections is 6.3 millimetres, somewhat narrower than the 7.5 millimetre mean width for Independence I blade sections and more in line with the mean width of blades from slightly later occupations. The chert debitage in Feature 1 reflected the variety of materials noted in the finished forms, except for the greenish chert points, which may have been made elsewhere.

A small needle fragment was not very diagnostic, being fairly flat on one side and rounded on the other.

The tool kit used by the occupants of Feature 1 was clearly different from the Independence I assemblages, but we needed more evidence to settle the questions of who these people were and when they had used the Bight site. The evidence was only a few hundred metres away in the form of a very deteriorated dwelling, Feature 2. Soil movement had disturbed the original dwelling so much that we were not able to retrieve much information about the structure itself. On the other hand, the artifact yield was good and even included a harpoon head fragment. As far we could tell, the dwelling had measured about 3 by 4 metres and contained a slightly raised circular gravel wall. We excavated about 70 percent of the dwelling, encountering bedrock in several areas. There were small concentrations of charred remains, mostly bone, but no evidence of constructed fire hearths. The interior was crisscrossed by frost cracks, which undoubtedly had resulted in an artificial concentration of artifacts and debris.

Although the artifacts were fairly similar to the ones from Feature 1, some interesting differences pointed to a later occupation period. The shouldering of the projectile points was a little more pronounced. The harpoon head fragment of bone contained an off-centre line hole, an attribute seen on recently excavated Saqqaq harpoon heads from the Disko Bay area in West Greenland.[7] The stone tools were made from a variety of lithic sources, including argillite, a material very common in Greenlandic Saqqaq assemblages, where it is usually referred to as *angmaq*. Seven out of nine burins were ground and polished, compared to only one out of eight in Feature 1. Two needle fragments from Feature 2 had round eyes and a generally flat cross-section, elements that are characteristic of later ASTt assemblages.

Rather than clarifying the picture, the radiocarbon dates from the two features caused more confusion. The first date was run on driftwood charcoal from Feature 1. Although we were aware of the problem driftwood dates could present, we had little choice; charred sea mammal bones were thought to be even more unreliable. The small driftwood sample produced a date of about 1850 B.C. Many years later a muskox bone from the refuse area of Feature 1 was dated to about 1650 B.C., using the accelerator technique. The dates at least confirmed our conjecture that the Bight site had been occupied several centuries after the Independence I people had used the Lakeview and the Campview sites. Our assumption that Feature 2 had been used a good deal later than Feature 1 was not verified by radiocarbon dating. Just the opposite: the accelerator date of a muskox bone from Feature 2 gave us a date of about 1900 B.C. Had the dates been reversed, we would have been most pleased.

Regardless of the dates, the importance of the Bight site findings was the fact that we had identified an early Palaeoeskimo occupation distinctly different from Independence I and more closely related to the West Greenland Saqqaq complex. We were also intrigued by the fact that we had found no evidence of Independence I occupations in the vicinity of the Flagler Bay polynya. It is conceivable that the polynya did not exist at that time, or that warmer climatic conditions may have caused it to be much less important, with the surrounding seas and lakes becoming ice free much earlier in the spring.

Over the years we have located other sites in the area related to the Saqqaq people—not in great numbers, but enough to indicate that for many centuries the central east coast of Ellesmere Island was used occasionally by these

0   3 cm

A small assortment of tool types from Feature 2 on the Bight site. From left to right, top row: two shouldered, leaf-shaped points and a thin, straight-based and ground endblade; bottom row: a broken adze blade and a partially ground burin.

people as they shifted their settlements and hunting areas back and forth across Smith Sound and Kane Basin. We have found remains of their settlements as far south as Cape Faraday,[8] which suggests that their territorial expansion into the Canadian High Arctic may have extended at least as far south as Jones Sound.[9] In fact it was the discovery of some of these Saqqaq-related sites with rectangular, gravel-walled dwelling structures at Cape Faraday that made us return to a site on Thorvald Peninsula we had visited many years before. At the time of the first visit, we didn't understand its significance. Now we did, but that story belongs in the next chapter.

It can certainly be argued that we are splitting hairs when we separate Independence I and Saqqaq. After all, the Palaeoeskimos from these two complexes were basically part of the same initial migration eastward from Alaska.

But, as I stressed earlier, new environments and human inventiveness have a way of changing the cultural make-up. Small, perhaps seemingly insignificant, traits become the mold for all subsequent developments not influenced from the outside. What the Bight site evidence tells us is that at some stage, probably within a century or two of the initial High Arctic appearance of the ASTt, some degree of intermingling of Independence I and Saqqaq took place in the Smith Sound region. So far, there is no evidence of this amalgamation north of the Bache Peninsula region or in the far northern regions of Greenland. Those areas appear to have been abandoned early in the Palaeoeskimo continuum. The Smith Sound region and the Greenlandic side of Baffin Bay were economically more viable and capable of sustaining scattered Palaeoeskimo groups between 1800 and 1100 B.C.

We know something about the lives of these Palaeoeskimo pioneers, the Independence I and the Saqqaq people. We are familiar with their tool kits and dwelling styles, the animals they hunted, and the ones they didn't. The last point is as important as the first, because it speaks directly to one of the topics that fascinates us; how ready were these Arctic pioneers to live in the environment they chose to enter? At least one measure of such readiness is the extent to which they hunted the available animal species. We suspect some deficiencies and know of others. During the first three thousand years or more of human occupation in the Arctic, the large bowhead whales were in no danger of being actively pursued. As far as we can tell, the Palaeoeskimo hunters did not have the technology required to hunt large whales in the open sea. The carcass of a dead whale, drifted ashore, was undoubtedly utilized as much as possible; but as a rule, that major food resource was beyond reach. Muskoxen and caribou were relatively easy prey as long as good bows and lances were available. The remaining terrestrial animals could be trapped or snared. Smaller sea mammals, like ringed seals, were harpooned from skin boats or at the breathing holes or the ice edge. A quick look at refuse bones from early Palaeoeskimo middens proves how important the smaller seals were. Hunting larger sea mammals like walrus, beluga, and narwhals required more sophisticated watercraft skills, but was occasionally done.

The location of the early Palaeoeskimo sites in the Bache Peninsula region reflects a predominant reliance on sea mammal hunting, particularly ringed seals. The often acclaimed Independence I emphasis on muskox hunting is clearly a phenomenon limited geographically to areas that can support these animals.

In a relatively marginal region like the High Arctic, it is unlikely that prehistoric hunters would have dared to rely so heavily on an animal scarce in numbers and easy to kill off.

The Palaeoeskimo summer camps were usually located on older, elevated beach terraces that were exposed to the weather, but provided good views of the surrounding ice and seas. Also associated with summer activities are single, slab-lined box hearths, usually filled with boiling stones. The more substantial house remains, slightly excavated into the ground and surrounded by raised gravel walls, were used later in the fall, when protection from the elements was important, as were light and heat from interior hearths. We can speculate on the extent to which any of these early Palaeoeskimo groups used snow houses. Since they did not appear to cache any substantial supplies of food near their fall camps, the use of snow houses closer to the ice edge later in the winter seems plausible.

The total Palaeoeskimo population in the Far North was undoubtedly small; this was a danger in itself, as the accidental loss of one or more of the best hunters could easily threaten the survival of the group. Nothing gives you much sense of security in the lives of these people: no permanency, no large settlements, usually one or two extended families travelling and hunting together. Even at the best of times, the peril of starvation was never far away; it was a most challenging existence, truly on the edge of survival. Luckily for the Palaeoeskimo people as a whole, conditions were not quite that severe in all Arctic regions. Had they been, the whole cultural tradition would probably have ended within a few centuries after leaving Alaska. The pioneering ASTt people who decided to cross Smith Sound and head southward along the west coast of Greenland entered a much more ecologically viable environment. In southeast and particularly southwest Greenland, the Saqqaq culture thrived for at least 1100 years, until about 900 B.C. when it seems to have disappeared. According to Danish archaeologists like Bjarne Grønnow and Jørgen Meldgaard, there appears to have been an interruption in cultural continuity in West Greenland between 900 and 500 B.C.[10] When cultural materials appeared once again, there was a clear-cut change in tool types, suggesting an arrival of the Dorset people. If we shift our attention back to Ellesmere Island, we can see that the picture is not altogether dissimilar. The Saqqaq-related sites gave way to late Pre-Dorset occupations about 1100 to 1000 B.C.; a transition followed, which culminated in the arrival about 800 B.C. of the early Dorset Palaeoeskimos, whose occupation of the Bache region terminated about 700 to 600 B.C. In time, I suspect—as do some of the Danish archaeologists—that prehistoric sites spanning the Saqqaq to Pre-Dorset to early Dorset transition will be found in West Greenland.

It is hardly a coincidence that the decline and termination of the Greenlandic Saqqaq period coincide with the first appearance of Pre-Dorset people on the east coast of Ellesmere Island. As the third branch of the pioneering ASTt family, these people had managed very well, particularly in ecologically rich areas such as the Igloolik region, southern Baffin Island and even the east coast of Labrador, where they initially rubbed shoulders with the Indians of the Maritime Archaic culture.[11]

It took a surprisingly long while for the Pre-Dorset Palaeoeskimos to be enticed into the Smith Sound region, particularly since older Pre-Dorset sites are known from northern Baffin Island[12] and parts of western and northeastern Devon Island.[13] Perhaps they needed the economic enticement created by better environmental conditions. As mentioned earlier, the end of the Climatic Optimum about 5000 years ago brought the Northern Hemisphere into a long, slow cooling trend. Occasionally conditions improved, the result of normal oscillations in the climatic record. One of these episodes was a relatively short-lived, but significant warming trend, which may have improved hunting conditions enough to tempt the Pre-Dorset hunters to migrate northward along the east coast of Ellesmere Island. For reasons not easily understood, this same time period did not favour the Saqqaq people. Their lengthy occupation in Greenland was coming to an end. Perhaps they suffered a fate similar to their Independence I cousins, whom they themselves had assimilated in the High Arctic. Conceivably the Saqqaq people were assimilated by the Pre-Dorset and early Dorset Palaeoeskimos.

6

The Arctic Renaissance

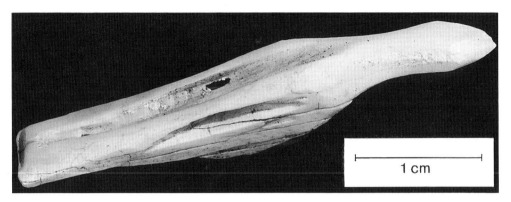

1 cm

A 30-millimetre-long ivory figurine from the late Pre-Dorset Ridge site, Feature 2. The more than 3000-year-old carving may portray a falcon in flight and may originally have had two moveable wings set into the grooved and perforated sides of the carving.

The falcon was curious enough to swoop down low over the camp one more time. An old man looked up and smiled before concentrating once again on the tiny ivory figurine he was carving. Last year he had spotted the falcon's nest high up on a cliff wall but had failed to reach it. No doubt the falcon had learned to be wary of humans. The old man held out the carving, studying the incised grooves where the short, thin wings would be attached.

Few hunters frequented the east coast of Ellesmere Island between 1500 and 1100 B.C. Occasionally one or two Saqqaq families travelled across Smith Sound from Greenland, but they left few traces. They may not have been around when the first Pre-Dorset families arrived in the Bache Peninsula region. Since we have found many Pre-Dorset sites that show no evidence of interaction with Saqqaq hunters, it may have been decades before the two groups met.

The northward movement of the Pre-Dorset Palaeoeskimos took place at a time of considerable cultural activity in the Canadian Arctic. Artifact styles and settlement patterns underwent relatively fast changes as people migrated farther afield than before. The late stage of the Pre-Dorset period was about to evolve into what archaeologists have termed the Dorset culture. The separation of one cultural stage from another within the same tradition is often somewhat arbitrary.

In a highly mobile society, where survival is based on seasonal and longer-term migrations from one region to another, cultural changes must be analyzed using a very broad database. One archaeological site or even a number of sites in a region will rarely provide a full picture of past cultural developments. In the case of Pre-Dorset and Dorset, most Arctic archaeologists feel that a sufficient number of cultural elements changed to warrant the distinction.[1] For the first time since the initial arrival of Palaeoeskimos on the east coast of Ellesmere Island, the Smith Sound region was again occupied by ASTt families from the central and eastern Canadian Arctic. It seems that once this old migration route had been reactivated, cultural impulses continued to flow northward for several centuries, reaching well beyond Smith Sound into northeast Greenland and down the west coast south of Melville Bay.

In many ways, this period of heightened cultural activity is one of the more difficult to understand, not only in the High Arctic but throughout the Palaeoeskimo territory, from Labrador and Newfoundland in the east to Banks Island in the west. Cultural developments which had been progressing at a conservative rate shifted into higher gear. People were on the move, reoccupying old territories and venturing into new ones. All this commotion was bound to result in encounters between peoples whose material, social, and spiritual ways were different—some populations, like the Saqqaq people, had lived for centuries in their own isolated world. Apparently the westward extension of Palaeoeskimo territory also resulted in renewed contact with people representing Alaskan cultural developments.[2] Although we need additional empirical data to be certain, a western influence in the Pre-Dorset/Dorset transition remains a strong possibility.

We discovered the first evidence of Pre-Dorset people on the shores of the Flagler Bay polynya in 1978. The Ridge site, we called it—a fairly unimaginative name, once we dropped the original prefix "mosquito" after discovering that the midsummer plague of these pests was far worse on most other sites in the area. The Ridge site features were located in several gently sloping gullies leading up from shore. Surface finds from dwelling structures located between 14 and 24 metres above sea level encouraged us to work extensively on the site. Cultural features ranged from barely discernible stone and boulder tent ring outlines to slightly more notable structures, isolated hearths, and food caches. The most prominent structure, the one that first caught our attention, was Feature 2, a large, circular dwelling nearly 6 metres in diameter. Although many of the stones and boulders were no longer in their original position, we could perceive some

Outline of the dwelling structure, Feature 2 on Ridge site overlooking the Flagler Bay polynya.

sort of axial configuration in the interior; nothing like the distinctive, slab-lined axial dwellings from Independence I sites, but an interior spatial arrangement that divided the circular structure into halves. We found no clear evidence of definable hearth structures, only small concentrations of charcoal both inside and outside the dwelling. Over several seasons we excavated the entire structure, as well as a large part of the adjacent midden. Within the dwelling, artifacts were found from the surface to a depth of 8 centimetres, generally scattered throughout except for a distinct concentration of tool fragments and waste flakes located along the northeast and southwest peripheries of the structure. We were intrigued by the style and relative numbers of certain artifacts in Feature 2. For one thing, we found that microblades and burins constituted 58 percent of the total assemblage, in sharp contrast to the Saqqaq sites, where microblades were almost nonexistent. And, unlike the Saqqaq people, who used a variety of lithic sources, the Ridge site toolmakers used light- to medium-grey cherts almost exclusively: an interesting return to the same conservative use of lithic material we had noticed on Independence I sites.

The large number of used microblades in Feature 2 indicated that the inhabitants had been busy manufacturing clothing. Another diagnostic attribute was the considerable variety in size and shape of burins and the fact that not a single one showed the slightest evidence of grinding, which easily distinguished them from most Saqqaq specimens. The many scraping implements were all unifacial (retouched on one side only), and included triangular endscrapers and asymmetric and concave sidescrapers. We found four sideblades—thinly retouched flakes used as cutting blades inset in grooved antler or bone handles. The needle fragments were primarily flat in cross section, although a couple of specimens were of a more rounded form. One needle section with an eye was flat and pointed. The eye was incised and elongated, another attribute identifying the assemblage as late Pre-Dorset. Feature 2 also yielded a sharpened hare tooth (incisor) and the beautifully carved ivory bird figurine illustrated at the beginning of the chapter. Carvings from this time period are rare and important as fragile testaments to the artistic abilities from this period, which led to the Dorset culture, renowned for its skillful expressions of spirituality.

In spite of poor organic preservation, we collected over 400 bone fragments, of which we could identify nearly half. About 80 percent were from small seals. The number of bird bones was remarkably small, suggesting a late fall occupation when the polynya was no longer teeming with waterfowl. The situation was remarkably similar to the one we had discovered on the Bight site only half a kilometre away. With the exception of one small skull fragment in a nearby feature, walrus bones were missing, although a few ivory chips and the bird carving indicated some exploitation of walrus, perhaps elsewhere at some other stage of the seasonal cycle.

We excavated another Pre-Dorset construction on the Ridge site: not a dwelling, but an interesting series of hearths and meat platforms built up with flat stones, conveniently sheltered behind a vertical cliff wall not far below Feature 2. I mention this feature because, later in time, the use of extensive rows of hearths and platforms became an impressive part of the cultural life of the late Dorset people. The idea of using joint cooking units obviously went far back in time. Two radiocarbon dates from the interior of Feature 2 gave us more headaches than clarity. The first, run on charred bone, produced a date of about 750 B.C., while the second, run on charred willow, resulted in a date of about 1500 B.C. Neither date matches the material evidence, which suggests an occupation between 1100 and 1000 B.C.

The distribution of Pre-Dorset sites indicates that, as in earlier times, people camped close to the sea. Not surprisingly, bone remains in the middens show no real change in subsistence practices. Sea mammals, especially small ringed seals, continued to provide the primary food source. The lifeways of the Pre-Dorset and the Saqqaq people were obviously not as different as their tool kits. As we have seen, the Saqqaq people had little use for microblades. There may be a good explanation for the latter phenomenon. On their way south along the west coast of Greenland, they would undoubtedly have come across several large iron meteorites in the vicinity of Cape York. We can speculate that, as cutting blades, pieces of meteoritic iron supplanted chert microblades. The Pre-Dorset people, being new to the Smith Sound region, had yet to encounter the meteoritic iron or the people familiar with it.

There is no way of knowing how long it took before the two Palaeoeskimo groups met, although evidence from Cape Faraday and the Bache Peninsula region suggests that they did, perhaps not long after the Ridge site occupations.[3] We first discovered the Beacon site on Thorvald Peninsula in 1978. Twelve years went by before we understood the significance of the site and returned to excavate one of the dwelling features. The incentive to revisit the Beacon site resulted from the excavation and testing of several unusual, subrectangular, gravel-walled house structures at Cape Faraday in 1989. Not only were the Cape Faraday dwellings a bit unusual, but the associated artifacts showed an interesting mixture of Saqqaq and Pre-Dorset elements. A look through old field notes confirmed that the earliest Beacon dwellings were very similar to the Cape Faraday features. Now we wanted to see if the artifacts also pointed to a similar Saqqaq/Pre-Dorset interaction.

The Beacon site had been used on many different occasions. The features we were interested in were located on a gently sloping plateau between 20 and 28 metres above sea level, which provided a splendid view of Buchanan Bay. On the east side, the plateau ends in a series of steep cliffs, while on the north side, a more gently angled path provides easier access to the site. Eight of the features were easily separated into four units, each consisting of two dwellings and associated middens. On a fairly random basis we chose to excavate Feature 8, a rectangular, gravel-walled dwelling measuring 3.5 by 3.0 metres. There was no evidence of any central hearth construction, but, as in the case of the excavated Cape Faraday house, there was a well-defined and fairly deep "hearth pit" in the centre of Feature 8. A large number of small pieces of charred driftwood were found within a 1 metre radius of the pit. The refuse area below Feature 8 also contained large amounts of driftwood charcoal and only a few charred pieces of

Eric Damkjar and Karen McCullough excavating Feature 10A on one of the largest Palaeoeskimo sites at Cape Faraday. Artifacts from this structure verified a strong Saqqaq influence of the Palaeoeskimo occupations of eastern Ellesmere Island.

bone—a sharp contrast to earlier Palaeoeskimo sites, where bone seemed to have been the primary fuel source. The chance of driftwood appearing in the Bache region is closely related to the extent of open water in the fall. Warmer climatic episodes with longer periods of open water undoubtedly resulted in greater amounts of driftwood being deposited in the inner bays and fiords. This scenario fits very well with the timing of the Beacon site occupation, which was radiocarbon dated on charred willow to about 1200 B.C. Since dates on willow are often too old, it is possible that the Beacon and the Ridge site occupations overlapped.[4]

With the arrival of the Pre-Dorset Palaeoeskimos, the High Arctic entered a period of cultural blossoming that involved the diffusion of traits and probably the amalgamation of populations associated with the final stages of the Saqqaq and the Pre-Dorset episodes. The people involved in these amalgamations didn't cease being Palaeoeskimos; they just blended cultural traits they had developed during the more than 1000-year interval since their geographical separation took place. Our attempt to interpret the rapid cultural developments of this period in the Smith Sound region was further complicated by the appearance of additional cultural impulses from the central and eastern Canadian Arctic, which culminated with the appearance of early Dorset people. The blending of all these elements over a relatively short time created a distinctive High Arctic transitional culture which some investigators refer to as Independence II.[5]

To distinguish the origin of cultural elements such as house styles and tool types in a specific area, it is crucial to locate "uncontaminated" sites: sites occupied by people who have just arrived in a new area and have yet to mingle with anyone else in the region. The Ridge site was such a location. We were equally fortunate to find a similarly undisturbed "pioneering" site used by early Dorset immigrants to the Smith Sound region. Remarkably enough, the site was one of the first ones we had discovered in 1978. Having landed all our equipment and food supplies at the Alexandra Fiord RCMP station, we had a couple of days to spend before the helicopter arrived to transfer everything to the base camp at Knud Peninsula. We decided to look for sites along the coast east of the station and set out on a pleasant walk along a beach terrace fronting the broad Twin Glacier valley. Our destination was a rocky headland and several small islands that had provided shelter for Nares's two ships, the *Alert* and the *Discovery*, during their one-night stay on the coast in 1875.[6] Without too much difficulty, we crossed a wide river delta dissected by numerous meltwater channels fed by the two massive glaciers at the head of the valley. Later in the season, the crossing became a real challenge as the 24-hour summer sun transformed glacial ice into torrents of milky white meltwater.

Past the delta we noticed a prominent, old beach ridge just below the steep cliffs that are part of the eastern mountain range framing the valley. The gravel ridge was bordered by reddish, Precambrian bedrock that formed a series of terraces down toward the first open leads in the bright, frozen ocean. We could see that when the ice broke up, there would be easy access to the sea regardless of the state of the tide. The place had been used in more recent times, probably during the occupation of the RCMP station. Scattered among the cliffs and boulders we found several disarticulated walrus skeletons, which included several large baculi, or penis bones, as they are more commonly known; thus, the Baculum site was named. The most prominent ridge, about 12 metres above sea level, was covered with chert flakes and old bone fragments. No sooner had we settled down to brew some tea and eat a bit of lunch, than the sunshine and the pleasantly mild breezes from the valley gave way to clouds and shifting winds, bringing a chill wind from the frozen sea. Although we didn't know it at the time, it was an omen; from then on, it seemed as though whenever we worked on the Baculum site, we were cold. It isn't just a matter of poor memory; photos from the site always show us at work, clad in every warm piece of clothing we had brought along.

We set out two main test grids covering areas particularly rich in debris. There were no clear signs of dwellings, just concentrations of stone chips and

pieces of bone in, around, and beneath boulders of all sizes and shapes. Only the year before we had found the first traces of early Dorset occupations in the High Arctic on a small island between Little Cornwallis and Bathurst Islands;[7] now we were about to repeat the discovery, this time within sight of Greenland. We didn't have long to wait. On the second day, we recovered the evidence we needed in the shape of a very deteriorated, but recognizable harpoon head of ivory and the tip of a perfectly ground burin. It was a great day, which even the cold wind couldn't spoil. There was enough left of the harpoon head to identify it as a type called Tyara Sliced II, originally discovered by William E. Taylor, Jr. on the early Dorset Tyara site in northern Ungava, and thought to date to about 800 B.C.[8] Similar harpoon heads had also been recovered in the Igloolik region, where they are likewise thought to be from about 800 B.C.

2cm

The Tyara Sliced harpoon head found at the Baculum site.

The Baculum site had provided hunters with easy and relatively early access to open water between the main coast and Skraeling Island, just north of the site. Not surprisingly, sea mammal bones constituted by far the largest percentage of faunal remains on the site. The Tyara and another large harpoon head indicated that the hunters sought larger sea mammals, like beluga or narwhal, which we had occasionally observed in these waters in early August. Bird bones and the seemingly unsheltered workshops suggested that the site had been used as a hunting camp during late summer and early fall. As was the case on the Ridge site, microblades again turned out to be the largest artifact category on the Baculum site. The blades were narrower, with a mean width of only 5.9 millimetres, and more than 30 percent showed clear evidence of use. We also found a great variety of burins, from completely flaked to mostly ground specimens. The burin spalls reflected the same variation. On such a terrace, you can never be absolutely certain that you are not picking up a few artifacts from earlier occupations. The different burin types could be the result of multiple site use; however, they could also reflect the transitional nature of burin manufacture at this time. Either way, there was a strong link between the late Pre-Dorset finds from the Ridge site and the early Dorset material from the Baculum site. Several bifacially flaked points with shallow notching and flared, straight, or slightly concave bases strengthened the connection to the earlier Ridge site occupation. The distinctiveness of the Baculum assemblage was also evident from the lack of some early Dorset elements usually seen in the central Arctic, such as triangular, tip-fluted endblades and implements made of slate. Over 84 percent of the waste flakes on the site consisted of small retouch flakes, indicating extensive rejuvenation and final retouch work. A radiocarbon date on charred plant material came out at about 800 B.C. Judging by the harpoon head types, give or take a hundred years, the date is probably a good estimate for the occupation of the site.

The discovery of the Baculum site was followed by the location of many other early Dorset sites, especially on nearby Skraeling Island.[9] On the AST #5 site, we could see how the early Dorset people, like their Pre-Dorset predecessors, were being influenced by Saqqaq elements. It took some time before we understood the full importance of this site, which was initially not much to look at: small concentrations of waste flakes, fragments of microblades, and the vague outline of an old tent ring. That impression changed one evening. Our camp routine often included an evening hike to look for new sites when the low angle of the night sun cast longer shadows, revealing constructions not readily seen during the day. We were just about to walk past AST #5 when we noticed two, thin, parallel stone edges barely sticking out of the sandy ground. Subsequent excavation revealed a rectangular, box-like structure, about 1.7 metres long and 65 centimetres wide, with sides made from thin, upright stone slabs. Inside, two small flagged platforms were separated by grease-saturated soil and fine sand, making this undoubtedly the hearth feature. Pieces of charred wood and bone were found scattered within and outside the structure. In Pearyland, northeast Greenland, Eigil Knuth had found similar "hearth passages," as he called them, some associated with Independence I and some associated with his Independence II culture.[10]

The second excavated feature on AST #5 was a round-to-oval, vaguely defined axial structure measuring about 2.5 by 3.0 metres. The central portion contained

The Flagler Bay polynya in early June—an Arctic oasis with dependable food resources.

Lonesome George, a regular visitor to our excavations on Knud Peninsula.

Our base camp on the north shore of Knud Peninsula.

A late Dorset tool cache from Knud Peninsula.

The upper section of a 68-metre-long late Dorset hearth row on Longhouse site.

Using a bipod to photograph hearth row features.

The 1990 joint Greenlandic and Canadian team excavating a late Dorset communal structure on Knud Peninsula.

The excavated box-hearth feature on site AST#5, Skraeling Island. The excavation is one metre wide.

the remains of what appeared to be a collapsed hearth structure. The following season we located another ASTt site on Skraeling Island with a similar combination of features, suggesting contemporaneity of these two structural types.

The discovery of early Dorset sites in the Bache Peninsula region shows that Palaeoeskimos continued to move between the Central and the High Arctic after the initial late Pre-Dorset migration. There are strong indications that both the Pre-Dorset and the early Dorset people came into contact and probably amalgamated with the Saqqaq people, producing the hybrid Palaeoeskimo culture sometimes referred to as Independence II. Usage of the designation "Independence II," however, tends to obscure a very significant period of Palaeoeskimo history, when long-distance migrations along the shores of Ellesmere Island and North Greenland resulted in the meeting of Palaeoeskimo groups who had previously lived in isolation from each other. Independence II did not simply evolve directly out of Independence I, as the name implies; it required the important intermediary evolution of the Saqqaq culture and eventually the infusion of Pre-Dorset and early Dorset traits from the central and eastern Canadian Arctic. It is a distinct possibility that the fusion of Pre-Dorset, early Dorset, and Saqqaq elements in the Smith Sound region or elsewhere in the Far North trickled southward along the west coast of Greenland, replacing what had been a distinctive Saqqaq culture.

What were some of the important factors that triggered this extraordinary level of human activity in the Far North? One ingredient has already been alluded to: climate change. There is good evidence that the Northern Hemisphere experienced a fairly short-lived warming trend sometime between 1000 and 700 B.C.[11] That this warming occurred at about the time of the Pre-Dorset/ early Dorset cultural florescence cannot be only a coincidence. Within a few centuries, however, the climate swung back to earlier, colder patterns. Months, years, and decades became less and less sympathetic to the hunters and their families. Eventually the far northern regions could no longer sustain even small groups of Palaeoeskimos. The time of impressive long-distance travels to remote and distant regions in the Far North was over for the time being. The High Arctic renaissance turned into a truly dark age as far as the Palaeoeskimos were concerned; the comparatively richer shores of West Greenland were eventually abandoned a few centuries later. Campsites remained silent year after year, century after century. From the perspective of an overpopulated world, it is remarkable that the Bache Peninsula region and probably most of the High Arctic and northern Greenland witnessed no human activity during the following 1200 years.

7

Silent Shores

"RINGED PLOVER"
Brenda Carter

It had been a strenuous flight all the way from Africa. The ringed plover was lucky to reach open water late in the spring; even now the polynya was not very large, and the lakes were still frozen over. The plover rested on top of a large pile of built-up stones, one of many along the shore. Once, a long time ago, humans had obviously lived in the area. During their absence, the Chou Dynasty came to an end, and Lao-Tse speculated about the reality of dreams and butterflies. Buddhism spread to Japan, Mayan astronomy reached its peak, Plato delivered his dialogues, Alexander the Great invaded India, and the Great Wall was completed in China. There was not a human to be found on Ellesmere Island when Jesus Christ was born, or when the Romans invaded Britain and Attila invaded Italy— not even when the Goths reached Rome and the Norwegians settled the Shetland and Orkney Islands.

To say that the High Arctic shores were silent just because people were absent is of course an appalling distortion of the truth; a reflection, perhaps, of the times we live in, when most noise is related to human activities. Ellesmere Island was far from silent, especially in the summer, when the shores of the polynya reverberated with the intimidating bellowing of lustful walrus drifting back and forth on soiled ice floes. Loons flying overhead still

81

sounded like cranky, old motors refusing to run smoothly, while the seductive cooing of eiders and distinctive call of oldsquaws filled the calm, sunlit summer nights. Long before the arrival of other long-distance flyers, the snow buntings heard the first drops of melting snow, the first trickle of running water, the first rush of wind through exposed sedges.

High in the cliffs sat the permanent resident of silent places, the black guardian of spirits and souls, the raven, watching them all. Indifferent to the changing seasons, when others fled, it was well aware that even in the dead of winter the shores were far from silent. The eternal movement of tides worked constantly and noisily to break the grip of the frozen sea as it clung tenaciously to rocky shores. In the fall, errant icebergs, descendants of Greenlandic glaciers, were led astray by currents and drifted into Buchanan Bay. Some escaped; others were held back by rocky ledges, grounded until thickening fast ice imprisoned them for the winter. The contact point between berg and fast ice was rarely silent, constantly fractured by the eternal fall and rise of the tides, a favourite haunt for polar bears hoping to catch an inattentive seal coming up for air.

For some time after the last people had left, foxes and bears visited the abandoned camps in search of scraps of food scattered about. The smell from abandoned houses and middens would have sent a signal far and wide. On more than one occasion, we have arrived in the spring to find that last year's excavations of Thule culture dwellings had been visited by bears and foxes. One would not have thought 800-year-old food remains to be much of a meal.

The land and the seas were not silent; there were just no human ears to hear the sounds. For centuries, winds swept the old campsites, covering them in cold, dry winter snow until the sun's rays warmed the land during brief summer intervals. While flowers exploded in brilliant colours, seasonal visitors flew in from distant places to join the hectic summer activities, courting, nesting, hatching, guarding, and encouraging flight before escape was no longer an option and water again turned to ice. With disappointing haste, heather and willow leaves were painted a golden brown, a warning and a signal for many to chase the sun on its journey south. Year after year, century after century, the routine was the same, and still, spring did not entice human hunters to the polynya. Only polar bears waited patiently at the breathing holes while foxes kept their distance, hoping to scavenge a morsel or two if the hunt was successful. There were no children chasing seagulls or building playhouses near the shore; no women busily preparing skins and sewing warm garments for the coming winter. The old campsites were silent.

Kayak supports on the south shore of the Flagler Bay polynya.

The earth spun on its axis, held onto the moon, and danced around the sun while growing a little older. Centuries rolled by while humanity carried on in its usual haphazard fashion, variously brilliant and brutal: stimulated intellectually and spiritually, while enslaved by barbaric conquests and power struggles.

But there were changes on the horizon. The Northern Hemisphere was about to shake off its long dominance by colder conditions. Perhaps it is no coincidence that the world was entering a new climatic phase, the Neo-Atlantic, about the time Vikings set sail for the shores of England and Ireland.[1] Although not as pronounced and long-lived as the Climatic Optimum, the Neo-Atlantic period between A.D. 800 and 1200 was warmer than the present, resulting in a greater extent and duration of open water in the Arctic, conditions favourable for larger sea mammals like whales and walrus.[2] For the ringed seals, however, warmer conditions meant less fast ice suitable for breeding and denning, resulting in smaller population numbers and individual sizes. Once again the tree line moved northward, and more Siberian driftwood reached the High Arctic shores.

Nearly 1200 years had passed since the last Palaeoeskimo families had camped on the shores of the High Arctic and Greenland. If anyone did enter the Far North during this long cultural hiatus, we have found no evidence of their presence. Yet in the central and eastern Arctic and Subarctic, as far away as Labrador and Newfoundland, the Dorset culture had continued to evolve.[3] The Palaeoeskimo tradition was transmitted from generation to generation while the far northern settlements lay abandoned. The varied territorial range of the Dorset people, their migratory habits, and their societal structures enabled them to survive. Their numbers were sufficient to carry on and transmit their cultural knowledge from family to family, from one region to the next, even when a significant part of their territory became too marginal to sustain them. In time, dwelling styles and tools, particularly harpoon heads, looked a little different, while the ceremonial and spiritual aspects of their lives became greatly ritualized. In the High Arctic, the stage was set for the final appearance of the Palaeoeskimos.

8

The Shamans Gather

BAIRD'S SANDPIPER"

The sandpiper flew quickly over the many people gathered along a long row of smoking hearths and landed on the sandy shore of a nearby lake. An old man sat quietly on a large boulder. They watched each other. The man was clad in a long, greasy skin coat decorated with many small ivory figurines. The sandpiper was worn out by its long journey from the steamy, hot jungles far to the south. In the large urban centres on the coast of Peru, the pre-Inca Chimu empire was showing signs of decline. Farther north, Mayan temples and cities were flourishing, even though excessive warfare between city states and resource exploitation threatened the general welfare of the society.

It was early August 1977; the midnight sun barely escaped the mountain peaks on the northern horizon. Our helicopter survey flight was coming to an end when I asked if we could spend just a few more minutes looking for the site Otto Sverdrup had called Eskimobyen.[1] It was supposed to be situated on the northeast coast of the peninsula now directly beneath us. Ahead was the dark blue water of the polynya. The pilot, Greg Curtis, was an old acquaintance who had once accompanied me on an archaeological field trip in Cumberland Sound. As he brought the helicopter around, we were low enough to excite a bundled mass of walrus on the ice floes below us. All along the shore we noticed tent rings, kayak supports, and large stone caches. We were looking at a very special place, rich in both food resources and cultural remains. Suddenly we passed directly over a heavily vegetated area full of large sod house ruins and bleached whale bones, probably the site mentioned by Sverdrup. We flew another couple of kilometres along the coast before deciding to turn back to have a closer look at Eskimobyen. Greg banked the helicopter sharply to the left, the side I was on. As we turned, I found myself staring directly down at a most unusual, stone-walled structure: obviously not a natural arrangement of stones. The descent was rather fast; Greg was as eager as the rest of us to have a closer look. As soon as it was safe to duck under the slowing rotor blades, we rushed over to the mysterious structure, which stood out distinctly in the long midnight shadows. A few bleached harpoon heads on the ground told the story; we had found the occupation that brought an end to the long cultural silence in the High Arctic. Before us were the remains of one of the largest late Dorset communal structures ever found in the Arctic.[2] On our reluctant return to the helicopter, we noticed a long row of stone features, but could not guess its purpose.

That late-night flight in 1977 and the discovery of what we later called the Longhouse site set the stage for many exciting seasons of fieldwork along the adjacent coast. The setting of our base camp on Knud Peninsula was a barren, rocky, sun-baked landscape dotted with countless small lakes ready to deliver a horrific population of mosquitos as soon as the water temperatures rose sufficiently to encourage them to take flight. Usually that didn't take long. By early July, the northeast coast of Knud Peninsula became a surprisingly hot and sunny place. On days when no wind stirred, only an escape out onto the ice foot, attached to the rocky shoreline, provided temporary relief from the mosquitos. Here we could sit for a while watching the eager little pests suddenly lose energy as they reached the cool air over the ice—a minor but important victory.

It was late evening by the time the first base camp was set up in 1978. Our equipment and supplies had been placed in a large rope net and transported from Alexandra Fiord to Knud Peninsula by helicopter. As soon as the tents were pitched and the gear was sorted, we set out in the soft light of the Arctic summer night. Our first destination was the large, stone-walled structure Tore and I had visited ever so briefly the previous August. Along the way, we came across an endless number of ancient camp remains, tent rings, hearths, caches, and kayak supports. Not far from our own camp, we discovered the remains of yet another stone-walled, late Dorset communal structure. Other amazing features in the rocky landscape were long rows of stones—not just the one we had seen on the first visit, but many others in various stages of completeness. During the winter, we had often speculated about what they could be. We hiked up the gentle slope of a small ridge that separated us from the area where we had seen the longhouse the year before; it had not been a late-night, imaginary vision; the long stone walls were as outstanding as I remembered them. Just as we started down toward the structure, we stumbled over a long row of stones and boulders. This row was particularly distinct, extending in a long, slightly curved line down a gentle gravel slope. The function of this row was obvious. Before us was a series of rectangular, slab-lined cooking hearths, each with its own adjoining stone platform, probably for the meat about to be cooked. One unit joined the next, sometimes platform against platform, at other times hearth against hearth. Such features had never been reported from late Dorset sites; yet in this area they were numerous and clearly associated with large communal structures. Filled with new impressions, we hiked up to the top of a prominent ridge behind the lowlands where all the sites appeared to be concentrated. Even on the old terrace, far above sea level, we found remains of human activity in the form of large stone caches. For the longest time we sat silently, marveling at the spectacular landscape before us. The dark blue waters of the polynya teemed with eiders, oldsquaws, terns, and gulls. While some walrus floated on the surface, filling their lungs with air for the next feeding rush to the bottom, others rested in big heaps on ice floes, drifting slowly with the tidal currents. Three loons flew low overhead with their strident calls reverberating off the cliff walls of a small lake near our camp. The lake was instantly named Echo Lake. We should have called it Three Loon Lake, because every summer the lake was home to three noisy red-throated loons.

The night was vibrant with the sounds of life; small wonder people had chosen this as their annual gathering place year after year. Below us, among cliffs and boulders, was our own little cluster of brightly coloured tents. It had been difficult to find a spot not used by ancient campers. When we did find a

Overhead view of the most prominent hearth row on Longhouse site.

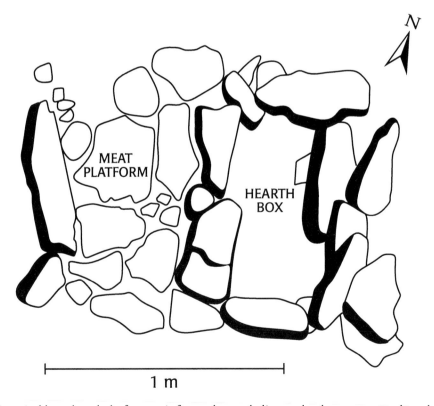

A typical hearth and platform unit from what we believe to be the most recent hearth row on Longhouse site.

"clean" location, we wondered why no one had used it before. Was there something wrong with the place? Was this akin to the experience in Cumberland Sound, when the small, grass-covered bench below steep cliffs became the bottom of a waterfall during a rainy night? No; the Knud Peninsula base camp turned out to be just fine and remained so for many years.

By the time we returned to camp, the sun was well on its way into the eastern sky. Every field season it took us a little while to become accustomed to sunlit nights. Without darkness, there were no stars to be seen and only occasionally the faint glimpse of a pale moon. It was tempting to let all thought of time fade away, as it would without some kind of regular schedule to provide structure to the 24 hours. But we had been outfitted with just that; our link to the outside world was PCSP headquarters in Resolute Bay. Safely tucked into a corner of our cook tent sat the SBX-11 radio. In the centre of camp, the radio antenna doubled as mast for a small Canadian flag, our personal display of sovereignty.

Breakfast calls were greeted with various levels of enthusiasm. A reluctant departure from a warm sleeping bag was followed by a quick run to the hills before we crowded into the warm cook tent, enticed by the aroma of fresh coffee and fried bacon. It was a wonderful, comfortable routine. Whoever was on cooking duty for the day was responsible for checking the screened weather station, recording the temperature, dew point, barometer, wind speed, and direction; and then figuring out the cloud types overhead. The last business could take a while and was often the topic of much merriment on the radio when some poor soul got it all wrong. At 7:00 a.m. our world expanded temporarily. Part of the arrangement with PCSP was our twice-daily delivery of the weather report and any other communication we might have. "Knud Peninsula, this is Resolute, how do you copy?" The High Arctic morning show was under way. Station after station reported in. Most of us knew each other, sometimes only as distant voices on the radio. "This is Truelove. Our weather: fog, drizzle, minus two degrees, zero visibility. Guess we won't be pulled out today?" "Guess you won't unless you come up with better weather," came the dry reply from Resolute. Neophytes stammered their way through the report, clicking the microphone on and off, terrified that their estimates of cloud type and height would be questioned. A stern voice from Resolute would patiently explain: "Altocumulus clouds don't usually occur at 2000 feet." Their error had been broadcast to the Arctic world. Then there were those who had obviously just awakened and barely stuck their heads outside the tent: a growly voice reporting zero visibility in 10/10 fog. The PCSP morning and evening shows were entertaining and informative, providing a welcome link to scientists scattered over thousands of kilometres. There was no regular news. Week after week, the rest of the world was shut out. It was marvelous.

The daily weather reports from different High Arctic research camps were often tremendously variable. The Bache Peninsula region and northern Ellesmere Island in general were usually blessed with excellent weather in contrast to areas farther south. Some of the warmest temperatures in the High Arctic were consistently reported from Fosheim Peninsula and the Lake Hazen area on Ellesmere Island. Considering the dependable occurrence of open water, abundant wildlife, and good weather, it was easy to understand why the Flagler Bay polynya had been such an attractive spring destination for the Dorset people. We were eager to learn as much as we could about these fascinating people who had built large communal structures and long rows of cooking hearths. When had they arrived in the Smith Sound region? Why had they migrated north? What happened to them?

To date, we have discovered five longhouses near the Flagler Bay polynya, two at Cape Faraday, and we know of two others just north of Etah on the Greenland side of Smith Sound. Mapping the polynya sites, especially the huge Longhouse site, took a long time. The 45-metre-long structure was located on a fairly level plateau between 7 and 9 metres above sea level. The ground was littered with refuse bones and fragments of stone, ivory, and bone tools. To accurately record the location of all the finds we set out a 400×400 metre grid system (200x–200y) with a solid stone cairn marking the centre point. As a matter of visual convenience, we ran the 200y line parallel to the west wall of the communal structure. Setting out the coordinates was tedious business, but absolutely essential for carrying out a professional excavation; each excavator would know precisely which unit he or she was working in, so that all finds could be accurately recorded. It was one occasion when the infamous Topometer came in handy.

When the grid system had been laid out, we noticed that the long parallel walls of the communal structure ran almost precisely along a true north/south noon meridian line. Was it a coincidence, or had the Dorset builders planned it that way? The question was answered when we found other communal structures, each one extending in a different direction; obviously the placement had more to do with available space than with a celestial noon sun alignment. The

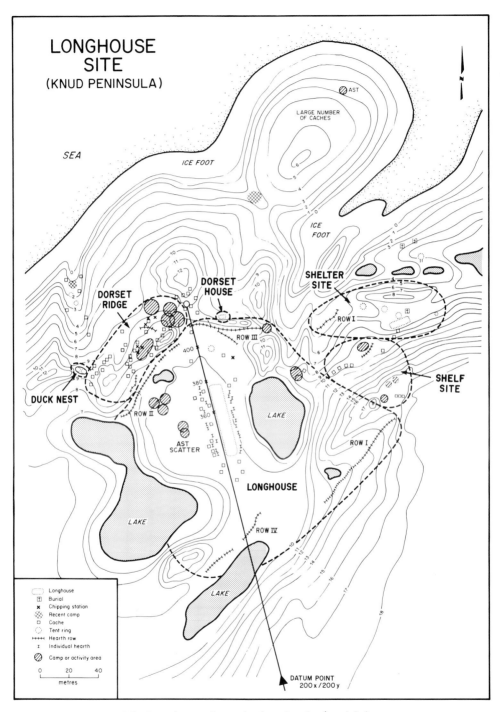

The Longhouse site and other sites in the vicinity.

communal structure on the Longhouse site is nearly
three times longer than any of the other communal
structures we have located on the central east coast of
Ellesmere Island. Could such a massive construction
have been completely roofed with skins? It seems most
unlikely. For some time we speculated that perhaps
individual family tents had been erected within the
walls. This scenario was depicted by our friend Brenda
Carter in a painting for the National Geographic.[3] The
tent idea had some merit, but was not entirely
convincing. We also considered the possibility that the
walls were symbolic only, or simply a protection from
cool winds and storms. I favour the idea that there
was some type of skin roof, but in the form of a lean-
to arrangement that extended from the top of the side
walls partway into the structure, possibly leaving the
centre open. Excavations confirmed our initial
impression that the interior had been divided into a
series of semicircular stone arrangements curving
inward from the side walls, possibly the space used by
each family, leaving a fairly narrow passage down
through the length of the structure. As information
was gathered from other, sometimes better-preserved,
communal structures, we learned that a number of
entrances had been located at evenly spaced intervals
along the side walls, probably one for each family. In
addition, each communal structure also had a front
entrance in the centre of the end wall, flanked by large
upright stones.

With each day and each season, working on
different sites, we learned more and more about the
late Dorset people who had once lived in this part of
the Arctic.[4] Refuse bones told us that the communal

Drawing of the 45-metre-long communal structure on Longhouse site based on overhead
photographs using a photographic bipod and a series of overhead shots taken from a hovering
helicopter.

Excellent preservation of the house walls of the longhouse at Cape Faraday confirmed our impression from the Longhouse site that these structures contained a number of evenly spaced entrances along the side walls in addition to the large main entrance.

sites had been used during the summer. We learned that the interior width fluctuated little from a standard of 4 metres, whereas the length was more variable. The five structures near the polynya varied in length from 6 to 45 metres, although those two measurements are the extreme sizes. The average length actually ranged between 10 and 13 metres. The variation in lengths undoubtedly reflects variations in the number of families using the structures. More evidence pointed to individual family activities: single units of hearths, platforms, and sometimes a small meat cache, constructed alongside the outer walls of the structure. Although the largest communual structure on Knud Peninsula produced no clear evidence of internal hearths, in several of the smaller communal structures, including the two at Cape Faraday, we found concentrations of charred material and stone slab features evenly spaced down the centre of the structures. We noted an interesting correlation between the number of external hearths and the length of the associated communal structure. In each case, the length of the structure divided by the number of individual family hearths suggested that each family occupied an interior space about two metres in length. The calculation gave us a good idea of the number of people at these annual gatherings: anywhere from about 20 to 120.

From the outset we had decided not to excavate the entire communal structure on the Longhouse site, to allow future researchers to test new ideas and methods at some later date. In all we excavated 77 square metre units, about 35 percent of the total interior space. We located 136 formed tools; fragments and waste material including wood shavings; ivory and bone chips; and hundreds of stone flakes. Considering the large number of excavated units, the artifact yield was actually quite small. That this was also the case in all the other communal structures strongly suggests that only a limited time was spent in them.

Karen McCullough and Eric Damkjar testing the interior of the most prominent Dorset communal structure in the land of the bears, Cape Faraday. Note the rifle leaning against the house wall, and the dense fog, which reduced visibility.

As far as we could tell, the communal structures were used for only a few seasons, perhaps only once. None of them appeared to have been lengthened or shortened to accommodate different numbers of people. However, the remains of many more hearth rows than communal structures might support an argument in favour of multiple communal structure use, or suggest that hearth row activities were not always associated with communal house use.

Interestingly enough, the shortest communal structure at the polynya was different from the others in having slightly raised side benches separated by a sunken central floor space that ran the length of the feature. This was also a distinctive feature of a communal structure at Cape Faraday.[5] Our friend and colleague Eric Damkjar, who has worked on similar structures in the central Canadian Arctic, has suggested that the side benches and sunken floor area are features found in the earliest communal structures.[6] If so, our small Narrows site structure may represent the initial gathering of late Dorset people at the polynya. This idea is appealing for several reasons. When the late Dorset people first arrived in the Smith Sound area, they were the first people to do so in well over a thousand years. They, like all pioneers, had to become familiar with the geography and the environment. Older sites undoubtedly gave them a clue to good hunting areas, but much can change in a thousand years, including favourable animal habitats. I suspect that the custom of arranging annual communal gatherings was well entrenched when these people moved north. To sustain such a gathering, it was crucial to find an area dependably rich in game, an arctic oasis of sorts. On their migration northward along the Ellesmere Island coast, they found such a location at Cape Faraday; yet nothing compared to the richness of the polynya they eventually discovered between Bache and Knud Peninsulas. As the number of Dorset families in the area increased, the annual gathering became a larger affair. The size of the communal or ceremonial structures increased accordingly, until the final gathering took place on the Longhouse site. On that occasion, there were probably well over a hundred people on the site. That final gathering may be correlated with the use of the upper 18 segments of the best-preserved hearth row in the area. The estimated presence of eighteen extended families, averaging about five to seven persons per family, suggests that the largest number of late Dorset people gathered at the polynya was somewhere between 90 and 126. Even if the population was slightly greater than that, and assuming that the spring event assembled most or all of the late Dorset people in the Smith Sound region, the population was not very large. In fact the number is reminiscent of the Polar Eskimo population estimates made by the explorers Elisha Kent Kane and Isaac Hayes, less than fifty years after John Ross first encountered the Inughuit in 1818.[7]

The Dorset people ate well at the polynya. An analysis of bone refuse from the interior of the largest communal structure gave us a good idea of the variety of animals utilized: small seals (54 percent), birds (33 percent), arctic fox (5 percent), walrus (3 percent), large seals (3 percent), polar bear (1 percent), and arctic hare (1 percent). There were hardly any fish bones, a few muskox, and a few wolf or dog bones. If they indeed are dog bones, they are unique. It is a peculiar fact that dog bones never show up on late Dorset sites anywhere in the Arctic. We know that dogs were used by the early Palaeoeskimos, so why not by the Dorset people? Dogs were important for hauling sleds, chasing and corralling polar bears, and finding seal breathing holes in the ice. Without dogs, winter and spring travel would have been considerably restricted by the man-hauling of small sledge loads; that is perhaps one reason that few late Dorset people ever crossed the immense Melville Bay south of Cape York.

Dogs may have been missing, but the spiritual side of life was not. The late Dorset culture is known for its beautiful ivory carvings: delicate, anatomically detailed figurines representing nearly all the animals in their world, creatures whose spirits had to be appeased at all costs. The more important (and perhaps dangerous) the animal was, the more carvings were made of it. Not surprisingly, the most common figurines are those of polar bears and humans. The less important food animals, like hares, had been missing from the Dorset carving inventory until one fine day when Karen McCullough found not only a flawless bear head carving, but the first hare figurine documented in the Arctic.

Dorset carvings are represented either in complete form or, occasionally, in single anatomical elements, such as caribou and muskox hoofs. The human form is most often depicted by facial carvings, sometimes clustered in large numbers on a single piece of antler or bone. A most peculiar and disturbing figurine, always carved in wood (often bark), shows the top half of an armless body, pierced through the chest with a sharp instrument. A ritual killing? If so, who was the intended victim or victims?

Most of the carvings were found inside or in close proximity to the communal structures, usually closer to the walls than to the centre. Without exception, the workmanship of the carvings is perfect. Each specimen is decorated with a series of short, incised lines—an external "skeletal motif" representing long bones, ribs, and vertebrae. Most of the carvings also have an incised suspension hole for attachment as a talisman to the shaman's or the hunter's coat. When you look at the carvings, several questions come to mind. Where are the less-than-perfect specimens, the ones that might show an apprentice's first attempt? I doubt that anybody can suddenly produce a perfect miniature carving of a bear's head. Yet, there are no mangled pieces or anything less than the flawless examples before us. Did they destroy anything less than the perfect pieces? Was the artisan an 'ordinary' man or woman, or was the artistic excellence a product of the spiritual messengers, the shamans? During the summer of 1995, we did locate a couple of carvings in a refuse area associated with a small, single-family late Dorset dwelling. The miniature carving representing a walrus was far from perfect, which suggested that only perfect specimens were used in the ceremonial activities in the communal structures.

One artifact apparently took on great significance: the harpoon head. Many of them, found near the centre of the communal structure, had been anthropomorphized with small incisions representing eyes and mouth. In our work, we have never found these in any context other than the communal longhouses. As one of the most important tools in the hunter's kit, the harpoon head brought in the greatest amount of food. So, not only was it important to placate the animal spirit, but the tool used to hunt the animal had to be treated with great respect. The crisscrossing of incised lines on the face of the harpoon heads may have been ownership markings, although we can't know that for certain. Many of the harpoon heads and some of the small ivory handles from the Longhouse site exhibit several parallel, diagonally incised lines that may also have served as ownership markings.

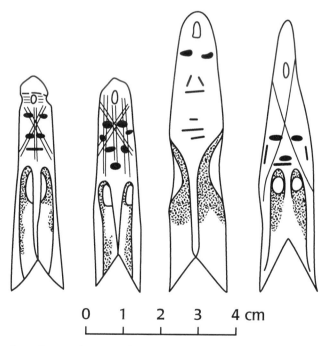

0 1 2 3 4 cm

Late Dorset harpoon heads showing the crisscrossing of incised lines and anthropomorphized facial features representing eyes and mouth.

We noted a great scarcity of stone cutting and incising tools, like the microblades and burins so important during the late Pre-Dorset and early Dorset period. The minimal use of these stone tools may reflect the use of meteoritic iron, as it probably did during the Saqqaq period. Meteoritic iron and native copper blades have been identified on many late Dorset sites in the Arctic.[8] There are other interesting details about the materials tools were made from. For the first time, we see quartz crystal being used regularly, and ground burins are often made from green nephrite. Surprisingly, the Dorset people did not use the bow drill; all perforations are incised or gouged.

As soon as the excavation of the communal structures was well under way it was time to have a closer look at the hearth rows. Since their discovery on Ellesmere Island, hearth rows have been identified on several other Dorset sites in the Arctic: Creswell Bay,[9] Little Cornwallis Island, and Brooman Point.[10] All of these site locations are associated with polynyas or at least exceptionally good hunting areas. During a brief visit to North Greenland in 1990, Karen McCullough and I had the good fortune to discover an eight-unit hearth row at a place called Nûgdlît, located halfway between the Thule Air Base and Qaanaaq. A radiocarbon date on charred material from one of the hearths suggested that the hearths were used between 1200 and 1300 years ago.[11] As much as we searched the surrounding area we could not find any clear evidence of a communal structure, although we did discover some peculiar stone walls in the cliffs above the hearth row location. It is quite possible that hearth rows occasionally were used independently of communal structures, which would also explain the comparatively greater number of them near the Flagler Bay polynya.

As we became more familiar with the hearth rows from Knud Peninsula, it became obvious that they were far less uniform than we had first thought. In their most "developed" form, they consisted of joint units of rectangular, slab-lined hearth boxes and flagged meat platforms. In other instances, the rows appeared to be much less elaborate, consisting instead of a series of equally spaced, single hearth-type structures, without the associated meat platforms. It took a while before we fully understood another peculiarity about these rows. Parallel to most of the more complete rows we noted what appeared to be a broken-up row of fairly evenly spaced single hearths, not associated with any kind of platform. At first, we speculated that they were remnants of older rows; then we realized that each of the parallel hearths matched the position of a hearth in the complete row. We now suspect that the parallel features weren't

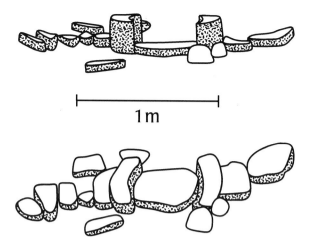

We now believe that the single, solidly built stone "hearth" features located parallel to the hearth rows were designed to hold skin containers, used for boiling food with hot boiling stones heated in the adjacent hearth.

hearths at all, but rather supports for boiling bags placed in convenient proximity to the hearths where the boiling stones were heated.

We have already seen that the use of outdoor communal cooking arrangements goes back to Pre-Dorset times on the Ridge site. On the late Dorset sites, the practice of "communal cooking" had obviously taken on great ceremonial importance, considering the fact that we find both single family hearths for ordinary use and hearth rows used by the same people during the same season. The most complete and probably last-used hearth row on the Longhouse site is truly impressive. Its overall length of 68 metres contains 26 units separated into three segments, probably representing three different periods of use. Four hearths in the upper row were excavated, producing large samples of charred bone mixed with smaller quantities of charred willow and driftwood. Averaging four radiocarbon dates from these hearths gave us a date of about A.D. 850. The excavation of the hearth units did not produce many artifacts, but there were enough to prove the late Dorset connection.

There is an extraordinary sameness to the material culture of the late Dorset period throughout the Arctic. The faultless carvings, the harpoon heads, and the lithic artifacts are almost identical wherever they are found, suggesting fairly rapid, long-range diffusion. The locations of settlements attest to a population very much at ease with open-water hunting. The Dorset people placed great value on the annual spring and summer gathering, which was made possible by identifying exceptionally rich and predictable hunting localities. Having established that the Flagler Bay polynya was indeed a reliable, regularly recurring phenomenon with sufficient resources to sustain relatively large numbers of people, the Dorset people chose it as their primary place of seasonal gathering and ceremonial activities. The annual assemblage was an important social occasion, a fertile ground for exchanging ideas, finding marriage partners, and strengthening cultural identity. The exquisitely carved ivory figurines from this time period have caught the public interest to a far greater extent than most collections of lithic tools ever could, no matter how well they were made.[12] The carvings, whether natural or highly stylized, have accentuated the mystique about the Dorset people who paid so much attention to being on good terms with the spiritual powers that controlled their world. Geographically, late Dorset population movements and trait diffusion reached farther than any prior Palaeoeskimo expansion: from Labrador in the south to Victoria Island in the west and the Kane Basin region in the north.

Did the last great gathering on the Longhouse site signal the end of the Dorset people's presence in the High Arctic? We don't believe so. Radiocarbon dates from two late Dorset sites, Mist and Oldsquaw on Skraeling Island, suggest

Oldsquaw Site, Feature 3 on Skraeling Island.

that Dorset families continued to use the area after the end of the communal gatherings at the polynya. The Mist and Oldsquaw sites are about a hundred years more recent than the Longhouse communal site. It is possible that a few Palaeoeskimo families lived and hunted in the Smith Sound region as late as a thousand years ago, perhaps even a few generations after that.

Naturally this leaves us with a great mystery. The termination of the Dorset period is as inexplicable in the High Arctic as in most other regions where the Dorset people once thrived. We can reasonably correlate the appearance of the pioneering Palaeoeskimos with a climatic warming trend even if the migration took place towards the end of that episode. Similarly, the pronounced increase in cultural activities marked by the arrival in the Smith Sound region of Pre-Dorset families was also associated with a brief climatic warming trend. The arrival of the late Dorset people in the High Arctic also coincides reasonably well with the onset of the Neo-Atlantic climatic warming episode, which lasted about three centuries. During that interval, the boreal forest advanced northward, and less drift ice appeared in the waters around Iceland and southern Greenland.[13] While the warming trend may have produced favourable hunting conditions that encouraged the northward movement of the Dorset people, we have to wonder: what caused their disappearance? They vanished from the Smith Sound region well before climatic conditions worsened. I have already suggested that the size of the late Dorset population in the Far North may have been relatively small, even at the best of times. A small population of any kind can be endangered in a number of ways, particularly in a region easily affected by minor environmental and ecological conditions. One disastrous hunting season or the accidental death of the best hunters could have led to starvation and the demise of a small group of people.

In the Ungava Peninsula region, rich in late Dorset communal longhouse sites,[14] the Dorset people are thought to have carried on well into the thirteenth century A.D. Even in more southerly parts of the High Arctic, such as Little Cornwallis Island, indications are that Dorset settlements were used as late as A.D. 1200,[15] in other words, very close to the time when the Thule culture Inuit arrived from the west. In East Greenland, the Dorset people may have survived long enough to encounter Thule Inuit groups, although the archaeological data to support such an event remain inconclusive.

Taken as a whole, the evidence for Dorset/Thule interaction remains surprisingly weak. The only thing we can say with certainty is that the opportunities for encounters between the two groups, at least in the central and eastern Arctic, must have been plentiful, considering the lengthy time span during which they occupied the same territory.

So far, our own data suggest that the late Dorset people disappeared from the Smith Sound region at least a century before the first Thule culture Inuit arrived. Whatever the cause, the disappearance of the Dorset people or their assimilation with the Thule culture Inuit brought to an end the long-lived Arctic Small Tool tradition. The Dorset people were the last descendants of the true High Arctic pioneers, the last Palaeoeskimos. This time, however, the disappearance of one group of people didn't result in a long period of human abandonment. Instead, the Smith Sound region became the domain of the Thule culture Inuit, the Arctic whale hunters.

1 cm

The small wooden figurine, perforated in the chest area, has been found on many Dorset sites in the Arctic. One can only wonder if the "ritual stabbing" is related to some magical activity, perhaps a wishful spell against the invading Thule Inuit?

B.C. 2500	
	Independence I (*Lakeview and Campview sites*)
2000	
	Independence I/Saqqaq (*Bight site*)
	Palaeoeskimo
1500	Saqqaq (*Topo site*)
	(*Beacon site*) **Period**
	Late Pre-Dorset (*Ridge site*)
1000	Transition (Independence II)
	Early Dorset (*Baculum site*)
	Abandonment of the High Arctic
500	
A.D. 0	
500	
	Late Dorset (*Longhouse and Oldsquaw sites*)
1000	
	Early Thule Culture /Norse Contact
	(*Skraeling Island Thule site*)
	Neoeskimo and
1500	
	Historic Period
	Late Thule/Western Contact (*Haa Island site*)
	Qitdlarssuaq's Journey
1900	RCMP posts established in the High Arctic
2000	

A chronological chart of the human presence in the Smith Sound region.

9

The Arctic Whale Hunters

"LONG-TAILED JAEGER"
Brenda Carter

The long-tailed jaeger watched the people in a large skin boat, poling their way through the pack ice toward the island with three peaks. People had not been seen in the Far North for many decades. The jaeger was resting after a journey that had nearly ended its life. On its northward migration, fierce storms had blown the jaeger far inland, where brutal battles were being fought near the Toltec capital of Tula. Farther north the jaeger flew over towns built into the sides of steep cliffs. Here, a quick stop to nibble at some corn had made it the centre of a stone-throwing competition by small children. After that, the jaeger had made few stops before reaching this High Arctic island. Some of the newcomers were erecting skin tents, while others paddled out to sea in small, narrow skin boats, in pursuit of the walrus feeding in the shallow waters. The Thule culture people had arrived on the east coast of Ellesmere Island, far from their western homeland in the region of the Bering and Chukchi Seas.

The Thule Expeditions came to life shortly after Knud Rasmussen and Peter Freuchen established their trading post near the old settlement of Uummannaq in North Greenland in 1909.[1] The station was called *Thule*, the 4th-century B.C. Greek scholar Pytheas's designation for the northernmost part of the habitable world.[2] Today, the name is better known in reference to the enormous American Thule military base, constructed in the early 1950s only a few kilometres from the old Thule trading post. Although the post was established essentially to provide the Polar Eskimos with the western goods they had come to rely on during the American Robert Peary's many years of exploration in the region, Rasmussen was determined to accomplish much more. Before long the first scientific "Thule" expedition was under way. Ancient artifacts gathered on the initial expeditions were assigned to what was called the Thule Culture.

Towards the end of the Palaeoeskimo era, significant cultural developments were taking place in the Chukchi and Bering Sea regions. For centuries this part of the Arctic had been the stage for the development of superbly efficient, maritime-oriented cultures known as Okvik, Old Bering Sea, and Punuk.[3] In large skin boats called *umiaks*, hunters pursued, harpooned, and lanced fifty-ton bowhead whales. They hunted walrus for the hide, meat, blubber, and ivory and lived in comfortable sod, whale bone, and driftwood houses. Their villages were large and dominated by the *umialiqs*, or whaling captains, whose umiaks were used in the whale hunt. The ability to secure large amounts of meat and blubber not only attained social stature within the community, but enabled hunters to keep large teams of dogs. Summer and winter, they were a very mobile people, an enormous advantage in an environment where chasing down game on land and at sea was a matter of survival. About 900 years ago, towards the latter part of the Neo-Atlantic warming episode, groups of these Arctic whale hunters began to move eastward in search of new hunting areas. In the literature they are occasionally referred to as *Neoeskimos*, the direct ancestors of all present-day Inuit in Canada and Greenland.

Although the scientific objectives of the Fifth Thule expedition were quite broad, it was Knud Rasmussen's ambition to place particular emphasis on exploring the question of Eskimo origins.[4] The Danish research team included two university-trained members: Kaj Birket-Smith, anthropologist and ethnographer, and Therkel Mathiassen, who carried out the first systematic excavations of ancient habitation sites in the central Canadian Arctic. Expedition

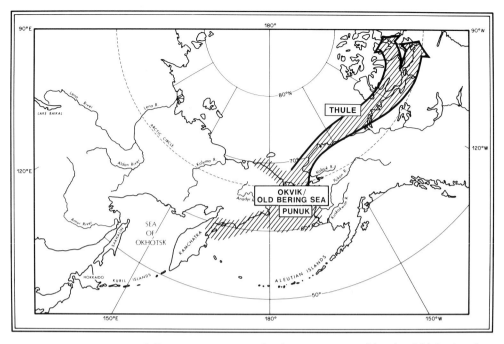

About 2200 years ago, a fully maritime-oriented culture represented by the Old Bering Sea and Okvik phases appeared in the Bering Strait region. These phases mark the beginning of the Neoeskimo stage of Arctic prehistory, which also encompasses the Birnirk, Punuk and Thule cultures. It was during the early Thule culture stage that an eastward migration brought the direct ancestors of all the Inuit presently living in Canada and Greenland.

headquarters was established just north of Southampton Island, near the northwest coast of Hudson Bay.[5] From there, the members set out on a variety of excursions, including Rasmussen's exceptional journey, accompanied by two Polar Eskimos, to the west coast of Alaska.[6] As they travelled further and further westward, they realized that all the Inuit along this vast stretch of territory, from Greenland to northern Alaska, spoke various dialects of the same Inuktitut language. That knowledge alone implied a considerable, not too ancient interaction between the different tribes and a relatively recent eastward migration of the ancestral Inuit from Alaska. Therkel Mathiassen, assisted by the Greenlander Jacob Olsen, excavated numerous Thule culture sites in the central and eastern Arctic, collecting data for the first meaningful picture of Inuit prehistory. The Naujan site near Repulse Bay provided much of this data, including skeletal material that was returned to its original location in 1991.[7]

When we arrived at Alexandra Fiord in 1977, we actually knew more about the Thule culture in the Far North than about the earlier Palaeoeskimo periods, mostly thanks to the work of Henry Collins near Resolute Bay on Cornwallis

Annual migration of Copper Inuit families in the central Arctic.(Photo credit: The Canadian Museum of Civilization)

A Copper Inuit family preparing a snow house shelter on a rocky Arctic shore. In the foreground is their heavily loaded *komatik* (sled). (Photo credit: The Canadian Museum of Civilization)

Island in the 1950s[8] and Erik Holtved in North Greenland in the 1930s and 1940s.[9] Even so, there were plenty of unanswered questions and problems that needed clarification. High on the list was the question of when the Thule culture Inuit first arrived in the High Arctic and Greenland. There was the question of the precise association of Norse artifacts discovered by Holtved in the 1930s in Thule culture winter dwellings on Ruin Island in North Greenland; the question of Polar Eskimo ancestry; and the timing and reasons for the final abandonment of the Canadian High Arctic. Our task was to locate sites and house ruins that would provide the data we needed to answer these and other questions. Otto Sverdrup's journals and maps had already pointed to the presence of large prehistoric sites, and our own 1977 survey had given us every reason to be optimistic. Sverdrup's Eskimopolis and Eskimobyen sites were clearly associated with the Thule culture. It was obvious that the Bache Peninsula region had been a major Thule culture settlement area for hundreds of years.

For decades it has been customary to state, rather dogmatically, that the Thule culture entered the High Arctic and northern Greenland about A.D. 940—in other words, prior to the arrival of Norsemen in the south. It has also been generally stated that the first Inuit/Norse contact took place in West Greenland about A.D. 1250.[10] The 300-year span between the two events has long puzzled some of us. Why should it have taken the Inuit centuries to head south along the west coast of Greenland? To explore that question, we needed good, solid, empirical data relevant to the time of arrival of the Thule Inuit in the High Arctic. In 1978, we knew precisely where to search for that information. Our brief visit to Skraeling Island the year before had led to the discovery of two large Thule culture sites containing over 40 winter house ruins from the early Thule culture period. The Skraeling Island site, located on the southeastern tip of the island, appeared to be the earliest. Here we found 23 winter house ruins scattered over a wide, beautifully vegetated plateau surrounding a small shallow lake. The Sverdrup site, situated on the northwestern tip of the island, contained nearly as many house ruins, with lots of whale bone sticking out from a generous carpet of grass and moss. Not only had Sverdrup and his men camped on this site, they had obviously spent a few hours digging into some of the ancient ruins. Luckily for us, Thule culture winter house ruins are not easily disturbed by transient visitors unless they have enough time to wait for the ground to thaw—a slow process in the High Arctic.

It was with great anticipation that we shifted our base camp from Knud Peninsula to Skraeling Island about mid-July in 1978; finally, we could get a closer look at the old house ruins. Camp was set up near the small bight where we had landed the year before, just about the only decent camp area that had not been used in the past. The spot was nicely sheltered from a steady, cool northeast wind, and the sandy ground gave us an unusually comfortable base for the tents. Brackish lakes and the lack of even the tiniest brook on the island sent us to the small meltwater pools on the ice foot for fresh water until we

A contemporaneous unit of four Thule culture winter houses on Skraeling Island following excavation. The large, squarish structure on the right is a gathering place or *karigi*.

could reach nearby creeks on the Johan Peninsula coast by boat. The ice foot, welded to the cliffs along the shore until late fall storms and high tides broke it apart, served as a convenient pathway and access to the sea. The view from camp was magnificent: Alexandra Fiord, bordered by tall mountains shouldering massive ice caps and glaciers and filled with sparkling sheets of pack ice drifting back and forth with tide and wind in dark blue waters. A tall, prominent island to the west was named Stiles Island, in honour of the constable who organized the construction of the Alexandra Fiord RCMP post. Other researchers have since renamed the island "Sphinx Island," because of its shape when viewed from the RCMP station. Over the past 4000 years, features in the landscape have been named and renamed countless times. It is only now, as names are placed on printed maps, that they take on any kind of permanency.

Knowing that the work on Thule culture winter house ruins would be more labour-intensive, we had arranged for additional crew members to join us during the second half of the field season. From the Grise Fiord community on the south coast of Ellesmere Island, we were pleased to have the assistance of Jimmy Nowra and Jarloo Kigutaq. Not until his arrival did we know that this was a homecoming for Jimmy. In 1962, Jimmy's family had lived at the Alexandra Fiord station, while his father served as Special Constable to the RCMP. It was the last year the station was in operation.

No sooner had we set up camp on Skraeling Island, eager to get to work, when the northern sky turned a menacing dark violet. Everything grew quiet; even the constantly nattering terns were subdued. We prepared for a great blow that never came. Instead, we woke up to find the ground covered in heavy, wet snow: time to stay in the cozy cook tent, drinking coffee or tea and eating hard pilot biscuits liberally topped with peanut butter and jam. It gave us an opportunity to talk about the results of Thule culture excavations elsewhere and discuss our own objectives, so that everyone understood the task ahead.

We had already noticed that most of the house ruins on the Skraeling Island site featured a distinctive, separate kitchen room, connected to the main dwelling by a very short tunnel. This feature alone identified them as belonging to Erik Holtved's so-called "Ruin Island phase."[11] Considering the large number of dwellings on the site, we decided that each person should be responsible for one primary house ruin while also testing others. Because of the slow rate of ground thawing, it would take more than one season to completely excavate each house.

There are several ways to approach the excavation of a large sod, stone, and whale bone house. Usually a combination of techniques works best. The first order of business is setting out a square metre grid system, over either the whole site or a portion of it. Each unit can then be excavated by arbitrary levels until enough identifiable elements, such as sleeping platforms, central floor, and cooking areas appear; these can then be worked by feature rather than by arbitrary levels. One of the trickier jobs is to judge which stones and boulders to remove along the way—intrusive materials derived from a collapsed wall or roof, or debris thrown in by later site users. Because it is easy to make a mistake and remove what turns out to be a structural part of the original dwelling, meticulous notes, drawings, and photographs must accompany every stage of the excavation. It is the only way to reconstruct what has been taken apart.

During the final days of the 1978 field season, the most exciting finds appeared. Karen McCullough was completing the final troweling of a test pit in one of the larger winter houses when an ivory harpoon head fragment came out of the dirt. It was precisely what we needed; the specimen had the shape and the ornamentation of the very earliest Thule culture forms found anywhere in

The late Dorset arctic hare figurine from Knud Peninsula.

Late Dorset snow goose and seal carvings from Knud Peninsula.

The late Dorset dwelling on the Franklin Pierce site.

A late Dorset knife blade of meteoritic iron.

Whale bone supports protruding from a Thule culture winter house on Bathurst Island.

An 800-year-old sealskin mitt from House 3, Skraeling Island site.

An ivory needle case found beneath the sleeping platform in the early Thule culture House 25 on Eskimobyen site.

An ivory harpoon head on the floor of House 14, Eskimobyen site.

Two separate hearth platforms in the kitchen room of House 3 on the Skraeling Island Thule site. Note the harpoon heads on the right-hand hearth platform and the section of whale vertebrae stacked up against the kitchen wall. The kitchen was entered from the main room through a short, narrow tunnel. (Photo credit: Karen McCullough)

the High Arctic and Greenland. During the following seasons, we discovered many more of these beautifully decorated harpoon heads, and other intriguing pieces of evidence that pointed to a rapid migration from the western Arctic. In several houses, we found fragments of clay pottery decorated with a circular motif well-known from northern Alaska. Not only did the fragments look as though they had come from the west; but later analyses of the clay and temper showed that the pottery most likely had been made there.[12] The occupants of several houses had also attempted to make local pottery, but with limited success. We found sections of poorly fired clay vessels, crumbling to the touch. In Alaska there had been no shortage of driftwood to fire clay vessels. In the High Arctic, wood was a scarce resource one could not squander on making clay pottery. Before long, lamps and cooking vessels were carved from blocks of soapstone.

Organic artifacts of wood, bone, antler, and ivory were excellently preserved in the early Thule culture winter houses. We also recovered many skin items, including mitts, boots, waterproof parkas, caps, and bags made of sealskin and gut.

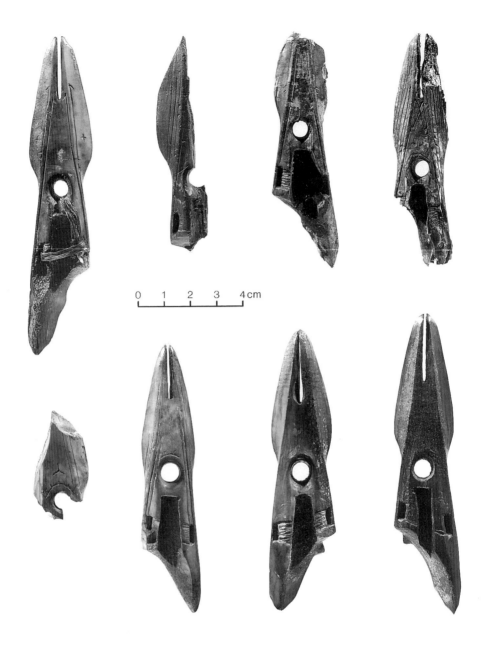

Early Thule culture harpoon heads from winter house ruins on the Skraeling Island site.

Karen McCullough accepted the challenge of putting all our information about the pioneering Thule culture Inuit together in one comprehensive Ph.D. dissertation. In a thorough analysis of the data, primarily from Skraeling Island, she traced the first Thule culture Inuit to the west coast of Alaska, most likely to the region surrounding Kotzebue Sound.[13] The migration had been swift, facilitated by the use of umiaks and kayaks during the open water season, or by heavily loaded sleds drawn by large dog teams in early spring. Although the immediate western origin of these people was beyond dispute, the time of their arrival in the High Arctic and Greenland turned out to be a contentious issue. To determine when the winter houses on Skraeling Island were occupied, we ran a total of 17 radiocarbon dates on a variety of materials from the floor and sleeping platform areas. The radiocarbon dates indicated that the earliest Thule culture Inuit did not set foot in the Smith Sound region until sometime between A.D. 1150 and 1200, long after the Norsemen had settled Greenland. The Thule culture Inuit may have entered more southerly Arctic regions before that, but not the High Arctic and not Greenland. This fact is significant, because it provides a reasonable explanation for the mid-thirteenth century

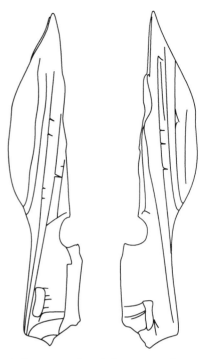

A harpoon head fragment from House 9 on the Skraeling Island site. The finely incised line motif links this specimen to similar harpoon head types from Alaska.

first contact between Inuit and Norse settlers in West Greenland. It has never seemed reasonable that a highly mobile people like the Thule Inuit, who covered the distance from Alaska to Smith Sound in a generation or two, should have paused there for centuries before heading southward along the west coast of Greenland. The later dates from the Skraeling Island houses also widen the gap between the last period of Dorset activities in the Smith Sound region and the arrival of the Arctic whale hunters.

The Thule culture Inuit had not just spent the winter in the Bache Peninsula region; summer sites were even more numerous, and very large. On nearly every approachable stretch of coast we located tent rings, meat caches, stone supports for kayaks and umiaks and children's playhouses. Summer camp remains are most abundant in areas bordering secondary polynyas, where the sea ice breaks up early in the summer. Near the summer camps and in the surrounding hills, we found large numbers of fox traps constructed of stones and boulders. Many of the broad, grass- and sedge-covered valleys contained hare-snare arrangements,

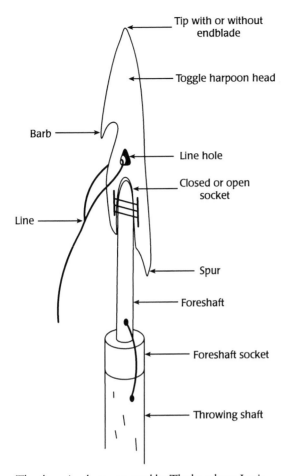

Tip with or without
endblade

Toggle harpoon head

Barb

Line hole

Closed or open
socket

Line

Spur

Foreshaft

Foreshaft socket

Throwing shaft

The throwing harpoon used by Thule culture Inuit for open-water sea mammal hunting consisted of several interrelated elements. The many attributes of the harpoon head itself, such as the open or closed socket, the self-bladed or inset endblade, the number of barbs, and the spur configuration changed through time and space. The essential elements of the toggle harpoon were the head itself; the foreshaft, connecting the head to the throwing shaft; and the sealskin line, which led to an inflated sealskin float. Once the harpoon head penetrated the animal, tension on the line would pivot or toggle the head, thereby firmly securing the animal, which could then be killed with a lance.

consisting of long lines of small boulders divided every two metres or so by larger upright stones. The most extensive of these hare-snare systems was located on top of a rounded hill far inland in Sverdrup Pass. Ethnographic accounts from North Greenland describe how leather thongs were stretched between each upright stone and the next.[14] Hanging down from these taut lines was a series of loops, which would snare the animals as they jumped over the smaller boulders. The large number of hare bones found in the house ruins attest to the success of the snare arrangements. Arctic hares were important because they remained in the Far North—no quick southern escape for them. It was different with waterfowl such as eiders, whose eggs were considered a great seasonal delicacy. In many places we found nesting locations obviously constructed by human hands: a few well-placed rocks provided sufficient shelter from the wind to entice an eider duck to nest. Interestingly enough, the Norsemen were also known to construct eider duck nests in both Iceland and Greenland.[15]

The Thule culture Inuit did not restrict their trapping activities to foxes and hares. We will never know who thought of it first, but someone had the great idea of constructing giant versions of the fox traps in which to capture polar bears. On a small rocky promontory on the Johan Peninsula coast, we located two of these bear traps built about five metres apart. The traps were nearly identical to ones I had seen during a field trip to the south coast of Ellesmere Island in 1974, with my colleague Robert McGhee.[16] At the time, our conclusion that the massive stone features were used to trap bears was highly criticized by some researchers. Nevertheless, late nineteenth-century ethno-

Fragment of a clay vessel found in House 3 on the Skraeling Island site. The curvilinear design and the analyzed composition of the clay and temper indicated that the vessel most likely had been made in Alaska and subsequently brought to Ellesmere Island.

graphic observations from North Greenland and Ellesmere Island confirmed the practice of trapping polar bears.[17] It is peculiar that, in all of the circumpolar world, bear traps of this kind appear to be confined to the eastern High Arctic and North Greenland. The construction of the trap began with the building of a solid, stone-walled chamber approximately three metres long, roofed with thick stone slabs. The chamber was then covered with a huge pile of boulders, highest in the front of the trap, where the stone-slab trap door hung suspended over the opening. The boulder mound tapered down towards the back, where strength was less important: only the head and the forelegs of the bear would reach that far, in an attempt to grab the bait tied to the tip of a protruding rock at the end of the chamber. The bear's pull on the bait would release the thong holding up the trap door, which would come crashing down behind the bear. The confined space within the chamber and the stretched posture of the bear undoubtedly prevented the animal from using its immense power to break free. By removing a top stones at the back of the trap, a hunter could dispatch the bear with a well-placed lance thrust.

When the Thule Inuit entered the Bache Peninsula region they must have literally stumbled over abandoned Dorset sites, particularly along the shores of the Flagler Bay polynya. The hearth rows and the impressive stone walls of the communal structures would have been even more outstanding than when we first saw them. I would imagine that the Inuit shamans knew they were treading

Torn gut skin parka from House 3, Skraeling Island site.

Skin boot from House 3, Skraeling Island site.

A sealskin bag from House 15, Skraeling Island site.

on sacred ground. They too built impressive, boulder-walled ceremonial gathering places to be used in the spring and summer. We have located three of these in the Bache region, each one a large, round structure with stone seats arranged along the inside of the wall. Wandering through the abandoned Dorset sites and ceremonial communal structures, the Thule Inuit undoubtedly picked

Stone fox traps are numerous along the shores of the Bache Peninsula region, particularly in the vicinity of large Thule culture summer camps, where meat caches must have presented a great attraction to the arctic fox. (Photo credit: Karen McCullough)

up many of the magnificent ivory carvings, undoubtedly appreciating the fine workmanship. Even though they too were excellent carvers, they produced nothing quite as exquisite and detailed as the Dorset figurines.

Every season we have found Dorset carvings and harpoon heads in Thule Inuit winter dwellings. For the most part we have attributed these finds to normal human inquisitiveness, artifacts from another culture brought home as a matter of curiosity. Dorset artifacts could also have fallen out of the sods cut for use in the construction of Thule winter houses built on older Dorset sites. But the possibility remains that some of these items, particularly the figurines, were collected for reasons other than esthetics. Like the Dorset shamans, the Thule medicine men and women came from a long tradition of spiritual practitioners who understood the need to be on good terms with animal spirits. Perhaps a greater connection to the sacred world could be attained by securing the spiritual power of the ancient Dorset or *Tunnit* shamans through their carvings? Throughout the Inuit world there are many legends about encounters with the *Tunnits*, a somewhat ignorant and backward, yet powerful people, not to be trusted. These legends are thought to relate to Inuit encounters with the Dorset

The author sitting at the entrance to a polar bear trap on the south coast of Ellesmere Island. (Photo credit: Robert McGhee)

people. Did the Inuit shamans occasionally seek the power of the Dorset spirit helpers? On a grey, chilly, overcast day on Skraeling Island, we found the answer to that question.

The early Thule culture Inuit used communal structures both summer and winter. The large sod, stone, and whale bone *karigi*, or gathering houses, differed from regular family dwellings by not having any sleeping platforms or cooking areas. Their entrance tunnels were relatively short and wide, and in many instances a large part of the central floor area was paved with well-fitted stone slabs. Large amounts of wood shavings, bone and ivory chips, and other debris on the floor suggested that the *karigi* had been used not only for drum dancing and various games and shamanistic rituals, but also as a busy workplace for hunters and possibly their wives. We spent many summers excavating these winter communal houses on Skraeling Island. On the Sverdrup site we excavated a large, round structure with an enormous whale skull placed over the tunnel entrance. Working our way down through collapsed roof material and thick layers of debris, we discovered a row of joined stone slab seats constructed along the perimeter of the wall, all facing the central floor area, where a deep pit full

A Thule culture communal structure used during the spring and summer.

The interior of House 2, a Thule culture *karigi* on the Sverdrup site. Excavation has reached debris. An arrangement of stone seats has been exposed along the periphery of the wall. A small paving of stones can be seen on the floor in front of the second seat from the right. We found the wooden Dorset face under the largest of these stones.

of blubber-saturated sand, charred pieces of wood, and bones had been dug. There didn't seem to be any particular difference in the size of the seats, although on closer inspection we could see that some of them had actually served as lamp platforms. Then, one day, while clearing the last layer of floor debris, I found that the floor immediately in front of one seat had been paved with small, stone slabs. I lifted each in turn, brushing away the sand and gravel underneath. Suddenly, two black, hollow eyes stared at me from the distant past. Gently, I

lifted up the ghostly image with its inset wooden slivers sticking out from many parts of the face. A carved oval mouth was twisted into a frozen *Tunnit* scream. What was a truly dramatic Dorset spirit doing in a Thule culture ceremonial house? It had not been brought in just as a curio; this was a powerful spirit helper, used by the Thule shaman during his own seances. The Dorset people might have disappeared, but their powerful allegiance with the spirit world remained very much alive and was absorbed by the Thule shamans.

Jimmy Nowra told us many stories about ghosts and spirits. He recalled vividly how they had haunted him as a boy, when his family was living at Alexandra Fiord. A long detour was always taken around a small wooden house where caribou and bear skins were scraped. According to Jimmy, that house was especially full of ghosts. Jimmy's English was fairly good under ordinary circumstances, but when he imitated characters from old gangster movies he had seen, we were all in stitches—the accent was perfect. We were looking forward to a second season with Jimmy

The wooden Dorset figurine located beneath a stone slab in House 2 on the Sverdrup site. (Photo credit: Sisse Brimberg)

when we heard the tragic news that he had been killed in a hunting accident. There was little we could do except name a site in his memory. I will always remember him sitting in the warmth of the evening sun behind our little camp on Skraeling Island, talking to our Norwegian teammate, Tore. It struck me as a scene from a very distant past when Norsemen and Inuit had first met. Following the 1978 field season, the question of Norse/Inuit contact was uppermost in our minds. Jimmy had participated in the initial discovery; it saddened us all that he would not be there for the rest of the adventure.

Jimmy Nowra and Tore Bjørgo at our 1978 base camp on Skraeling Island. Did their respective ancestors meet on the island more than 700 years ago?

10

Vikings in the High Arctic

A Viking ship rivet from House 6 on the Skraeling Island site.

I had just exposed the stone edging of a round meat pit when the trowel made contact with a solid, dirt-encrusted lump of some kind. Carefully I picked it up, brushed it lightly, and stared at a mass of small, rusty, interlocking iron rings. It took a while to register: it had to be—it could only be—a piece of medieval chain mail! A short while later, I was nearing the bottom of the meat pit when the trowel struck something hard—again the now familiar sound of metal against metal. Dirt was carefully brushed away to reveal an iron ship rivet—a Viking ship rivet!

As far as we know, Norse Greenlanders were the first people of European origin to contact Thule culture Inuit. When the quick-tempered Icelander Eirik the Red was sentenced to three years' banishment from his homeland in A.D. 982, he promptly headed westward to explore the land Bjarne had reported.[1] For three years Eirik explored immense fiord systems fanning out from an ice-capped interior. Impressed with the lush vegetation covering the inner fiord areas and uplands, he named the land Greenland. The southern region where he built his own farm, Brattahlid, supported an impressive growth of dwarf birch and tall willow.[2] The uplands were dotted with lakes and grassy meadows that made superb sheep pasture. Countless streams cascaded over cliff sides and meandered through lowlands, a water source easily diverted through irrigation ditches to the home fields close to byres and stables. Not only was it a bountiful land he explored; it was uninhabited. In Iceland, the Norsemen had found it necessary to oust or enslave Celtic monks. In Greenland, Eirik met no one. Fiord after fiord was explored with a keen eye for settlement potential. He was well aware of the excitement his discoveries would generate among chieftains back home, where good land had become a scarce commodity.

No sooner had he returned from his exile than plans for a major land taking (*Landnam*) in Greenland were well under way. In the spring of 986, a fleet of 34 vessels set sail for Greenland. The powerful chieftains would make their land selections first; some would have whole fiords named after them.[3] According to the sagas, only 14 ships completed the first major crossing, undoubtedly a good reflection of the dangers encountered in the stormy waters between Iceland and Greenland. The Norsemen found evidence of old settlements and parts of boats, but who these older sites might have belonged to we don't know. Although it has been speculated that they were the remains of Palaeoeskimo camps, I am equally inclined to believe that some of these remains are related to activities of the Irish, who had frequented the region many decades before the Norsemen. At the time of the Norse *Landnam*, Dorset people were certainly present on Ellesmere Island and in northern Greenland. They may also have occupied part of the east coast of Greenland. According to the Floamanna saga, Torgils Orrabeinfostre was wrecked on the east coast of Greenland around A.D. 1000. It took him several years to reach the Norse settlements, during which time he supposedly encountered witches, conceivably Natives.[4] At that time, the only indigenous people in Greenland would have been the Dorset.

The two largest Norse settlement areas in Greenland were called Østerbygd (the Eastern Settlement) and Vesterbygd (the Western Settlement). Østerbygd farms were scattered throughout the southwestern part of Greenland, while the Vesterbygd settlement took in the fiord system near the present-day capital of Greenland, Nuuk. A smaller number of farms were located between these two major centres. It is estimated that by about A.D. 1250, probably the pinnacle of the Norse period in Greenland, the settlements included at least 280 farms, 17 parish churches, including the bishop's cathedral at Gardar in Østerbygd, and 2 monasteries. Population estimates vary considerably, ranging between 4000 and 5000 inhabitants.[5] As far as we know, the Norsemen had not encountered any Native people (Skraelings) in Greenland before the early part of the thirteenth century. It had been a very different story on the North American continent to the west, initially explored by Eirik the Red's son Leif Eiriksson and the Norwegian merchant Thorfinn Karlsefni. In Vinland and Markland (the Gulf of Saint Lawrence region and Labrador), they had encountered fierce opposition to their presence from local Indian groups, whom they also referred to as Skraelings.[6] It is not inconceivable that some of these Skraelings, particularly in Labrador, may have been Dorset people.

Although the Norse Greenlanders were excellent hunters as well as farmers, they still needed to trade for many of their needs, such as iron, grain, and whatever luxuries they could afford. With the exception of walrus hides and ivory, narwhal tusks, woolen cloth, and live falcons, the Norse Greenlanders could offer little of value when the Norwegian trade vessel, the *knarr*, arrived from Bergen. The pursuit of walrus and narwhals took place far north of Vesterbygd in an area they called Nordrsetur, most likely the region around Disko Bay. Hunting pressure and diminishing returns undoubtedly caused the Nordrsetur hunters to head farther and father north until they faced the immense, ice-choked vastness of Melville Bay. By A.D. 1250, they were about to encounter the first of the pioneering Thule Inuit families who had crossed Smith Sound and were now advancing steadily southward along the west Greenland coast.

Meanwhile, the Catholic Church and the Norwegian Crown were exerting increasing pressure on the Greenland Freestate, extracting ever-increasing amounts of taxes and tithe payments. In A.D. 1260, King Haakonsson of Norway brought Greenland under his rule and declared exclusive trading rights with the distant colony. It was the beginning of a long decline for the Norse settlements, which ended with the abandonment of Østerbygd about A.D. 1450. The farms of Vesterbygd had been abandoned about a hundred years earlier.[7]

When we started excavating the early Thule culture winter house ruins on Skraeling Island, we didn't expect to find artifacts of Norse origin. We were proceeding on the assumption that the thirteenth-century Norse items found by Erik Holtved in Thule culture house ruins on Ruin Island in Inglefield Land were intrusive, that somehow they had been left in the house ruins long after the houses were first occupied. If the Norse artifacts were not intrusive, the popular theory of a tenth-century arrival of the Thule culture Inuit in North Greenland was definitely in jeopardy. This background made what happened on Skraeling Island that much more exciting.

Because I spent a fair amount of time each day assisting and checking on the other excavations on the site, I had chosen to work on a smaller house ruin close to camp, ably assisted by Jimmy Nowra. We had removed the sod cover from the entire dwelling and were excavating our way down towards the floor when I uncovered the chain mail just below the outside edge of a meat pit. Nearby, I found a thick, flat piece of iron very different from the thin sections of meteoritic iron we had come across before. The finding of a complete ship rivet suggested that it had been removed from the ship by splitting or burning the ship's planking. On the floor, near the back of the house, Jimmy had located a peculiar-looking ivory needle case, decorated with two figurines. It was a type matched by needle cases from Alaska. After a long and lively discussion with the rest of the team over lunch, Jimmy and I returned to House 6, now dubbed the chain mail house.

Overhead photo of House 6 on the Skraeling Island site. The chain mail was found adjacent to the stone-lined meat pit in which the first ship rivet was found. The meat pit is situated just left of the entrance to the separate kitchen.

The Viking ship rivet as it was discovered near the bottom of the meat pit in House 6 on the Skraeling Island site.

During the following field seasons, more than 50 items of Norse origin were found in early Thule culture winter houses in the Bache Peninsula region. The finds included two pieces of woven woolen cloth, a carpenter's plane, barrel bottom sections, a gaming piece, more ship rivets, knife and spear blades, iron wedges, and numerous pieces of iron and copper. Experts in Denmark concluded that the two pieces of woolen cloth, from House 15, most likely had been spun in Greenland. An analysis of the plane, found by Peter Francis in the same house, indicated that the carpenter's tool had been shaped from a piece of birch, *Betula pubescens* ssp. *tortuosa*, most probably obtained in the inner fiord areas of Østerbygd.[8] The use of a thin, crooked branch of birch for the plane may suggest that decent wood had become difficult to find in the Norse settlement.

On Skraeling Island and other early Thule sites in the Bache region, there was no doubt about the provenience of the Norse artifacts; every one of them had been left behind by the people who occupied the dwellings. A piece of charred oak from the cooking hearth in the chain mail house gave a radiocarbon date of about A.D. 1260. The woolen cloth from House 15 on Skraeling Island produced a date of about A.D. 1200.

Items believed to be of Norse origin have shown up elsewhere in the Arctic. A section of a bronze balance, supposedly of Norse origin, was located in a tent ring on the west coast of Ellesmere Island.[9] Several pieces of terrestrial iron have been found in house ruins dated to the twelfth or thirteenth centuries on the west coast of Hudson Bay.[10] A piece of smelted iron and part of a cast bronze bowl were located on Devon Island in house ruins thought to date to the fifteenth century. House ruins on Bathurst Island, believed to date to the twelfth century, yielded pieces of smelted copper, meteoritic iron, and a small bronze pendant.[11] In 1949, Eigil Knuth located the frame of an old Thule culture umiak at Herlufsholm Strand in Northeast Greenland.[12] A small piece of

Two ivory needle cases located on the floor in the rear section of House 6 on the Skraeling Island site. The style of the needle cases is directly linked to similar finds in western Alaska.

the boat's gunwale turned out to be oak, and was subsequently dated to about A.D. 1230, similar in age to the charred oak from the chain mail house on Skraeling Island.

We had proven that the Norse artifacts on Skraeling Island had been in the hands of some of the pioneering Thule culture families to reach the Smith Sound region from Alaska. But how did the artifacts get there? There were essentially two ways: the items could have been brought northward by Thule people who had obtained them through barter with Norsemen in West Greenland; or, they were brought to the Smith Sound region by venturesome Norsemen in search of better walrus and narwhal hunting grounds. Although it is difficult to prove, I very much favour the last explanation. As articles of long-distance trade, the woolen cloth pieces, the chain mail rings, the carpenter's plane, the barrel bottom sections, and the gaming piece would have offered little more than esoteric value. The woolen cloth sections had been thrown into a corner of House 15 together with what looked like scrap pieces of skin. The Norse carpenter's plane had likewise been cast aside after the iron blade was removed. Of the Viking ship rivets, only two had been reworked and used as harpoon end blades or

A large piece of woven, woolen cloth found on the floor of House 15 on the Skraeling Island site. Experts in Copenhagen believe the cloth was originally woven on one of the Norse farms in southern Greenland.

A well-preserved iron knife blade from House 5 on the Skraeling Island site. The metal analysis of the iron indicated that it originated in Norway.

arrow points; the remaining clinch nails were intact. The knife blade, spear point, and three sturdy iron wedges would have been worthwhile trade items; one wonders why they too were left behind when the Inuit moved on. Was leaving behind something of special value a way of securing good luck on the next winter site, or perhaps a way of thanking the spirits for the use of a favourable winter site?

Perhaps the best indication of an actual Norse presence on Skraeling Island came to light one afternoon in House 22, when Diane Lyons noticed what looked like cut marks on a small piece of driftwood. From under a thin layer of dirt and grease, there appeared the facial features of a distinctly non-Inuit person. Was it the depiction of a guest in the winter house, or did the Inuit carver shape the wood to a likeness of someone he or she had seen somewhere else? Averaging the radiocarbon dates from House 22 and the adjoining House 21 gave us a date of about A.D. 1240 for the use of these dwellings.

I have already alluded to some of the other, more controversial pieces of evidence occasionally presented as proof of a Norse presence in the High Arctic.

The eider duck shelters are a feature known to have been used by Norsemen in Iceland and Norway. Is it a long stretch to suggest that the idea of enticing eider ducks to nest in certain locations was introduced to the High Arctic Inuit by the Norsemen? Perhaps. The questionable association of eider duck nests and Norsemen leads us to the equally debatable connection between polar bear traps and Norsemen. It is alleged that Norse Greenlanders on rare occasions shipped live polar bears to kings and bishops in Europe,[13] but would this practice have involved the use of large traps? It is most unlikely. The catching and transport of bears to Europe must have involved young cubs taken from dens after the mother was killed, certainly not grown bears. The Inuit, on the other hand, had at least two good reasons for trapping bears; one was food and the hide; the other might have been a matter of convenience. Polar bears, like foxes, were a great nuisance in areas where meat had been stored for the winter, and they could do considerably more damage to the stone caches. If one could trap foxes, why not bears?

The Norse Greenlanders had much better reasons to travel far north of Disko Bay than searching for eiders and bears. As mentioned earlier, by A.D. 1250 increasing demand for tusks and hides as trade commodities had placed considerable strain on the northern hunting areas. To add to that problem, the Norsemen were now facing competition of a very different kind: marvelously skilled Inuit hunters from North Greenland.

Before meeting the Skraelings, Norse hunters might have been reluctant to cross the rather intimidating Melville Bay. Initial encounters between Inuit and Norsemen in Nordrsetur and Inuit stories of excellent narwhal and walrus hunting north of that area may have been the motivation needed to set out on voyages of exploration to the Far North. Once the Norsemen reached Smith Sound, the magnificent mountains and enticing shores of Ellesmere Island were only 45 kilometres away, a quick crossing by sail under the right conditions. There are references in the Norse sagas to such northern voyages. One of these mentions a voyage of the priests of Østerbygd, the centre of Church power and the home of the Greenlandic bishop. Not only was the Church keenly interested in ivory, but a voyage to the Far North would also give members of the clergy a firsthand impression of the newly discovered heathens in those remote regions. Unfortunately little is known about the voyage, mentioned only briefly in a letter to the Greenlandic bishop who was visiting Iceland. Another fascinating reference to an ancient voyage of exploration to northern Greenland tells of the expedition of the mathematician and Carmelite Nicholas of Lynne, who is thought to have made such a journey around A.D. 1350. Nicholas apparently described the voyage in a book entitled *Inventio Fortunatae*, which has since been lost. The book was mentioned by an English merchant, John Day, in a letter to the Grand Lord Admiral of Spain (possibly Columbus) in 1497. In his letter, John Day states that the book could no longer be found. Even so, in 1577, the cartographer Mercator reproduced a map supposedly originating from that book.[14] If Nicholas of Lynne's account of his travels is ever found, it may shed some light on the abandonment of the Norsemen's Vesterbygd. Presently we only have the brief words of Ivar Bårdsson (Bardum) to go by. About A.D. 1350, Bårdsson, the bishop's deputy at the episcopal church of Gardar, was sent north to Vesterbygd by the Lawspeaker to investigate rumours about difficulties between Norsemen and Skraelings. When he reached the settlement, he found cattle and sheep roaming the fields but no sign of either Norsemen or Heathens (Skraelings). To this day the disappearance of the Norsemen from Vesterbygd remains an unsolved mystery. If the plague, which at that time was ravaging Norway and the trade centre at Bergen, had not wiped out the Norse settlers, where had they gone? No records exist of an influx of Vesterbygd refugees in Iceland or any other Atlantic destinations. Did they choose to head west to known regions in Markland or Vinland? We may never know.

Norse activities in the Far North were probably limited because of the considerable distance to Smith Sound, even from Disko Bay, and the hazardous ice conditions along the way. It is possible that most of the Norse artifacts found in the region originated from a single expedition. Having crossed Smith Sound, the Norse voyagers may have proceeded northward along the east coast of Ellesmere Island until ice conditions prevented any further progress. The northernmost evidence for such a voyage may have existed on top of a prominent island overlooking Kane Basin—Washington Irving Island.

On the eve of August 12th, 1875, the British explorer Captain George S. Nares and several of his men climbed the steep scree-slope to the top of Washington Irving Island, located off the east coast of Ellesmere Island, about 79°33′N. Heavy pack ice had temporarily halted the progress of Nares's ships the *Alert* and the *Discovery* en route to the northeast coast of Ellesmere Island, farther north than any Westerner had ever journeyed. On top of the prominent southern plateau, they discovered two ancient, lichen-covered stone cairns.[15]

It was the American explorer Dr. Elisha Kent Kane who saw the distant island during his 1853–55 expedition and named it after his favourite author, Washington Irving.[16] Kane's discovery and naming of the island appear to have gone unnoticed by Nares, normally a stickler for geographical accuracy, who referred to the island as "Sphinx Island" in his expedition records. As a man who regularly erected cairns and deposited messages along his route, Nares was obviously intrigued with the two cairns. He asked his ship's surgeon, Edward Moss, to make a drawing of them. Nares correctly assumed that the Inuit were not in the habit of erecting cairns on prominent points high above sea level. To mark particular, epic achievements far away from home was an activity typical of Western explorers. For the Polar Eskimos (Inughuit), this part of the world was home; to be there was a matter of everyday life, not an occasion to be celebrated by erecting cairns.

In the fall of 1876, Nares revisited Washington Irving Island, following his overwintering near the northeastern tip of Ellesmere Island. His account of the second visit is very confusing, alluding not only to the cairn built by his own men, but to a reexamination of the two old, lichen-covered cairns. We can only assume that he was referring to an examination of the *location* of the two old cairns, since both had apparently been torn down the year before.

Drawing of two ancient cairns on top of Washington Irving Island by Edward Moss of the 1875–76 Nares expedition to the High Arctic (From Moss, 1878). The two cairns were most probably constructed by members of a Norse expedition exploring the Kane Basin area in the thirteenth century.

The next recorded visit to the island was by members of the ill-fated United States Lady Franklin Bay Expedition of 1881-84, under the command of General A. W. Greely.[17] On their voyage northward through Kane Basin, members of the Greely expedition visited the island, retrieved the original Nares record from the cairn, and left a copy behind, together with a record of their own progress. Two years later, during their desperate southward retreat, one of Greely's men, Sergeant Rice, checked the Washington Irving Island cairn once again and reported it untouched since their last visit. Strangely enough, there is no indication that Otto Sverdrup, the champion of everything Norwegian and Norse, visited the cairns during his wintering near Pim Island between 1898 and 1899. Since he also ignored Nares's original naming of Skraeling Island, one wonders if he had read the English captain's journals. The fact that Peary, who wintered even closer to Washington Irving Island, didn't bother to investigate it comes as no surprise. His obsession with reaching the North Pole left little room for other interests.

As far as I know, there are no other recorded visits to the island until 1939. In March of that year, RCMP Constable L. T. Fyfe and two Inuit assistants, Nookapunguaq and Sikeuse, set out on a 500-kilometre-long sled patrol from the Royal Canadian Mounted Police post at Craig Harbour on the southeast coast of Ellesmere Island.[18] Their destination was Washington Irving Island, where they hoped to locate the cairns and search for evidence to prove that they were indeed of Norse origin. When they reached the island they found only one cairn, which they described as being about eight feet high. It is not clear whether they knew that this was Nares's construction and not one of the old cairns. A tin can containing the written record of Nares's visit was found on the ground near the cairn. Constable Fyfe makes no mention of finding the message Greely left in it, but reports that he collected Nares's message, and left in its place a record of his own visit to the island. Nor does he indicate that the Nares message he found was a copy of the original, which supposedly had been removed by Greely's men. Sometime between 1883 and 1939, somebody visited the Nares cairn, went through the message tin, and dropped it on the ground. There can be little doubt that this visit was made by Inughuit hunters who had spotted the prominent Nares cairn during their travels past the island.

In Greenland, the first solid evidence of Norse voyages far north of Vesterbygd came to light early in the nineteenth century, when a stone with runic inscriptions was located near three cairns on Kingigtorssuaq Island, northwest of Upernavik, about 72°55′N. The small, dark-grey stone (10 by 4 centimetres) had been found by an Inuk, Pelimut, and presented to the Danish Lieutenant Commander, W. A. Graah in 1824. The inscription reads: *Erling Sigvatsson, Bjarne Tordsson and Eindride Oddsson erected these cairns on the Saturday before Rogation Day, and runed well.* The rune message is fairly securely dated to a spring day (the Saturday before Rogation Day) between A.D. 1250 and 1350, and less reliably to A.D. 1333.[19]

With that discovery in mind, we were keen to explore Washington Irving Island, the first visit since 1939, or so we believed. A helicopter flight was arranged with the PCSP during the summer of 1979, and it was with great anticipation that we lifted off from Skraeling Island, heading out over a wide-open Buchanan Bay. Just as we approached the south coast of Bache Peninsula, we spotted several pods of narwhal congregating in the deep, dark waters far below us. They all appeared to be male narwhal, positioned in several large circular formations with tusks pointing inward, like a group of medieval knights crossing lances before the joust. After photographing the peculiar narwhal behaviour below us, we crossed Bache Peninsula and Princess Marie Bay, skirting spectacular, precipitous headlands that soared hundreds of metres straight up from narrow shorelines. Along the way we spotted two of Peary's old coal depots, left behind during one of his many attempts to reach the Pole.

The island came into view: vertical cliffs supporting a broad, gently sloping southern plateau where the cairn was supposed to be. As the helicopter circled the plateau, we spotted what appeared to be a small cairn; even from the air it looked frustratingly recent. On the ground our impression was confirmed; with disappointment, we noted the 1975 Canadian Hydrographic Survey marker embedded in the ground next to a heap of boulders. To add to our frustration, gathering storm clouds were fast closing in on us; the pilot was anxious to leave the island. A quick search of the plateau revealed a concentration of lichen-covered boulders some distance north of the hydrographic cairn; was this the remains of one of the two cairns seen by Nares? We photographed what there was to see and left the island with more questions than answers. Subsequent meetings with members of the Hydrographic Survey in Ottawa gave us the impression that the stones and boulders piled around the hydrographic marker had come from a "nearby" cairn. We knew that we had to return to the island for a careful search of the south plateau.

Sixteen years later we found the opportunity. This time the weather was on our side; we stepped out of the helicopter on top of Washington Irving Island under clear blue skies, with barely a wind stirring. As soon as our field gear and supplies were secured, the helicopter took off for other destinations. The sound of the engine diminished until all we could hear was an enormous silence. The vista was spectacular—to the south and east, tightly packed drift ice in Kane Basin stretched as far as the eye could see. Small wonder that early explorers had made the arduous climb to the top to see what conditions were like.

The southern plateau of Washington Irving Island, 194 metres above sea level. "a" marks the location of a recent Canadian Hydrographic Survey stake and the remains of Nares's 1875 cairn; "b" marks the location of the remains of one of the ancient Norse cairns.

For one full day we investigated the entire plateau, measuring and photographing obvious and not-so-obvious remains of cairns. The heap of boulders next to the hydrographic marker had diminished since our previous visit, revealing the very base of the original Nares cairn, including the tin message box. The Canadian Forces had used most of the remaining boulders to lay out a cloth marker as part of an aerial photography project. A study of the old drawing of the two cairns strongly suggested that the scatter of boulders we had noticed years before was indeed the remains of one of the two original cairns.

The author standing next to the remains of Nares's 1875 cairn and the hydrographic marker on Washington Irving Island. "b" marks the location of the remains of one of the ancient Norse cairns. (Photo credit: Karen McCullough)

The second had probably stood just about where we found the remains of the Nares cairn. For hours we searched every major stone and boulder on the plateau for any evidence of a Norse presence; a small runic stone like the one from Upernavik in Greenland would have been rewarding. We knew it was a long shot and were not surprised to leave the island empty-handed. Even without such evidence, I am convinced that the two cairns discovered by Nares were built by Norse voyagers. Including the finds made by Holtved, we now have nearly 80 items of Norse origin from the Smith Sound region. Most of the finds were made in almost identical-looking Thule culture winter house ruins, with the greatest concentration located on Skraeling Island.

I believe that one or more Norse vessels entered the Smith Sound region on a voyage of exploration, sometime in the late thirteenth century. Heavy pack ice in Kane Basin forced the Norsemen to sail close to the Ellesmere Island coast as they attempted to penetrate farther northward. It was a route followed by all subsequent expeditions trying to get north of Kane Basin. The cairns on

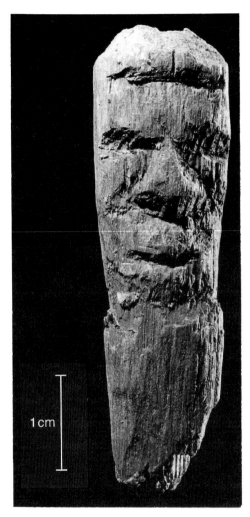

Wooden carving of a face with distinctly non-Inuit features, found in House 22 on the Skraeling Island site.

Washington Irving Island may have marked the farthest north achieved by the Norsemen before they turned towards home. Their vessel or vessels may have been crushed in the ice; the survivors may have lived with the Inuit on Skraeling Island for a winter or two; the face, so delicately carved on a small piece of driftwood and left behind in House 22 on Skraeling Island, may have been a portrait of one of the survivors. The possible scenarios are many and will remain totally speculative until we find those voices in stone, the carefully inscribed runic message.

Towards the end of the fifteenth century, Neoeskimos occupied most of the coastal regions of Greenland, including the land that had supported Norse farmers for nearly five centuries. The last of the valuable church bells in Østerbygd had been taken down by the priest and loaded on the departing *knarr* a decade or two before Columbus landed on San Salvador. Unfortunately for the Native population of the New World, he would succeed where the Norsemen had failed. Although the increasing presence of Inuit in southern Greenland may have hastened the Norse abandonment, there were many other contributing causes: increasing isolation from Europe, climatic deterioration, soil erosion, poor hay yields for domestic animals, decline of societal cohesion brought about by greedy Church officials and Norwegian kings, possible pirate attacks, and diseases. No single reason can explain the final collapse of Europe's most westerly outpost. Unfortunately for the Norsemen, there were many evils to choose from.

11

Death and Abandonment

A dismal scene greeted Jens Munk as he staggered to the railing of the Unicorn *and gazed out over Munk's Harbour and the land he had named Nova Dania on the southwest coast of Hudson Bay. It was June 1620. The Danish explorer had just penned his final will and testament. As far as he knew, the entire crew had died from scurvy; there seemed little reason to believe that he would ever see the shores of Denmark again. Then, suddenly, he spotted two men walking near the smaller vessel* Lamprey, *dragged up on shore the previous fall. Haunted by the spectacle of their dead comrades, the three men worked feverishly to ready the vessel for escape. On July 16 they pushed her into the shallow waters of the bay and headed for home. For 67 days they struggled through ice-infested, storm-swept seas, crossed Hudson Bay, sailed through the Strait, rounded Cape Farvel on the southeast tip of Greenland and entered the North Atlantic. On September 20, the master mariner spotted distant mountains on the west coast of Norway; they had completed a sea voyage no less epic than any carried out by their Viking ancestors.*

In contrast to Martin Frobisher and Henry Hudson, who had experienced several violent encounters with Thule culture Inuit on Baffin Island, Jens Munk and his men had met no one during their wintering on the west coast of Hudson Bay.[1] A few decades later the Northern Hemisphere entered a period of colder climatic conditions, which culminated in the Little Ice Age between A.D. 1650 and 1850. Glaciers advanced, fast-ice areas became more extensive, and the tundra pushed the tree line southward.[2] The effects of these environmental and ecological changes were felt most keenly by the Thule culture Inuit living in the more central regions of the Canadian Arctic.[3] The winter settlements of large, semipermanent, sod and whale bone houses gave way to winter snow house communities easily abandoned and reestablished as the need to find new hunting areas arose. Open-water hunting of large sea mammals became less important than breathing-hole hunting of ringed seals. Although the coast of Labrador and the more southerly regions of eastern and western Greenland were less severely influenced by the deteriorating climatic conditions,

A large, early twentieth-century snow house winter village on the sea ice in the central Canadian Arctic. (Photo credit: Canadian Museum of Civilization)

cultural responses took place nevertheless. The most impressive of these was a fairly rapid shift in the size of winter houses. The earlier settlements had consisted of a number of one- or two-platform houses occupied by extended families. This pattern gave way to the use of large, rectangular dwellings that sometimes housed the entire settlement of 30 to 40 people. As mentioned earlier, I cut my first Thule sods on one of those giant structures in Saglek Bay on the central coast of Labrador. As we unearthed the large dwelling from under thick layers of sod, I was amazed to see that the interior arrangements were essentially identical to late Thule communal houses in Greenland. The raised sleeping platform, extending all along the back and sides of the interior, faced a flagged central floor area and the entrance tunnel. Jutting out at regular intervals from the edge of the platform were smaller lamp and cooking platforms, one for each family occupying the platform. The large roof structure had been supported by driftwood logs.[4] An excellent description of the living arrangements in the Greenlandic communal houses was made by the Danish naval officer Gustav Holm, who led an umiak expedition up the southeast coast of Greenland in 1884.[5] According to his observations, each family group occupied a specific section of the platform, separated from its neighbours by a piece of hide or sealskin.

In 1771, the Moravian missionary Jens Haven entered a large communal dwelling in Saglek Bay, possibly the one we excavated two hundred years later.[6] His puritanical reaction to a large group of Natives going about their communal lifestyle in limited attire, with little regard for Moravian modesty, led to a concerted effort by the Moravians to convince the Inuit to return to winter life in smaller family dwellings. My work in Labrador showed that the missionaries eventually achieved their objective; towards the end of the eighteenth century, the Inuit winter houses in Labrador reverted to a smaller, single-family form.[7]

On Baffin Island, the Inuit followed the same trend towards wintering in large, communal-type dwellings; but their houses were of a different style. Probably because access to driftwood was limited, the Baffinlanders continued to use bowhead whale ribs and jaws for roof supports, which resulted in large, cloverleaf-shaped houses with three sleeping platforms facing a central floor area.[8] Why the change in house style? What encouraged people to move under one roof instead of many? As usual there is no single explanation, but rather the coming together of a series of challenges. The move to a communal lifestyle may have been a response to deteriorating climatic conditions, which reduced the availability of larger sea mammals. Communal residence would encourage greater sharing of resources brought to camp and reduce the amount of blubber needed for heat, light, and cooking.[9] At an earlier stage, Norse settlers in Greenland responded in a similar way by constructing multiroom farm dwellings, in which nearly all activity areas were concentrated.

Interestingly enough, the idea of spending the winter in a communal setting was never far from the Thule Inuit mind. Perhaps all that was needed was a real incentive to do so. The early Thule culture winter sites in the Bache Peninsula region, particularly on Skraeling Island, consisted of several extended family dwellings associated with a larger communal dwelling. In Alaska, these gathering houses, referred to as *karigi*, served primarily as places where men worked on their hunting equipment, received guests, and socialized. Women brought food several times during the day and participated in some of the dances and ceremonies.[10] This particular arrangement was an essential part of the social structure that guided the lives of the early Thule culture Inuit. As they migrated eastward, they encountered new environments and new challenges that required different solutions. Given the small size of the winter communities on Skraeling Island, women may have been involved to a greater extent in *karigi* activities than was the case in Alaska.[11] Even so, the tradition of preparing meals in the family dwellings and bringing them to the *karigi* continued, at least for a while.

Although guided by certain taboos, rules, and accepted codes of behaviour, people still remain pragmatic, especially in an area like the High Arctic. We have already noted the switch from clay to soapstone vessels. The tradition of cooking over open fires in separate kitchen rooms was soon abandoned in favour of using seal-oil lamps for heat, light, and cooking on small platforms within the main dwelling. Fastidious use of limited energy resources was an essential element of survival. It would not have taken a great leap of imagination for the

Thule Inuit to decide to use the communal house on a 24-hour basis instead of maintaining a number of individual households. The move required only some physical restructuring, such as incorporating sleeping platforms and cooking areas. On the social level, life in a communal winter house undoubtedly encouraged greater prominence of one or more leaders in the community.

When George Nares sailed into Buchanan Bay in the fall of 1875, he did not see or encounter any Inuit. In fact, he did not meet up with any Inuit along the northeast coast of Ellesmere Island. The same was unfortunately true for Greely, whose men might have been saved had some of the Inughuit from North Greenland wintered in the Bache Peninsula region in 1883. Otto Sverdrup and his men encountered a few Inughuit while wintering in Fram Harbour near Pim Island between 1898 and 1899.[12] The Inughuit he met were involved with Peary's exploration activities, as were most of the Inughuit population at one time or another. With the exception of that encounter, Sverdrup and his men did not meet up with any Inuit during their four years of exploring the Arctic Islands. This was altogether puzzling. Ellesmere Island had been a major winter and summer settlement area for the Thule culture Inuit for hundreds of years. Why was it abandoned, and when?

It was nearly midnight when we first saw the steep, rocky island at the juncture of three great fiords, Hayes, Jokel, and Beitstad. Approaching the almost vertical cliffs on the east side of the island, we couldn't see enough level land anywhere to hold a Thule culture winter settlement. But as we flew around to the west side, a gently sloping, narrow valley and low headland came into view. The remains of large, sod-walled winter house ruins were immediately visible. This was Sverdrup's Haa Island and, as we discovered through later excavations, it was also the last major winter settlement of the Thule culture Inuit in the Bache Peninsula region and possibly on Ellesmere Island.

Haa Island is in the centre of prime breathing-hole hunting of ringed seals in the winter and basking seal hunting in the spring. In the summer, walrus and beluga whales frequent the area, as bowhead once did. The island is also situated near a convenient route via Beitstad Fiord to muskox and caribou hunting areas in and beyond Sverdrup Pass. We were impressed, not only with the dimensions of the site, but with the size of the many large, cloverleaf-shaped sod and whale bone houses, each with three prominent sleeping platforms. I was quite familiar with this style of dwelling from Cumberland Sound on Baffin Island.

Work on Haa Island turned out to be a difficult logistic undertaking. With our hands full on Skraeling Island and Knud Peninsula, we could not establish a permanent base camp on Haa Island. Instead, we decided to operate brief out-camps on the island, working intensively for short periods of time. Although the heavily vegetated site was quite wet, preservation of organic materials was excellent, no doubt reflecting the relatively recent occupation of the site. There was little doubt that the excavations would shed light on the late Thule culture activities in the area. The location of the large settlement was by itself an indication of change, as it was the only winter site situated that far from the winter floe edge of the open North Water.

Overhead photo of one of the largest and perhaps last occupied of the Haa Island communal winter houses, House 10. The structure was unusual in having the three raised sleeping platforms constructed in a row rather than in a cloverleaf-shape as in the other communal houses on the site. The sub-rectangular outline of House 10 is more reminiscent of the Labrador and Greenland communal dwellings. The total length of House 10, about 9 metres, was difficult to estimate since the right side, including part of the right sleeping platform, had been greatly disturbed.

We tested a number of dwellings and excavated the better part of one of the largest, House 10, which also appeared to be the last one occupied, judging by the large number of whale bones scattered in and around the dwelling. On

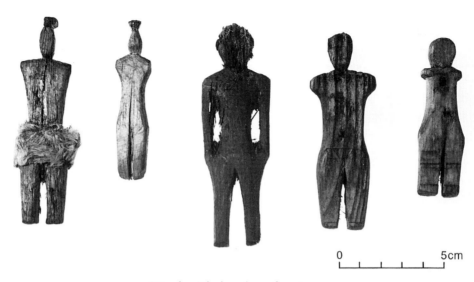

Wooden Thule culture figurines.

large Thule culture winter sites, whale ribs and jaws were repeatedly removed from older house ruins and used in new constructions. We have often speculated that many of these winter sites probably started with the beaching of a large whale, the eventual source of important building material that was then used and re-used for hundreds of years. The last dwellings to be occupied on a site would be full of bones. Excavations on Haa Island revealed that most of the houses had several distinct floor levels; they had been occupied on several occasions. That in itself was not unusual, but the fact that, in almost every instance, the last occupation was represented by only a shallow layer of refuse and the entrance tunnel had not been used was different from what we had observed on other sites. These final occupations looked very much like "autumn houses" (*quarmats*) I had seen on late Thule culture sites on Baffin Island. The fall structures usually consisted of single- or double-layered skin tents covering older sod house foundations. The autumn house eventually replaced the sod, stone, and bone house as the primary winter dwelling.

The inner fiord location of the Haa Island site indicated that the inhabitants had a strong preference for hunting seals at their winter and spring breathing holes in areas of extensive fast ice. This significant shift away from open-water hunting had already taken place in many central Arctic regions in response to environmental changes brought about by the Little Ice Age. A study of harpoon heads from the Haa Island dwellings and a radiocarbon date on charred wood from the floor area of House 10 suggested that the site had been used extensively

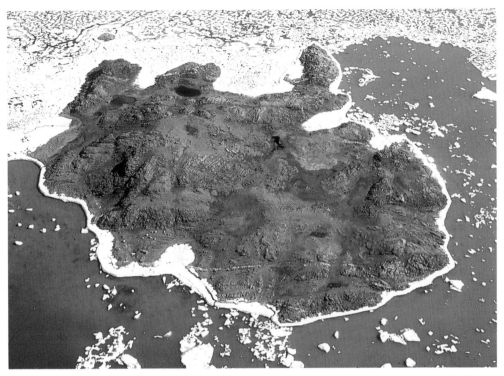

The southern portion of Skraeling Island looking northeast. Our base camp is situated adjacent to a small, ice-covered bight on the southwest shore.

The Thule culture *karigi*, House 2, on Sverdrup site, Skraeling Island.

The author uncovering the Norse woolen cloth in House 15, Skraeling Island site (Photo credit: Karen McCullough).

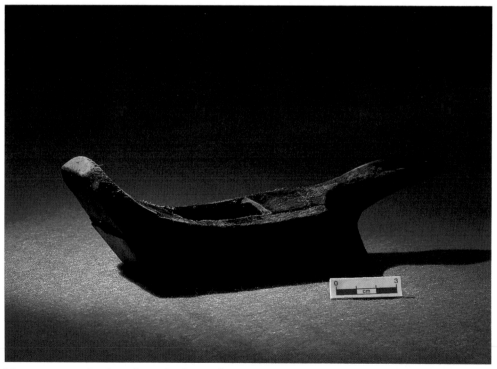

Norse carpenter's plane from the floor of House 15, Skraeling Island site (Photo credit: Jim Peacock).

Peary's huts at Fort Conger, Ellesmere Island.

Cross and cairn erected near Fram Harbour in memory of Johan Svendsen, physician on the Second Norwegian Fram Expedition, who killed himself on Knud Peninsula in 1899.

A Thule culture animal figurine from Skraeling Island. The carving depicts four different animals: polar bear, beluga, seal, and duck (Photo credit: Jim Peacock).

somewhere between A.D. 1650 and 1700. All evidence pointed to strong and direct cultural ties to more southerly regions of the central and eastern Canadian Arctic, especially Baffin Island. Was it possible that the direct ancestors of the Inughuit had arrived in the Smith Sound region much later than we thought?

For a long time it has been generally assumed that the Inughuit, who met Ross and Parry in 1818, traced their ancestry all the way back to the early Thule culture pioneers. This view was not seriously challenged until two Danish linguists came up with the hypothesis that the present-day Inughuit are the descendants of Thule culture Inuit who migrated to North Greenland from northern Canada, possibly as late as the eighteenth century.[13] It was an intriguing thought, and the more we studied the late Thule data from Haa Island, the more we were inclined to support the theory. What remains an enigma is the fact that nowhere in Inughuit myths and legends have we found references to a recent arrival into Greenland.

As we have learned from studying the Palaeoeskimo occupations in the High Arctic, cultural continuity in a marginal region is difficult to achieve, particularly with small populations. It makes sense that the Thule culture Inuit, even if they were much better adapted than the Palaeoeskimos to arctic conditions, experienced times when resources became too meagre to sustain the population. One result of colder climatic conditions during the Little Ice Age was the expansion and duration of fast ice, the favourite environment for ringed seals. The Inuit hunters who shifted their technology sufficiently to take advantage of breathing-hole hunting would do well; others would not. As the climatic conditions worsened in the Smith Sound and Baffin Bay area, Inuit families, descendants of the pioneering Arctic whale hunters, may have decided to seek better hunting conditions on the west coast of Greenland. The Inuit who migrated northward from the eastern Arctic and established the large winter settlement on Haa Island may have entered an abandoned or scarcely populated region. In addition to their well-developed techniques for hunting seals at breathing holes and their triple-platform house style, they brought with them a central/eastern Arctic dialect of Inuktitut. I suspect that they may also have been responsible for the appearance of another cultural trait: the practice of placing their dead in large stone-cairn burials. When I worked on Thule sites in Labrador and Cumberland Sound, I was amazed at the large number of cairn burials, both in and around the big winter and summer camps. In sharp contrast, on the east coast of Ellesmere Island such burials are quite rare and found only in close proximity to late Thule winter house ruins. Not surprisingly, the greatest concentration of such burials was found on Haa Island.

If this scenario is correct, then the northward migration of the late Thule culture Inuit from Baffin Island most likely represents the only time when deteriorating climatic conditions in the High Arctic actually favoured a prehistoric population movement. The size of their settlements and the multifamily winter houses on Ellesmere Island and in North Greenland suggests that these latecomers to the High Arctic were doing very well. They may have hunted and lived in the Bache Peninsula region intermittently for some time, shifting their activities back and forth between Ellesmere Island and Greenland. Hunting conditions may have been more favourable along the Greenland coast, where archaeologists have located many of their winter settlements between Inglefield Bay and Cape York.[14] Some of the later *quarmat* structures on Haa Island may reflect occasional return visits by Inughuit families, who crossed Smith Sound to spend the fall hunting muskoxen in Sverdrup Pass and beyond.

The Inughuit, when encountered by John Ross near Cape York, explained to Ross's Native interpreter Sacheuse that they lived in houses built entirely of stone and that each house sheltered several families. Ross was told that they no longer built kayaks, nor apparently fished or hunted with bow and arrow. It must be emphasized that Ross and his men met only a small number of Polar Eskimos. Did they in fact adequately represent the whole Inughuit population at the time? Several of the Inughuit had bravely come aboard Ross's ship. When asked if their country contained as many people as there were pieces of ice around the ship, they replied: "many more." According to Ross's account, there were perhaps as many as a thousand fragments floating around the ship.[15] Even if that number is greatly inflated, it leaves room for a substantial population in 1818. Yet, by the time Isaac Hayes wintered in North Greenland in 1860–61, the Inughuit population was down to about a hundred souls.[16] What had happened? Had a hundred or more years of severe climatic conditions reduced the Inughuit population to the point of near extinction, or had most families escaped to more southerly regions, like West Greenland and Baffin Island? I don't think so. I believe the answer may lie with the whalers, who followed Ross's ships, the *Alexander* and the *Isabella*, into Baffin Bay, keen to exploit the newly discovered whaling grounds. For the next 30 years, large numbers of whaling ships continued to "fish" regularly in Baffin Bay and Lancaster Sound.[17] Many of them touched the shores of North Greenland, unfortunately with catastrophic results for the Inughuit. Although the available references to such events are not many, they are telling enough.

Sherard Osborn, commander of the *Pioneer* during the 1850 Franklin searches, makes several interesting observations concerning the Polar Eskimos:

> *Old whale-fishermen say that, when in former days their pursuit carried them into the head of Baffin's Bay, they found the natives numerous; and it is undoubted that, in spite of an apparently severe mortality amongst these Arctic Highlanders, or Northern Esquimaux, the stock is not yet extinct. Every whaler who has visited the coast northward of Cape York during late years reports deserted villages and dead bodies, as if some sudden epidemic had cut down men and women suddenly and in their prime.*
>
> *The "Intrepid's" people found in the huts of the natives which were situated close to the winter quarters of the "North Star," in Wolstenholme Sound, numerous corpses, unburied, indeed, as if the poor creatures had been suddenly cut off, and their brethren had fled from them. Poor York, who, amongst the dead, recognised his own brother, described the malady of which they died as one of the chest and lungs: at any rate the mortality was great.*[18]

Leopold M'Clintock, commander of the 1857 expedition that recovered two written records from Sir John Franklin's disastrous 1845 expedition, made the following observations about the Polar Eskimos:

> *Of late years these Arctic Highlanders have become alarmed by the rapid diminution of their numbers through famine and disease, and have been less violent towards each other in their feuds and quarrels.*[19]

Elisha Kent Kane, in his personal narrative from the 1850 U.S. Grinnell Expedition in search of John Franklin, records a gruesome discovery made at Cape York in 1829 by boat crews from a whaler:

> *Grouped around an oilless lamp, in the attitudes of life, were four or five human corpses, with darkened lip and sunken eyeball; but all else preserved in perennial ice. The frozen dog lay beside his frozen*

master, and the child, stark and stiff, in the reindeer hood which enveloped the frozen mother. The cause was a mystery, for the hunting apparatus was near them, and the bay abounds with seals, the habitual food, and light, and fire of the Esquimaux. Perhaps the excessive cold had shut off their supplies perhaps an epidemic had stricken them. Some three or four huts that were near had the same melancholy furniture of extinct life.[20]

In an account of his expedition to the Smith Sound region from 1853 to 1855, Kane recorded his belief that the Polar Eskimo population was dying out:

I can already count eight settlements, including about one hundred and forty souls. There are more perhaps, but certainly not many. Out of these I can number five deaths since our arrival; and I am aware of hardships and disasters encountered by the survivors, which, repeated as they must be in the future, cannot fail to involve a larger mortality. Crime combines with disease and exposure to thin their numbers: I know of three murders with the past two years; and one infanticide occurred only a few months ago. They confirm a fearful conclusion which these poor wretches have themselves communicated to us—that they are dying out; not lingeringly, like the American tribes, but so rapidly as to be able to mark within a generation their progress toward extinction.[21]

These observations are most illuminating. It is probably fair to say that the reduction of the Inughuit population, the direct descendants of the late Thule culture Inuit, was not entirely the result of deteriorating climatic and environmental conditions and scarce resources. Without Western contact, the late Thule culture Inuit might have weathered the Little Ice Age quite well on Ellesmere Island and in North Greenland. But that was not to be their fate; contact with Westerners meant exposure to diseases against which the Inughuit had no immunity. Within a couple of decades, their numbers were drastically reduced and their old settlements and hunting grounds in the Smith Sound region mostly abandoned. It was a repeat of the momentous population decline experienced in West Greenland about a hundred years earlier, following the arrival of the Moravian missionary Hans Egede in 1721. It was the calamitous result of European contact that had damned indigenous populations in the New World since the days of the Spanish conquests of the Americas.

12

Land of the Bears

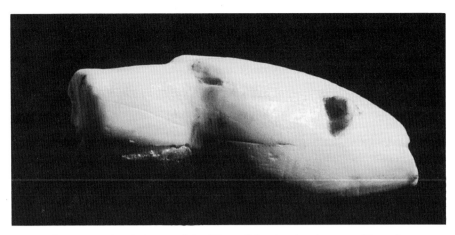

Dorset carving in ivory of the King of the Arctic, the great *Nanook*.

The Captain thought he heard someone calling and shouting from the ice and shortly thereafter he noticed figures moving about. We now realized that they were Eskimos and immediately sailed towards them, making fast to the ice edge near them. They were the first people we had met on the American side. Three men, three women and a couple of children immediately came on board; only four people remained on the ice. They were all dressed in reindeer clothing and looked much like our Greenlanders, just as their language was close to theirs. I noticed that the women were tattooed. The Eskimos couldn't tell me anything about lost ships that might relate to the Franklin expedition; however, they told me that they had often been on board English whaling ships. The Captain asked me to inquire about their earlier life and they told me that before, they had always lived in Ponds Bay [Pond Inlet]. Two years ago they had left with their dog sleds and crossed Lancaster Sound, but they knew nothing about the land farther north. In this area they were hunting narwhal and walrus. The oldest man among them was quite bald, which is very rare, and his name was Kre'tlak. Four years ago he had visited Captain Inglefield on board the Phoenix. *We left them after about half an hour, having given them needles and knives and pieces of wood.*

(Carl Petersen, 1860:92–93; translated by P. Schledermann)

148

This account by the Greenlander Carl Petersen, translator onboard the British explorer Leopold M'Clintock's vessel the *Fox*, introduces us to the bald Kre'tlak, who can be no other than Qitdlarssuaq, the man who decided to lead his people on a journey to Greenland sometime in the 1860s.[1] Qitdlarssuaq's story is a remarkable account of a long-distance migration as related by some of the participants, particularly Ittussaarsuaq, who lived the last years of her life in Siorapaluk, North Greenland, the northernmost settlement in the world.[2]

Several reasons have been advanced to explain Qitdlarssuaq's decision to head for Greenland, including fear of revenge from blood-feuds and the spiritual guidance of a powerful shaman. The truth is probably much less illusory. Having traded walrus and narwhal ivory with the whalers in the Pond Inlet area, Qitdlarssuaq had undoubtedly heard many stories about the Polar Eskimos in Greenland and decided to go there. Whatever the reasons, in the late 1850s Qitdlarssuaq and another powerful Inuit leader, Oqe, led a large number of Baffinland Inuit on a journey northward across Lancaster Sound to Devon Island, where they had already lived for two years when M'Clintock met them.[3] Somewhere along the way, Oqe convinced some of his followers to return to Baffin Island. The fact that M'Clintock saw only 12 people has led to the suggestion that the two Inuit leaders had already split up. Others have suggested that the two groups stayed together until they reached the central east coast of Ellesmere Island, where they spent the last winter together. The following spring, Oqe decided to bring his people back home to Baffin Island. It is not known if they ever got there. Qitdlarssuaq and his people continued their journey northward, eventually crossing Smith Sound to Greenland, where they met the Inughuit and reintroduced to them the bow and arrow, the kayak, and the fish spear. The meeting with M'Clintock took place in the early 1860s, suggesting that the migration had taken about four to five years. The Baffinlanders remained in Greenland six years, in several instances intermarrying with the Inughuit.

It says a lot for Qitdlarssuaq's strong leadership that when his health began to fail and he decided to return to Baffin Island, most of the Baffinlanders and a few Inughuit decided to join him. Unfortunately the return journey was a disaster. Qitdlarssuaq died shortly after the group had crossed Smith Sound. With the exception of one family, the group settled for the winter in the same place they had used on their way north. The family that had chosen not to stay with the rest spent the winter farther south in Makinson Inlet and returned the following spring with glowing reports of good hunting in that area. That summer the entire group decided to go to Makinson Inlet and the plentiful resources they had been told about. The capricious nature of the High Arctic environment decided against them; there was no game to be found. In desperation they divided into two groups, each trying to survive the long and bitter winter on the few, small fish they occasionally caught through holes in the ice of a large lake near their winter houses. Two of the men, Mattaaq and Minik, turned to cannibalism, killing and terrorizing the dwindling group until only Meqqusaaq, his wife and two children, and his brother Qumangaapik were left. Following a ghastly knife fight with one of the cannibals, in which Meqqusaaq lost an eye, Qumangaapik knew that only by fleeing would they have a chance to survive.

The tiny group struggled northward through the dark and frigid landscape, terrified that the cannibals would catch up to them. Totally exhausted, they finally stopped for the night when Qumangaapik found a place where strong winds had packed the snow hard enough to build an igloo. Hunger was taking its toll, especially on the two youngsters; there was nothing to eat but pieces of skin from their clothing. A violent storm kept Qumangaapik from returning to the breathing hole he had already visited without luck. When the weather finally improved, he crawled out through the snow tunnel, blocking it securely from the outside to keep bears out. This would be his last attempt; if he failed, they would all starve to death. Inside sat his young daughter, Ittussaarsuaq, chewing slowly on a piece of skin, waiting. That day her father's perseverance and endurance at the breathing hole were rewarded: one seal gave them life. In the spring they went back to get the sled they had abandoned and then headed north. They spent one more winter at the place they had used twice before and crossed over to Greenland the following summer. Ittussaarsuaq grew up among the Inughuit. When she died in 1939, she was the only survivor of the original Baffinland immigrants and great-great grandmother to nearly a fifth of the Inughuit population.[4]

In the Bache Peninsula region, we had found no evidence of Thule culture winter settlements from the nineteenth century. Not a trace. To what extent had prehistoric hunters, heading north along the rugged and inhospitable southeast coast of Ellesmere Island, crossed Smith Sound to Greenland without leaving a trace of their movements in the Bache Peninsula region north of Pim Island? Had Qitdlarssuaq unintentionally followed the path of most human migrations into the Smith Sound region and Greenland? There was only one way to answer those questions: we had to find a habitable spot, attractive to prehistoric hunters, along the mostly glaciated southeast coast of Ellesmere Island.

With our field season completed in August of 1979, we flew south along that wild stretch of coast, eyes straining and cameras ready as we passed over every headland along the way. When you know what you are looking for, it is amazing how much you can observe in the barren Arctic landscape. For a while we spotted only the usual tent rings and stone caches jammed onto small rocky promontories—nothing major until we flew in over a small island in Goding Bay. The most obvious evidence of prehistoric settlement activity is the clustered, heavily vegetated mounds of Thule culture winter house ruins, usually situated near shore. Orne Island contained at least one large Thule culture site. As we circled the island and photographed the main site, we noticed smaller clusters of house ruins. Since it was impossible to land the Twin Otter on the island, we flew west towards Cape Faraday. Coming in for a low approach along the southeast coast, we saw land dotted with small lakes and what appeared to be remarkably lush, green areas—Thule culture winter sites without a doubt. The brief overflight convinced us that the Goding Bay area had been used more extensively than any other place along the southeast coast of Ellesmere Island. Our study area had just been expanded; we would have to attempt a couple of field seasons around Goding Bay if at all possible. Logistically it would not be easy. From what we had observed, even the remarkable Twin Otter with its equally amazing pilots would be hard-pressed to land anywhere in the area. Most likely it would have to be a coordinated Twin Otter and helicopter approach.

Not until the summer of 1987 did we finally manage to set foot on Cape Faraday. We had only a few hours to survey the Cape, but it was a most encouraging visit. Aside from several large Thule culture winter settlements, the southeast coast was brimming with sites associated with much earlier occupations. It was precisely what we had hoped for. Not only did we discover two late Dorset communal houses, we felt convinced that one of the large Thule culture winter sites was of fairly recent vintage, possibly from the time of Qitdlarssuaq's journey to Greenland.

We flew back north to Alexandra Fiord, crossing massive glacier tongues that spilled out into the deep blue waters of northern Baffin Bay and Smith Sound. The task ahead would be difficult. We had spent enough time flying

Thule culture winter house ruins on the Brice Site, Cape Faraday.

survey flights on the outer coast of Ellesmere Island to realize how variable and unpredictable the weather could be from one area to the next. On Skraeling Island, we had often sat in beautiful, sunny, calm weather, looking at black, menacing storm clouds over Kane Basin. We had flown in calm conditions along the Johan Peninsula coast, only to be buffeted with sudden violence by savage winds streaking over Pim Island, whipping the ocean into a froth of crashing ice floes. The outer coast extended little mercy to passing intruders; storms struck without much warning and were brutal in their show of force. Another omnipresent concern was the significant number of polar bear tracks we had seen crisscrossing the sea ice between Orne Island and Cape Faraday.

Planning for the first field season at the Cape had to be guided by one overriding principle: keeping everything to a minimum—gear, food and, most especially, the size of the field party. In Resolute, the Polar Shelf people worked out the logistics. The Twin Otter would attempt a landing at the Cape; if unsuccessful, the plane would continue to Alexandra Fiord, where everything would be unloaded and later transported back south by helicopter. It was an excellent backup plan, although we still hoped it would be possible to land at the Cape. The flight from Resolute took us over Devon Island and the dark blue waters of the Hell Gate–Cardigan Strait polynya that separates Devon Island and Ellesmere Island. In 1974, Robert McGhee and I had investigated the shores of Cardigan Strait and the amazing series of beach ridges at Cape Storm on the south coast of Ellesmere Island. It was near Cape Storm that we had first located polar bear traps.

The Twin Otter crossed Makinson Inlet, making a low pass over the lake we believed Qitdlarssuaq's people had fished so desperately during their terrible starvation winter. Along a low ridge near shore we spotted several sod mounds, the remains of old winter houses, possibly the dwellings built by Qitdlarssuaq's people. North of Makinson Inlet, we flew over monstrous glaciers streaked with rock debris, picked up as the ice mass flowed towards its own demise at the calving grounds on the edge of the North Water. To the east the Greenland coast was clearly visible. Approaching Cape Faraday, the Twin Otter began a gradual descent; its capacity as a STOL (Short Take Off and Landing) craft would be tested to the limit. It didn't look promising. Again and again, the pilot slowly brought the plane low over the Cape, his experienced eyes searching for a place to land. The flaps were brought down, the Twin Otter slowed to a crawl in the air, and the stall buzzer activated: we were about to land. Seconds before the big balloon tires touched the gravel ridge, the pilot aborted the landing, straining the engines to climb over the nearest ridge. There was enough room to land, he explained, but not to take off again—a critical consideration, we all agreed.

By the time we reached Alexandra Fiord, the PCSP helicopter was already on its way to meet us. Slinging loads in a big net under the helicopter works well as long as the winds are reasonably light. However, the 100-kilometre flight line between Alexandra Fiord and Cape Faraday is notorious for sudden catabatic winds blowing down through broad glacier-covered valleys. John Pridie knew that his skill as a helicopter pilot would be tested. Fortunately the summer of 1988 was outstanding, clear and sunny day after day. The weather gods were on our side. By late afternoon the final sling load came into sight as we were busy setting up the main cook tent in a small protected gully at the Cape. The load was carefully lowered to the ground, the hook was released, and with a cheerful wave, John headed northward until all we could hear was the light flapping of tent canvas.

That first night we were too exhausted to do anything but cook up a hefty portion of brown beans and corned beef, stash our gear inside the cook tent, roll out the sleeping bags, and sleep the sleep of the dead. Outside, the eternal summer sun slipped silently around the northern horizon. The invisible tide lifted and lowered the fast ice, almost imperceptibly widening and narrowing long tidal cracks. Seals were hauled out on the ice near the cracks and breathing holes, occasionally scanning the horizon for any sign of movement, the approach of the mighty polar bear. For the first few nights we slept soundly enough; then we too began to sleep more like uneasy seals.

It was the beginning of two exciting if somewhat anxious field seasons: a time of tantalizing discoveries that brought out many additional nuances in the prehistoric picture. Evidence of human activity was abundant along the southeastern shore of the Cape. Sod mounds of Thule culture winter house ruins occurred in clusters containing from three to more than twenty houses. Summer activity was indicated by large numbers of tent rings, stone caches, and boulder stands for kayaks and umiaks. The successful pursuit of bowhead whales and walrus was easily demonstrated by skeletal remains and the sheer size of meat and blubber caches along the beaches. Palaeoeskimo sites dotted a series of gradually raised beach terraces extending from near shore to 35 metres above the present sea level—a superb chronology of Palaeoeskimo occupations from late Dorset back to the days of the true pioneers.

Day after day the sun beamed from a cloudless sky, to the point where we wished for overcast skies to soften the light and reduce the stark contrast. It was one of those rare High Arctic summers that would give the one-time visitor a most erroneous impression about the "usual" state of summer weather. We remarked on the extensive cover of black rock lichen, called "rock tripe" by unfortunate explorers who had boiled it to a gelatinous substance and consumed it when there was nothing else to eat. A profusion of this type of lichen generally indicates very wet summer conditions, through either rain or heavy fog. The following summer we were to discover firsthand why rock lichen grew so generously at the Cape.

Our first task was to survey, locate, and map as many prehistoric features as possible, which was no small undertaking for three people, considering the abundance of remains confronting us. One of our research questions was quickly answered; the Thule culture winter house site, located closest to the ice-covered shore, contained house ruins of a style I recognized from my earlier days in Cumberland Sound on Baffin Island. There, similar house ruins dated to the middle of the nineteenth century. Could these winter house ruins have been built and used by the Qitdlarssuaq group? The site, having been used on many occasions over the centuries, would have provided all the building material Qitdlarssuaq and his people needed. Two dwellings were earmarked for excavation the following summer.

In the Goding Bay area we had found solid evidence of a much-frequented migration route used by Palaeo- and Neoeskimo groups travelling back and forth between the southeast coast of Ellesmere Island and Greenland. A brief helicopter visit to nearby Orne Island, about 7 kilometres northeast of Cape Faraday, yielded many more sites, including the large Thule culture winter settlement we had seen from the air the year before. Thirteen kilometres northeast of Orne Island, at Cape Dunsterville, we visited the most unlikely site location I have ever seen. Along a narrow, boulder-filled ledge constituting the drop zone at the foot of a steep talus slope, we found a concentration of Thule culture winter houses and the remains of a polar bear trap. The cape towered over the site, and swells from the wide open North Water slammed against the cliffs, even on a calm day. I dreaded to think what the place would be like during a storm. The substantial polar bear trap was the fourth one we had found in the area. The old traps and the many bear tracks on the sea ice in Goding Bay were potent reminders of the presence of *Nanook*.

The first sighting of bears was pleasant enough. In the evening we usually clambered up to the top of the rocky ridge behind camp. The view was breathtaking. Just east of Orne Island the edge of the fast ice drew a sharp line against the dark, blue waters of the huge North Water. A good hundred kilometres farther east, on the Greenland side, towered the mighty, glacier-capped Northumberland Island. At an even greater distance, directly south, we could see the mountain range that makes up the southeastern part of Ellesmere Island; to the north, the waters of Smith Sound and Cape Alexander, the westernmost point of Greenland. Not only was the scenery stunning, but from this particular vantage point it was much easier to imagine human migrations over great distances. For people on the move, it would be natural enough to want to visit lands so clearly visible.

As a passionate birdwatcher, Karen McCullough habitually scanned the shore and the sea ice. That, of course, is also a sure way of spotting polar bears. The first sighting was a young bear intently interested in two seals: a small ringed seal swimming in an open lead and a much larger bearded seal—resting rather carelessly, we thought—on the edge of the lead a little farther south. The bear slid into the lead and became practically invisible except for its black snout, which stuck out of the water like a snake's head. Ever so smoothly, leaving hardly a ripple in the dark water, the bear made its way closer and closer to the frolicking seal, which seemed unaware of the oncoming danger. From our vantage point, the bear appeared to be right on top of the seal when a mad thrashing of flippers and paws shattered the evening quiet as the chase went under water. For a brief moment there was calm; then the bear returned to the surface empty-handed. The bearded seal had not moved during all the commotion. The bear decided to repeat the same tactic. Nose barely above water, it steadily closed the distance before leaping onto the ice just in time to see the bearded seal make a graceful rolling slide into the water. The bear followed with a splash, but returned soon after, having suffered a second blow to the ego. This all amused us greatly, until we remembered that the bear was still hungry and might think of trying an easier target. With that sobering thought, we hiked back to our camp and settled in for the night. We saw no more of that bear and were just beginning to relax when, a few days later, I came across fresh bear tracks not far from our tents. Obviously we had been under observation. That evening, we spotted several bears far out on the ice, going about their business of stalking and killing seals. By now we had pieced together a couple of observations; when there were bears in the area, we rarely saw any seals lying about on the ice. Conversely, when there were lots of seals around, we began to feel a bit more secure. Nevertheless each person slept with a loaded rifle beside his or her sleeping bag. For my part, in addition to a double-barreled shotgun with 12-gauge slugs, I also kept a knife ready in case it seemed prudent to make a hasty retreat through the back of the tent.

Early one morning, something woke me from a comfortable, sound sleep. As I struggled to gain consciousness, I realized that my tent was moving; yet there was no wind and no sound. Something large was pushing against the tent just above my head—a polar bear. My first reaction was to yell and hit the side of the tent, while struggling to get out of the sleeping bag and reaching for the gun. The tent was no longer moving. With some apprehension I unzipped the tent door and found myself staring directly at a young bear who was looking straight at me, its back against a low rocky outcrop less than 5 metres away. I don't know how long this staring contest went on. A few shouts made no obvious difference, except that I thought the bear looked a bit irritated. That's the trouble with young polar bears, they're too curious for their own good. They are also quite capable of knocking your head off with a well-placed blow. The bear appeared indecisive about what to do next, so I decided to encourage its departure by firing a shot just short of its left paw. The thundering noise not only created a lot of commotion in the other two tents; it also helped the bear make up its mind and take flight—a decision that pleased me greatly, since I had only one shot left.

That little incident changed our approach to working at Cape Faraday. It was also the beginning of many bear encounters during that season and the next, until we eventually abandoned the area. We learned a lot about bears and ourselves. Two days after the first close encounter, I stepped out of the cook tent after dinner to get a wash basin—just in time to unnerve two very adult-sized bears heading straight for the tent. The rifle we had decided to place inside the cook tent for such an occasion came in handy. A barrage of warning shots sent the two visitors hastily on their way.

From then on there was a fair amount of looking over our shoulders as we continued to work. The mapping was going well, and sod removal had been completed on several Thule culture house ruins we planned to excavate the following season. Arrangements had been made with PCSP for a helicopter to ferry our gear and ourselves back up to Skraeling Island, where we would finish the field season in familiar and friendlier surroundings. One incident a few days before we left Cape Faraday gave us an additional insight into the business of population movements and changed our perception of what is feasible under certain circumstances.

It was a most unusual encounter. To complete several small projects, we had bravely, or foolishly, decided to work independently that day. The sun was its usual brilliant self, sparkling in the cobalt blue and turquoise meltwater ponds that dotted the fast ice still surrounding the Cape. In spite of the beaming sun, a cool breeze off the ice kept me from shedding my red down parka. I was standing on top of an immense boulder looking at the remains of an old Thule culture summer camp full of lichen-covered tent rings, caches, and kayak supports. Being alone in bear country tunes one's ears to a fine pitch, but, so far, the only sound had come from the creaking ice pans as they lifted and pressed together with the movement of tide and swells from the North Water. I was sketching away when I thought I heard shouts coming from somewhere out between the ice ridges bordering the Cape. There was a repeat of a distant "hello," then two silhouetted figures appeared, waving enthusiastically. They seemed to be hauling something and were heading directly for me. We had not seen another human being for three weeks and certainly didn't expect company in this place, over 90 kilometres from the nearest community or research camp. The two strangers disappeared behind a long pressure ridge. The thought occurred to me that the whole incident was a hallucination, perhaps a ghostly apparition of Dorset hunters on a spirit journey from the past. But the figures on the ice turned out to be real enough; a couple from Minnesota, Jon and Christine, who were attempting to travel by sea kayak from the south coast of Ellesmere Island to Greenland. Having found no open water near land, they had hauled their kayaks over the ice for three weeks. Understandably enough they were tired, hungry, and interested in a bath in one of the many lakes on the Cape, luxuries indeed. We cooked up a huge serving of our favourite meal, corned beef and beans with bannock, followed by more bannock covered with peanut butter and jam. Later in the day we all hiked to the top of the Cape to get a good view of the ice and water separating Jon and Christine from their goal. Orne Island, to the east, was nearly clear of fast ice. Another seven kilometres of hauling and they would finally be able to slip their kayaks into the icy waters of Smith Sound. After a day of rest they pushed on, heading north towards Cape Herschel, where an old friend, Weston Blake Jr., had his geological research camp. A few days later, Wes radioed to tell us that the two adventurers had set out across a mirror-like Smith Sound to Greenland. In the fall Jon wrote that it had taken 17 hours of hard paddling and lots of incentive to get across before conditions changed. I think they knew how lucky they were. One week later the weather returned to more normal conditions, and we observed Smith Sound in a near-gale—an inferno of huge, crashing ice floes. Not a place for tiny sea kayaks.

It had been not only a fun visit, but a very informative one. We had learned that two people, hauling everything they needed, could cover the distance between the south coast of Ellesmere Island and Smith Sound in three weeks. From here, a long and undoubtedly demanding crossing brought them to the coast of Greenland and eventually to Siorapaluk and Qaanaaq, the northernmost settlements in the world. It provided us with a much better perspective about distances and potential human migrations in this part of the Arctic.

Our preparations for the 1989 field season at Cape Faraday included detailed planning on how we could guard against night visits by bears. When we next left Resolute for Cape Faraday, our field gear included rods, wire, batteries, a police siren, starter pistols with screamer and banger shells, shotguns, and lots of ammunition. The bear warning system had been adapted from a design by Jeffrey Marley in Calgary. We were ready to work in the land of bears again, at least so we thought.

The 1989 weather was as dreadful as the previous summer had been wonderful. Just getting to Cape Faraday turned out to be a logistic nightmare, during which the divided field party barely escaped being stranded in two separate locations. Only the marvelous work of helicopter pilot Lin Ho kept me from sitting by myself at Cape Faraday with some of the supplies, while Karen and our teammate Erik Damkjar were left with the remaining supplies on a cold, exposed beach at Gale Point, 30 kilometres to the north. As the pilot left me on the final trip to get the others, I watched with apprehension as the fog grew thicker and thicker. Light snow was already falling, and one by one the trapped icebergs in the surrounding fast ice vanished in the descending fog. Lin had to complete a 40 minute round trip, not including loading and refueling at the other end. Finally, with great relief, I heard the helicopter approaching the Cape. Even so, it took a long while before the machine appeared, crawling ahead a few feet off the ground through the thick weather. We had a happy reunion amidst a jumble of field gear and food boxes. The helicopter had barely lifted before it disappeared into the fog. The muffled engine sound vanished as we looked at our pile of gear slowly being covered in snow—July 1, Canada Day!

Our arrival at the Cape was an inauspicious start to a most demanding field season. When it didn't snow or rain during the next ten days, we were cloaked in pea-soup fog. As we suspected, it was the kind of summer weather the black rock lichen thrived in. I had selected a new campsite on the basis of our experiences with bears the previous summer. This time we picked a wider, reasonably level gravel terrace, surrounded by a scatter of boulders and protruding sections of bedrock. There was enough room for the tents and the bear warning fence in all directions but one, a spot where the fence wires ran close to a section of bedrock. At the time we didn't think much of it. Wires were run at two levels through clamps on fibreglass posts pounded into the ground around the perimeter of the camp. The wires were strung as tightly as possible and held in a pinched grip that would release with any further pressure. Battery wires connected the grip to a police siren we had mounted on top of the kitchen tent. Disconnection of the grip resulted in a horrific wailing of the siren, a sound

Our "secure" 1989 camp at Cape Faraday photographed by K. McCullough at midnight from the bear watch cliff behind camp.

that to this day makes me think of bears rather than emergency vehicles. With all that in place, we felt quite secure even though we couldn't see much of anything in the murk of snow, rain, and fog.

Late in the afternoon on the fifth day, we were sitting in the cook tent, thawing out after a fruitless attempt at mapping one of the nearby sites in thick fog. The shrill sound of the siren sent our heartbeats into high gear as we scurried around the confined space of the tent, grabbing the rifles and attempting to silence the horrific wailing, all the while expecting a bear to come tearing through the tent wall at any moment. We managed to stop the siren. There wasn't a sound from the outside. Carefully, we peered out. It was snowing heavily, there was not a bear in sight, and the fence was perfectly strung. With rifles at the ready, we checked the perimeter of the camp. Everything was in perfect order: no paw prints in the snow. We surmised that melting snow, covering the wire connections of the grip, had caused a short circuit, resulting in the false alarm. At least we now knew that the siren worked.

Finally the weather improved enough to melt the new snow. Unfortunately old snow still covered large portions of the Cape, including several of the features we wanted to excavate. A good deal of shoveling solved that problem, and eventually the excavations progressed as planned. Our contention that the Thule culture Inuit didn't arrive in the High Arctic until the late twelfth or early thirteenth century had not been easily accepted by other archaeologists. At Cape Faraday we were pleased to determine that the earliest evidence of the Thule culture corresponded to our findings on Skraeling Island. We found no evidence to support a Thule culture Inuit presence predating the early Ruin Island phase.

Along with work on Palaeoeskimo sites, we turned our attention to the excavation of the relatively recent sod house ruins on the site, hoping to connect them to the Qitdlarssuaq migration to Greenland. The two clusters of winter houses of identical type fit well with the migration story, which mentions two groups of people, one led by Qitdlarssuaq and the other by Oqe. We decided to open up one dwelling in each cluster, House 3 and House 13. Clearly House 13 had been rebuilt and used on several occasions. That also corresponded well with the account of the migration, in which this winter site was used on three different occasions, including the return trip by the survivors from Makinson Inlet.

Our work was finally going well. The weather had improved and the snow was melting—not as fast as we would have liked, but it was gradually

House 13 on the Brice site at Cape Faraday, quite possibly one of the winter houses used and re-used by Qitdlarssuaq and his people.

disappearing. Since the horrific, false siren blast, we had become less and less concerned about bears. When we first arrived, just before the bad weather completely obscured the landscape, we had noticed that the ice edge (*sina*) was located much farther east of the Cape than had been the case the year before. We assumed that the bears were hunting out along the *sina*, far from camp. But ten days had changed the landscape. On the first clear day, we could see that the *sina* had come much closer. In fact, it was skirting the outer shores of Orne Island, only about 8 kilometres away.

That evening while we were hard at work shoveling snow, we saw three bears out on the ice, an adult male trotting in big circles around a female and her two-year-old cub. Polar bears seem to have a maladaptive trait in their hereditary planning: the male bears often stalk and occasionally kill cubs, even their own offspring. This mother bear was in no mood to let that happen. She charged with surprising swiftness whenever he got a bit too close. We watched the drama for a long time, until the trio appeared to be heading away from the coast. Although it was tempting to linger in the bright, warm light of the night sun, we decided to return to camp to get some sleep. Much had been accomplished that day. House 13 had produced a small, well-used, iron-bladed knife with a smooth, worn antler handle. Qitdlarssuaq's knife perhaps? We had also found several pieces of old galvanized iron and a cut section of shot lead tied with a thin piece of sinew, most likely worn as an amulet.

The night was still. Not a wind rustled through the magnificent landscape. As the tide drew water away from under stranded icebergs, straining their unsupported mass, they cracked asunder with the booming sound of cannon fire. I read for a while, cozy in the warm sleeping bag, looking forward to what the next day might bring. Sleep came quickly.

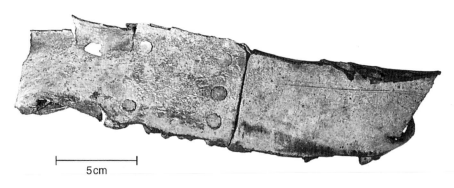

5cm

A section of galvanized iron found in House 3 on the Brice site at Cape Faraday.

A cut section of shot lead, most likely worn as an amulet, from House 3 on the Brice site.

There are many kinds of nightmares. I was having the one where you know something dreadful is about to happen, but you can't do anything about it—the slow motion, the deep, guttural, primeval scream. Anyway that's how my teammates later described it; I just wanted to wake up and come to terms with the realization that once again a polar bear's snout was lathering my tent with saliva just about six inches above my head! Like the year before, my first reaction was to strike out without concern for the possible consequences of smacking a bear on the nose. I yelled. Where were my friends? Why had I not heard the siren? Struggling to get out of the sleeping bag, I grabbed my high-powered rifle, unzipped the tent door partway, and fired the first volley up in the air. At this point the siren went off, loud and piercing. The bear decided to leave the unfriendly camp by tearing straight through the two strands of wire, snapping both like old elastic bands, and headed for its two compatriots down on the ice below camp. By now everyone was up and firing all manner of screamers, bangers, and bullets in the direction of the swiftly retreating young bear. This was the same little family we had observed earlier.

We kept firing until the bears got tired of all the racket and wandered out towards the *sina*. They weren't running by any means. There was no sign of fear, no sign that they had ever been hunted by anybody. It was time to check our defences. Somehow the young bear had got inside the warning fence without setting off the alarm. Only in one place could that have been accomplished—

the point where the fence wire ran too close to the cliff. The bear must have scouted the perimeter, listened with curiosity to one or more snoring individuals in their flimsy, nylon tents, then climbed up on the bedrock and soundlessly jumped inside.

That was the beginning of an increasing number of bear sightings and encounters. During the day, when we worked far away from camp, we always expected to hear the siren, but it never happened. The bears rarely bothered us during the day. Night was obviously their favourite roaming time. So we had little choice. If we were ever to get any sleep, we had to take turns being night guards. We decided on three-hour watches from a comfortable perch on the flat top of a tall rock pillar behind the camp. A thermos of tea or coffee, the spotting scope, binoculars, and a Walkman helped pass the time. The silence, the magnificent vista, and magical tones of Mozart coming through the earphones made night duty a very special time.

Several days passed without bear incidents, so we began to relax. Karen and I were busy with the Thule site excavations, while Eric was investigating the late Dorset site about a kilometre away. Suddenly we heard a shot. We ran towards camp, where we met up with Erik. He had left the Dorset site in a hurry, after firing a warning shot in the direction of a large male bear that was standing on its hind legs trying to get a better view of him—probably sizing him up for lunch.

Our daily radio reports to Resolute were being listened to with increasing interest, not only by the PCSP staff, but by many other isolated Arctic research camps. There was good news. An old friend of ours, the Canadian artist Brenda Carter, was coming for a visit. Brenda had joined our digs before on Knud Peninsula and Skraeling Island and she now wanted a chance to get some sketches from an area very rarely visited.

Even Brenda's arrival was marked by the appearance of an old polar bear, the only one no amount of firing and shouting could deter from approaching our camp. As the pilot, Lin Ho, brought his helicopter in for a landing, he spotted the bear behind the cliffs and boulders near camp. We unloaded the machine in a hurry and accompanied Lin as he chased the bear far away with the helicopter. Much to our relief, it did not come back.

With four of us, night watch was a little easier. We could now split up into teams of two when necessary. But time was running out. The weather was turning nasty again, the ground was no longer thawing, and we had accomplished our

The gang of four: the author, Karen McCullough, Brenda Carter, and Eric Damkjar. We were visited by five bears throughout our last night at Cape Faraday.

most immediate goals. It was time to consider an orderly retreat. By now the ice edge was only a few kilometres away from the Cape, and every bear in the Goding Bay–Talbot Inlet area, young or old, seemed to wander by regularly. So far, no one—bear or human—had been hurt, but sooner or later our luck would run out. During our final night on the Cape, the Goding Bay spirits decided to reinforce our decision to leave by sending in five bears at regularly spaced intervals. No one was able to sleep that night. We would barely get into our sleeping bags before the next call came from whoever was on watch: "Bear near camp—everybody up." We were glad to see the end of that night and the arrival of the helicopter. In all, we had 29 visits from polar bears during our final two weeks at Cape Faraday.

Cape Faraday will always have a special place in my list of interesting places I have worked. That place and Pim Island taught us more about the raw power of the High Arctic than anything we had experienced in the relative safety of Knud Peninsula, Skraeling Island and, of course, the outright luxury of safety around the old RCMP station at Alexandra Fiord.

13

A Question of Sovereignty

The Alexandra Fiord RCMP station. (Photo credit: Karen McCullough)

The first dusting of snow brushed the land, then quickly melted. Rust-coloured heather and golden willow had announced the arrival of fall when the Labrador *rounded Cape Sabine on Pim Island, pushed through loose pack ice in Kane Basin, and entered Buchanan Bay. Its destination was the northernmost outpost of the Royal Canadian Mounted Police at Alexandra Fiord. The skipper repeatedly checked the ship's position with reference to wooden beacons, erected on prominent headlands to guide him safely through otherwise uncharted waters. He signalled the engines to a crawl and maneuvered the vessel between Skraeling and Stiles Island. The anchor was dropped just offshore from the RCMP station where the flag would soon be lowered, folded, and put away for many years to come.*

Another chapter in the history of Canada's ambivalent relationship to its North was about to come to an end. For the second time in 40 years, the RCMP were abandoning the Bache Peninsula region on Ellesmere Island.[1]

Constable R. M. Coombs and Special Constables Joalamee and Nowra secured the last sheet of thick plywood over the north-facing kitchen window on the main building. Only a few narrow streaks of light penetrated the interior of the two main buildings, one for the RCMP constables, the other, with its raised sleeping platforms, for the Native assistants and their families. The two houses had been constructed on a broad terrace that overlooked the outer part of Alexandra Fiord and the two large islands in its centre. The smaller houses, closer to shore, had likewise been secured. The dog pen was silent. Coombs felt secure in the knowledge that everything had been done to protect the station from the violent storms that often came roaring down Twin Glacier Valley. Undoubtedly he had been looking forward to this day; yet now that it had arrived, he must have felt sad to leave. For two years the place had been his home, the landscape as familiar as any he had ever known; it would remain in his consciousness forever undiminished. He walked along the narrow gravel path lined with white-painted stones, down the steep hill to the buildings below and the barge landing they had laboriously cleared of boulders. Locks were checked one more time; not that there would be many visitors, at least not from the south. Come spring, Inughuit hunters from Greenland would stop by, but this time there would be no one to greet them with hot tea and biscuits. He stepped into the ship's dinghy and was rowed away from the land for the last time. As the *Labrador* picked up steam, he watched the abandoned buildings grow smaller and smaller. In his diary, he noted that it was Tuesday, September 3, 1963.

Western curiosity about the North American Arctic began long before the first spunky RCMP recruits applied for duty in what had to be some of the most isolated posts in the world. European interest in the Canadian Arctic had less to do with the land itself, than with finding a navigable passage through it—an uncontested path to profitable trade opportunities in the Far East. A few more southerly attempts had been made in the sixteenth and seventeenth centuries by people like Martin Frobisher, John Davis, Henry Hudson, and Jens Munk.[2] None of them were successful, and some were costly in human lives.

Except for the voyages of Norse Greenlanders and the English explorer William Baffin, European forays into the High Arctic lagged far behind events in more southerly regions. With the possible exception of Celtic explorers, the Norse Greenlanders were the first to investigate the southeast shores of Baffin Island (Helluland), the coast of Labrador (Markland), and the outer regions of the Gulf of St. Lawrence (Vinland), nearly a thousand years ago.[3]

In 1616, the Merchant Adventurers of England dispatched William Baffin and Robert Bylot to the far northern reaches of the Arctic in search of a passage to India. They used the 55-ton *Discovery*, the vessel Henry Hudson had commanded on his final, fateful voyage to Hudson Bay in 1610. In a remarkable display of excellent seamanship, Baffin took the *Discovery* north along the west coast of Greenland and far into the bay which would bear his name. He remarked on the large numbers of whales along the Greenland coast and named both Whale Sound and the impressive Northumberland Island we could see so clearly from Cape Faraday. After passing and naming the Carey Islands, he sailed far enough north to observe and name Sir Thomas Smith Sound before heading south, to sail past and name Jones and Lancaster Sounds. Even though Norsemen may have preceded him by several hundred years, Baffin made the first recorded landing by a Westerner on an eastern High Arctic Island.[4] He did not observe any Native people and was of the opinion that no passage to the Far East was to be found that far north. It was an extraordinary voyage; yet its results were scarcely believed in England and eventually ignored for the next 200 years.

In 1818, the British Admiralty launched a two-pronged attack on the Far North. Captain Buchan and his second-in-command, Lieutenant John Franklin, took the *Dorothea* and the *Trent* north to Spitsbergen with orders to proceed from there to the North Pole and beyond to the Bering Strait. Meanwhile, John Ross and his second-in-command, William Parry, were taking the *Alexander* and the *Isabella* northward along the west coast of Greenland in search of the Northwest Passage.[5] They were to navigate the Passage and meet up with Captain Buchan. In London, the plan may have seemed straightforward and not too complicated, particularly to a man like John Barrow, second secretary to the Admiralty, whose Arctic exposure was limited to a youthful experience on a whaler off the southwest coast of Greenland.

Retracing Baffin's route, John Ross was impressed with the accuracy of his predecessor's observations. Ross landed at Cape York, where he encountered the "Arctic Highlanders" before continuing his journey to the top of Baffin Bay. After crossing the North Water to Ellesmere Island, he headed south to investigate the two large sounds named by Baffin. Having dismissed Jones Sound as a possible route to the west, he entered the more promising Lancaster Sound. About 30 nautical miles up the sound, Ross was stopped by heavy fog and decided to let the slower *Alexander* catch up before proceeding. While he was waiting for Parry, the fog lifted briefly, allowing him to see a range of mountains that blocked access to the west, or so he insisted. He recorded them as the Croker Mountains, turned about, and headed for home, ordering the *Alexander* to follow.

The Buchan and Franklin North Pole expedition had been a fiasco. Now the Admiralty was faced with the failure of the second expedition. John Barrow, who had planned the two expeditions, demolished Ross's report. William Parry, who had been careful not to criticize John Ross's conclusions regarding Lancaster Sound too openly, waited for his chance. It was not long in coming. The following year, Parry completed his own impressive voyage through Lancaster Sound and Barrow Strait all the way to the south coast of Melville Island, where he cut his two ships, the *Hecla* and the *Griper*, into the fast ice at Winter Harbour. The expedition returned safely to England in the fall of 1820, having successfully crossed the 110 degrees west meridian and thus earning a parliamentary reward of five thousand pounds.[6]

Most of the subsequent British and occasionally American expeditions were dedicated to searching for lost passage seekers such as John Franklin, John Ross, and Robert M'Clure.[7] They rarely touched the shores of Ellesmere Island or went as far as Smith Sound, although occasionally it did happen. In 1852, during the height of the search for Franklin, Captain E. A. Inglefield, commanding the *Isabel*, set sail for northwest Greenland to investigate a rather spurious rumour that Franklin and his men had met their death at the hands of Inuit in Wolstenholme Fiord. As soon as that story had been laid to rest, Inglefield proceeded northward, making the first recorded entry into Smith Sound and establishing a farthest north latitude of 78°21′N. He named a few prominent landmarks before sailing southward to Lancaster Sound, where he joined the more promising Franklin search activities.[8] Two of his landmarks, Victoria Head and Cape Albert, have turned out to be the northeastern tip and the easternmost point of Bache Peninsula, which for many years was thought to be an island.

The limited American involvement in the Franklin searches resulted in further exploration of the Smith Sound region. The United States Grinnell Expedition was dispatched under the command of E. J. De Haven, who brought his two vessels, the *Advance* and the *Rescue*, to Lancaster Sound in August of 1850.[9]

The surgeon onboard, the spirited Dr. Elisha Kent Kane, became obsessed with the idea that Franklin had headed north to a much-debated figment of many people's imagination, the "open polar sea." His ideas and plans must have been well received in the right circles because in the spring of 1853, Kane received orders from the Secretary of the Navy to lead the Second United States Grinnell Expedition, which was to combine a search for Franklin with an attempt to reach the North Pole.

Once again walking the deck of the *Advance*, Kane set course for Smith Sound, convinced that from there he could reach the open polar sea and meet up with Franklin. Although he did not get very far, he managed to penetrate into the basin which now bears his name, and eventually placed his vessel in winter quarters in Rensselaer Bay on the Greenland coast. Several sledge parties were sent out, including one led by Dr. Isaac Israel Hayes, who reached Dobbin Bay on the Ellesmere Island coast before proceeding south to Cape Sabine on Pim Island and back east to the *Advance*. Another expedition member, Morton, was able to sled quite far north into Kennedy Channel, where he was stopped by open water along the ice foot. His report of open water was eagerly noted by Kane who saw it as proof of the open polar sea theory.[10]

Kane and his party spent a rather miserable two years solidly embedded in the ice at Rensselaer Bay. Only the repeated assistance of the Inughuit enabled anyone from the expedition to get home alive. Considering the hardships encountered during those two years, it is quite amazing that Isaac Hayes decided to organize his own expedition and return to the area in 1860. Haye's obsession is a good example of the bewitching web the Arctic can spin around a person's soul.

By the time Hayes sailed north in the *United States*, the fate of Franklin and his men had finally come to light. First, the extraordinary Hudson's Bay man, Dr. John Rae brought back to a disbelieving England stories of starving and dying white men seen by Natives near Back's Great Fish River south of King William Island.[11] Second, Leopold M'Clintock and Robert Hobson discovered the only message ever found from the ill-fated expedition.[12] Thus, Hayes could focus his sights entirely on reaching the North Pole. Now that the Franklin searches were over, others would soon follow him—the Pole had become the acknowledged goal of Arctic explorers and adventurers.

On his way north, Hayes stopped in Greenland to purchase sled dogs and hire Inuit hunters to aid the expedition. Near Cape York, he and his old teammate from the Kane Expedition, August Sonntag, met up with another former Kane employee, the Inughuit hunter Hans Hendrik, who eagerly came on board with his wife and baby. Severe ice conditions in Kane Basin prevented Hayes from wintering near Ellesmere Island, or Grinnell Land, as he called it. Instead he wintered in Port Foulke, just south of Etah on the northwest coast of Greenland. In most ways, the Hayes expedition turned out to be as full of misfortune as Kane's. In mid-winter, when the dogs began to die from disease, Hendrik and Sonntag were sent out to visit Inughuit settlements in search of fresh animals. Sonntag fell through the ice and died soon afterwards. Hendrik eventually returned to the ship.

In the spring, Hayes set out on a long, arduous sledge trip across Smith Sound. He was apparently convinced that the wide sound north of Pim Island (Buchanan Bay) continued westward, separating Inglefield's Ellesmere Island and his and Kane's Grinnell Land. There is no indication that he attempted to confirm this idea, although it would not have taken much of a side trip to find out that the so-called sound was a bay and that Bache Island was a peninsula. On May 11, he reached and named Cape Hawks, the impressive headland opposite Washington Irving Island. According to his records, he continued northward to latitude 81°35′N, the mouth of Lady Franklin Bay. This claim has been consistently questioned. In July 1861 he managed to extricate the *United States* from the ice and headed for home. When he stopped along the way to thank the Inughuit for their assistance, he noted that they now numbered only about a hundred souls. Before leaving Greenland, he received news that civil war had broken out in America. If he harboured further ambitions regarding polar exploration, the war certainly dampened them, at least for a while.

By the time Hayes reached Boston, another American explorer was on his way north. On board the *Rescue* stood "Captain" Charles Francis Hall, eagerly anticipating his planned search for further evidence related to the Franklin tragedy. In sharp contrast to his fellow explorers, Hall had resolved to live with the Inuit to study their language and ways of coping with the arctic environment.[13] On Baffin Island, he had the great fortune to meet Ebierbing and his wife Tookoolito (Joe and Hannah), who remained his most trusted Inuit companions to the day he died. The extraordinary couple had been to England, where they were introduced to Her Majesty Queen Victoria. Joe and Hannah accompanied Hall on a most arduous five-year search for Franklin evidence in the central Arctic.

Charles Francis Hall and his Inuit companions, Ebierbing and Tookoolito. (From *Harper's Weekly*, October 23, 1869, p. 677)

By the time Hall returned to the United States in 1869, the Civil War was over. Hall wasted little time drawing up plans for a new expedition to the Arctic aimed at reaching the North Pole. With inexhaustible energy, he set about securing the funding and having his plans approved by the government. All was well until Dr. Hayes suddenly renewed his polar ambitions and challenged Hall for the leadership of the expedition. Hall effectively prevented Hayes from taking over and was no doubt relieved when the *Polaris* headed for Kane Basin on June 10, 1871. Captain Buddington commanded the vessel, the seasoned whaler Captain Tyson was chief mate, and Dr. Emil Bessels was in charge of the scientific investigations. In addition to Hannah, Joe, and their daughter, the Greenlander Hans Hendrik and his family also accompanied the expedition.

Undoubtedly because of more favourable ice conditions than those experienced by Kane and Hayes, the *Polaris* reached the northern entrance to Robeson Channel before retreating to what became the expedition's winter quarters: Thank God Harbour, in Polaris Bay just south of 82°N. As was the case on so many Arctic expeditions, the wintering was marked by endless squabbles among the men. The antagonism was particularly vehement between Hall and Dr. Bessels. Returning from a two-week sled journey in late October, Hall complained of feeling ill soon after coming on board. He died on November 8, 1871, and was buried on the shores of the Polaris Promontory. Following a near disastrous encounter with pressing ice floes, the ship remained reasonably secure throughout the remaining winter. In mid-August 1872, the crew managed to free the ship and head south, but their troubles were far from over. At the height of a fierce storm in Smith Sound, it appeared that the *Polaris* was in great danger of sinking. Two whaleboats were lowered onto a large ice floe along with all the provisions people could get their hands on. The floe split, separating the party from the *Polaris*, which disappeared from view. Captain Tyson and 18 members of the expedition, including the two Inuit families, were marooned. During the next six months, Tyson's party drifted southward with the current through Baffin Bay and Davis Strait. Survival was very much in the hands of the Inuit, who kept everyone alive by hunting seals from their kayaks. Tyson had his hands full keeping tensions between members of the party from getting out of hand as they drifted farther and father south. After five months, the original floe began to break apart. One boat had already been used for firewood. Now, on April 1, they crammed themselves and whatever supplies they could salvage into the remaining boat. They searched desperately for another floe large enough to provide at least some safety. The choices were few. Three weeks went by before they saw a ship. Unfortunately, no one saw them. The following day another ship appeared and disappeared. Finally, on April 30, 1873, the Newfoundland barquentine *Tigress*, commanded by Captain Bartlett, appeared through the fog and rescued them. The party had drifted just over 2000 kilometres.[14]

As Tyson and his party had been drifting into Baffin Bay, the *Polaris* had been blown northward. The ship eventually reached Port Foulke, near Etah, where the crew constructed the "Polaris" house and spent the winter. In the spring, the men built two boats and made their way south.

If nothing else, the 1871 expedition had accomplished one thing: the myth of the open polar sea had been laid to rest along with Hall. The rumour that he was murdered by Dr. Bessels has persisted for a long time. In 1967, Chauncey Loomis opened Hall's shallow grave and removed a sample of hair for analysis. The results indicated a concentration of arsenic, giving some credence to the idea that Hall had been poisoned.[15]

In 1871, Bache Peninsula was still identified on exploration maps as an island, and fiords in the vicinity remained unexplored. While the Americans showed no immediate interest in launching new polar expeditions, the British decided to get into the act. Aware of the impossible ice conditions encountered by Kane and Hayes in the eastern part of Kane Basin, the British planned to push northward along the east coast of Ellesmere Island. The command of the expedition was entrusted to the resourceful and competent George Nares. In May 1875, he and his men left England in the *Alert* and the *Discovery*. Their precise goal was to push one or both ships as far north as possible through Robeson Channel, establish winter quarters, and sledge north, preferably all the way to the North Pole. Nares stopped in Greenland to take on dogs, provisions, and an Inuit assistant, the experienced expedition member Hans Hendrik.

I have already mentioned some of Nares's discoveries in the Bache Peninsula region. Our evening activities on Skraeling Island often included a hike up to a large boulder that rested on the highest point near base camp. From here we had a splendid view of the narrow, protected harbour used by Nares in the fall of 1875. Nares's journal entry of August 4, 1875 describes Alexandra Fiord:

> To the southward of us we had opened a long fiord, entirely free of ice, running to the S.W., about eight miles in depth and three and a half in width. Snow-capped hills upwards of 2,000 feet high with steep cliffs formed the shores of the fiord; glaciers occupied the higher portion of each of the valleys, but none of them appeared to reach the sea. This fiord is protected from the entry of any large floes by an

island at its mouth, to which was given the name of the Three Sisters, from a similar number of conspicuous conical hills rising from its base. Wishing to anchor at the entrance of the fiord ready to take advantage of any movement in the outer ice, we sounded our way towards the shore, opposite to a large valley, off which I expected to find a bank with shallow water. Instead of this we obtained no bottom with fifty fathoms at a distance of fifty yards from the beach. Not finding an anchorage, we retraced our course about a mile to a small rocky bay scarcely large enough to receive the two ships, situated at the extreme end of one of the spurs of the Prince of Wales Mountains. I named it Alexandra Haven.[16]

To say that the bay was "scarcely large enough," must have been the British naval understatement of 1875. To squeeze two relatively large ships in between the rocky islands that constituted the "bay" was indeed testimony to superb seamanship. Nares and his men explored and named the broad Twin Glacier Valley, but stayed only one night in Alexandra Haven; time was a precious commodity. The next morning they "made a stern board" out of the small harbour and continued their explorations. A landing was made on the outer part of the north shore of Thorvald Peninsula, where a small party reportedly climbed 1500 feet up the mountainside to try to ascertain whether Hayes Sound might be a passage to the west. The matter remained unresolved, as did the question of whether Bache was an island or a peninsula, although Nares correctly suspected the latter. How they could have failed to ascertain that Bache was a peninsula from the height they claimed to have attained remains a mystery. One can only assume that low clouds or fog obscured their view. Heading northward from Buchanan Bay, Nares observed that: *The names given to the headlands [Cape Albert and Victoria], undoubtedly discovered by Admiral Inglefield should not have been altered by Drs. Kane and Hayes, each of whom published very misleading delineations of the same coast.*[17] Nares would not have been pleased with Sverdrup's renaming of Three Sisters Island.

Following the discovery of the two cairns on Washington Irving Island, Nares guided his ships northward, eventually securing the *Discovery* in winter quarters in Discovery Harbour on the north shore of Lady Franklin Bay. With considerable luck, superb ice navigation, and a splendid show of courage, Nares brought the *Alert* to the very edge of the Polar Basin. The ship was frozen in for

One of Nares's ships, the *Discovery*, in winter quarters in Discovery Harbour on the north shore of Lady Franklin Bay, northeastern Ellesmere Island. (From *The Graphic Arctic Number*, November 8, 1876, p. 23)

the winter at Floeberg Beach just off Cape Sheridan, not far from the present-day military installation at Alert. Unfortunately, the British Navy had learned nothing since the days of the Franklin searches about preventing scurvy or travelling in polar conditions. Men and officers endured incredible hardships, man-hauling heavy sleds and boats over long distances, increasingly debilitated by the horrible effects of scurvy which had set in during the winter, months before the backbreaking work began. A good part of the north coasts of Ellesmere Island and Greenland were explored in this manner. Commander Markham managed a farthest north of 83°20′. The human cost was high. Nearly half of the 121 men on the two ships suffered from scurvy. Several men died, and many more were physically ruined for a long time, some for life. The men on the *Discovery* fared a little better in large measure because of Hans Hendrik's ability to supply the party with fresh seal meat.[18] In the fall of 1876, both ships were extracted from the ice and eventually reached England at the beginning of November.

This time the Americans were paying attention. Getting through Kane Basin and Kennedy Channel did not seem so difficult after all, particularly with steam-powered ships. At the Second International Polar Conference, held in Bern, Switzerland in 1880, the United States agreed to establish two polar research stations. One was to be at Point Barrow, Alaska; the second, at Lady Franklin Bay on the northeast coast of Ellesmere Island, the very place where the *Discovery* had wintered so successfully five years earlier. The station was to be named Fort Conger, and the man in charge would be Lieutenant Adolphus Washington Greely.[19] The party sailed north in the *Proteus*, stopping along the way to check on Nares's cairns and various food depots, including the one at Cape Hawks near Washington Irving Island. On August 11, 1881, the *Proteus*, under Captain Pike, anchored in Discovery Harbour, the location of natural coal deposits to be used as a fuel source. The *Proteus* was only the fourth ship to get beyond Kane Basin, and Captain Pike was eager to leave as soon as the cargo was unloaded. Although the party had encountered reasonably good ice conditions on the way north, Pike was well aware of the dangers lying ahead. As he prepared to leave, Greely announced that two members of the expedition would return south with the ship: Corporal Starr, on account of asthma, and Mr. Henry Clay, who had irreconcilable differences with Dr. Octave Pavy, the expedition doctor. Under other circumstances, Greely would undoubtedly have preferred to get rid of Pavy, who had already proven difficult and disrespectful of command (shades of Hall and Dr. Bessels). These and other incidents of strife and command rivalry between expedition leaders and doctors may have influenced the Norwegian explorer Roald Amundsen's decision never to bring doctors on any of his expeditions.

For three days the *Proteus* lay hemmed in by impenetrable pack ice in Discovery Harbour. Another man, Private Ryan, was added to the list of evacuees, having suffered an epileptic fit. At the last minute Second Lieutenant Kislingbury, at his own request, was relieved of duty and hurried down to shore with all his baggage. Unfortunately, his struggle to get over the hummocky ice went unnoticed on board. A lead had opened up and Captain Pike had instantly instructed the first officer, Mr. Norman, to seize the opportunity. Kislingbury could only watch as the *Proteus* slipped through the ice and headed south. He tried to take courage in the fact that the ship was scheduled to return the following year with supplies. Fortunately, no one on shore could know what fate had in store for them.

Greely's Fort Conger in Lady Franklin Bay, 1882. (Greely, 1888:Frontispiece)

The foundations of Fort Conger in 1990.

Scientific projects and extensive exploration journeys were carried out from Fort Conger. Lieutenant Lockwood was in charge of two of the longest journeys. The first headed eastward along the north coast of Greenland to Lockwood Island and a new farthest north of 83°42′N. In early September 1993, I had an opportunity to see this bleak and rugged coastline from a very different vantage point: the bridge of an 18,000 ton Russian icebreaker, *Kapitan Khlebnikov*, attempting the first circumnavigation of Greenland. Within sight of the northern tip of Ellesmere Island, we could make no further progress in the colossal masses of multiyear ice. For three days, the huge diesel engines, with a combined strength of 25,000 hp, struggled with the ice, to no avail. It took one of the most powerful icebreakers in the world, the Russian nuclear-powered *Yamal*, to break us free and lead us back the way we had come. For us, relief came quickly; not so for the Greely expedition.

Disappointment ran through the 26 men when the *Proteus* didn't show up as planned in the fall of 1882. There was no panic, however; they were well supplied, and easily resigned to another winter's activities. Lockwood set out on another long journey, this time heading southwest, and eventually reached the easternmost arm of Greely Fiord. Other scientific investigations included the discovery of Thule culture winter house ruins and artifacts. By late fall of 1883, it was obvious that, once again, the supply vessels had failed to reach them. Convinced that the relief ships had been stopped each season by heavy ice in Kane Basin and had unloaded their supplies as planned farther south along the Ellesmere Island coast, Greely decided to take his large party south. On August 9, 1883, everyone crowded into the launch and the three small boats in tow. They brought along enough rations for 40 days, expecting to shortly reach the supplies left for them by the relief parties. As the days went by, the retreat grew increasingly desperate. There were no messages or supplies other than the ones Nares had cached. At Cape Hawks they took what there was. The erratic drift of the pack ice in Kane Basin sent the despondent party on several lengthy detours before they finally managed to reach shore at a place called Wade Point (Eskimo Point), about 18 kilometres south of Pim Island. The diminishing hope of finding food caches that kept Greely on the Ellesmere side. Construction of two stone-walled houses began immediately, making good use of materials from several old Thule culture winter house ruins on the site. Two men were sent north to Cape Sabine on Pim Island, where they finally found a message from the second relief expedition, under Captain Garlington.

The news was not good. On July 23, 1883, the *Proteus* had been crushed in the ice off Bache Peninsula. The crew had managed to save some supplies in the short time available to them before the ship slipped to the bottom. A small portion of the salvaged goods had been left at Cape Sabine on Pim Island. Wrapped around some of the supplies were the pages from a newspaper article written by Mr. Clay, sharply critical of the lack of efforts being made to arrange a rescue expedition to Lady Franklin Bay. Greely remained ignorant of how inept and badly bungled the relief expeditions had been. There was the cowardly retreat by the captain of the 1882 supply vessel, who, without leaving a single ration behind, headed back to New York. Following the 1883 sinking of the *Proteus*, Garlington had taken as much of the salvaged food as he could manage, even though he knew his own rescue was close at hand. He had also failed to instruct Captain Wilde of the accompanying rescue vessel *Yantic*, to head north to Cape Sabine to leave his supplies for the Fort Conger party.

In spite of the progress already made on the wintering huts and the onset of severe winter conditions, Greely decided to move everyone north to Pim Island. At least it would get them nearer to the few supplies at Cape Sabine and, they hoped, an eventual rescue. Hungry, weak, and cold, the men struggled to reach the north shore of Pim Island. Once again they began the hard task of breaking from the frozen ground all the boulders needed to construct living quarters. The hut was roofed with an overturned boat supported by a number of oars stretching from the side walls across the low dwelling, which became their dreary, cramped home for the next eight months. Although Greely named the place Camp Clay, it is most often referred to, more appropriately, as Camp Starvation.

On our first visit, we were struck by the starkness of the rocky terrain. Evidence of the tragedy that had taken place among the red granitic rocks and steep cliffs was everywhere: rusty barrel hoops and empty tin cans, pieces of weathered rope, and fragments of tent canvas. A small mound of ashes marked the location of the cooking fire where the two cooks had prepared increasingly meagre meals with everyone looking on, slumped, two or three to a sleeping bag, along the stone walls. They were getting down to a daily food ration of six ounces per man and eventually consumed everything even remotely digestible, including seaweed, rock lichen, strips of sealskin, and the occasional treat of a tiny shrimp or two. As soon as light returned to the land, two men attempted to cross Smith Sound to Greenland, but were stopped by open water. Had they headed a little farther north before attempting to cross, they might have reached

The remains of Greely's hut at Camp Clay on Pim Island. A small mound of ashes from the central cooking area is still visible today, more than a hundred years after the deadly wintering between 1883 and 1884 during which most of the men starved to death.

solid ice on which to cross over. Help was not that far away; Etah, across from Pim Island, was used regularly by the Inughuit, who had plenty of experience saving White explorers.

By early spring of 1884, flooding had made their hut uninhabitable. Since January of that year, death had stalked the place with increasing frequency. At first the dead were buried on a raised gravel terrace above the hut, shining metal buttons showing through the thin layer of sand covering the shallow graves. When the living could no longer find strength to haul the dead to the ridge, the bodies were simply dumped into cracks in the shore ice. Lieutenant Kislingbury died on June 1. On June 6, Private Henry was executed for stealing supplies. This left only seven men alive when the rescue vessels, the *Thetis* and the *Bear*, under the command of Captain Schley of the U.S. Navy, rounded Cape Sabine anxiously looking for survivors. Shortly before, in a small cairn just south of the cape, they had found Greely's message and read, with great relief, that the Greely party was camped nearby with sufficient rations for a couple of months. Elation turned to dismay when they realized that the note was dated seven months earlier.[20]

A gale had been blowing for days. Back at Camp Clay, one man had just died, his body lying half-covered by the collapsed tent. No one had the strength to drag him any further. They were all within days of dying. Greely thought he heard a ship's whistle and implored two of the stronger men, Brainard and Long, to reach the hill and raise the flag. Brainard couldn't make it and returned to the collapsed tent convinced that what had sounded like a ship's whistle was a trick played on them by the wind. Long made it to the top of the hill and re-erected the flag that had blown down during the gale. Crouched against strong winds, he thought he heard the ship's whistle again. In disbelief he watched as the *Thetis* rounded the cape, heading directly for him. One of the first of the rescuers to reach the tent was Norman, first officer on the *Proteus* in 1881. Of the seven men rescued, one died when they reached the west coast of Greenland. The others were soon brought back to good health, including Greely, who lived to be 92 years old.

On our second visit to Pim Island, we set up base camp about a kilometre west of Camp Starvation. It was not as good a location, but somehow the thought of setting up camp on the Greely site seemed disrespectful, an offence to the spirits. I have not met anyone who wasn't touched by the sombre and mournful ambience of the scene; it is a place where you instinctively speak in hushed tones. I will never forget the dream I had when we returned to the RCMP station at Alexandra Fiord after our first visit to Camp Starvation. In the dream, I had been sleeping in the small, south-facing bedroom at the station when a strange noise from outside woke me up. Looking out of the window, I stared in shock at a bedraggled group of ill-clad, gaunt-looking men slowly making their way across the soggy tundra towards the station, their mouths pleading, their arms reaching out. I woke up in a cold sweat and looked out the window, half expecting to see Greely and his men on the tundra.

From our camp on Pim Island, we surveyed the rocky north shore and stopped for lunch at the Greely site, a place where one appreciates food more than usual. On each visit to the site, we have left small offerings of food, in memory of those who died over a century ago. We sat for a while on a rocky ridge overlooking Kane Basin and Smith Sound, enjoying the unusually calm, summer day. Beside us was the small stone cairn where the Greely party had erected its flag.

Back in our own camp, we read Greely's official account and reflected on the disaster, comparing the fate of the starving and dying men to the evidence of prehistoric activities we were finding along the coast: tent rings, meat caches, and other features associated with both Palaeoeskimo and Thule period occupations, mostly the latter. There is little doubt that many of the Westerners who chose to explore the High Arctic, particularly those associated with the British Navy, were ill-prepared to live off the land. Greely had brought along two native Greenlanders. Unfortunately they were from West Greenland, and had no familiarity with the Smith Sound region. Both had died in April, one from overexertion, the other drowned in a hunting accident.

We worked on Pim Island for a couple of days, using a zodiac to reach more distant locations along the coast. The weather was sunny with light winds, conditions not known to last very long in this area. Perhaps our small food offering on the Greely site had placated the spirits, permitting us to complete our work in peace. On several occasions, we remarked on the hefty size of boulders used by the Thule culture Inuit to hold down their summer tents. We also noted the construction of waist-high boulder walls on the land side of the summer camps and wondered what purpose they had served. The evening was dead calm. Not a cloud touched the deep blue sky when we crawled into our tents. The tranquillity lasted two more hours. Then a couple of sharp wind gusts slapped the tent walls, followed by a moment of silence before we were set upon by a screaming tempest, not from the ice-choked Kane Basin to the north, as we expected, but from the south. The gale blew directly over top of the island, then descended straight down the rocky cliffs, literally beating our small camp to pieces. One tent fly was shredded in no time and pieces were sent flying out over the fast-disappearing ice. We dressed in record time, collapsed and piled boulders on the tortured tents, then ran to save the large cook tent, already threatening to sail out over Kane Basin. The strength of the wind grew by the minute, until it was nearly impossible to stand up. Stung savagely by airborne sand and gravel, we made our way down to the shore, fearing that the zodiac had already been blown away. Luckily, out of old habit we had placed the heavy outboard motor and fuel tanks inside the boat after we had last used it. So far, that had been enough to keep it from taking off. Now we weighted it down further with several large boulders. If it moved, Pim Island itself would take off. The temperature dropped and blowing snow blended with flying sand and gravel. We crawled in under the collapsed cook tent to remove the radio before placing more boulders on the flapping canvas. At this point only one tent was standing, testimony to the splendid strength of the older Logan style, double-walled, canvas tents. As our last place of refuge, it received all our consideration: more boulders, more lines, and careful attention to the most vulnerable points where grommets and taut lines came together.

Having done what we could, we arranged ourselves around the centre pole of the madly flapping tent, hoping for a quick end to the storm. Hour after hour we listened to the roar of the wind and sand particles blasting the tent canvas. Occasionally we crawled out to check and adjust the straining lines, piling more boulders on top of tent pegs. The scene was stunning in its intensity and rage. The pack ice had been blown out of sight, leaving behind only a few grounded icebergs near shore. Back in the tent, we managed to make radio contact with two geologists working at Cape Herschel, just south of Pim Island. Looking out of the window of their solidly constructed frame building, they could see the wind picking up large propane gas bottles and tossing them about. The station instruments were recording over 100 kilometre-an-hour winds, and there was no sign of a letup. We buried ourselves in our sleeping bags and waited it out. Fifty-two hours after it began, the wind dropped as suddenly as it had begun. The calm was eerie. We crawled out of the tent, groggy and a bit stunned by the onslaught. Before us lay Kane Basin, ice-free as far north as the eye could see. We now knew the reason for the large tent ring boulders and shelter walls on the Thule culture summer sites.

Following the Greely disaster, the shores of the Bache Peninsula region were visited only occasionally by Inughuit hunters from Greenland. Fourteen years went by before Westerners again set foot on Ellesmere Island. In 1898, two very different parties established winter quarters in the Bache Peninsula region. The first arrived on the Norwegian expedition ship *Fram*, already renowned for its transpolar drift under Fridtjof Nansen and Otto Sverdrup. Now, in the fall of 1898, it was heading for Kane Basin as part of the Second Norwegian Polar Expedition, under the leadership of Sverdrup.[21] Unable to proceed very far into Kane Basin, Sverdrup brought the *Fram* into a small bight on the west side of Rice Strait and established winter quarters. From Fram Havn (Harbour), just across from Pim Island, Sverdrup and his team of scientists engaged in an extraordinary series of dog-drawn sled trips, surveying, mapping, and writing volumes on their botanical, geological, biological, and occasional archaeological observations. In every sense of the word it was a scientific expedition and, just as importantly, a claim of Norwegian sovereignty over the High Arctic Islands!

That same year, the American explorer Robert E. Peary entered Kane Basin. Peary had been drawn to the polar regions on many occasions since his first visit to the west coast of Greenland in 1886. He had completed several extraordinary and dangerous (some would say foolhardy) journeys across the northern part of the Inland Ice. To be the first man to stand on top of the world had become his obsession. With such single-mindedness, it is not surprising that he harboured great anxieties about any perceived competition in his quest for the Pole. Naturally, he found Sverdrup's presence in the Bache region most alarming; it must have seemed inconceivable to him that an expedition into these northern regions could have any other goal than his own. In the fall of 1898, Peary let his ship, *Windward*, freeze in for the winter in the fast ice just off Cape D'Urville, about 70 kilometres north of Pim Island and Fram Havn.[22]

There was no reason for Peary to worry. Sverdrup did not have the slightest interest in reaching the geographical North Pole. Most likely he had seen enough of the polar pack during his drift with Nansen; now he was leading a scientific expedition determined to map and investigate large portions of the High Arctic Islands. Although such activities didn't concern Peary in the least, they were a wake-up call for the Canadian Government; Sverdrup's claim to the Arctic Islands on behalf of the Norwegian Crown, however debatable, had to be countered. In 1903, one year after Sverdrup's return to Norway, the Canadian Government decided to show some presence in the suddenly disputed territory. In August of that year, the *Neptune*, under command of geologist A. P. Low, headed for Hudson Bay and a first wintering at Fullerton Harbour.[23] The following August, the *Neptune* arrived at Cape Herschel, just south of Pim Island. An official proclamation of possession was placed in a stone cairn at the Cape. In 1904, the *Arctic* sailed north on the first of four Arctic voyages under the command of Captain J. E. Bernier.[24] The last three touched the shores of the Queen Elizabeth Islands between 1906 and 1911. While these voyages proclaimed Canada's sovereignty over the High Arctic islands, Frederick Cook and Peary each claimed the attainment of the North Pole. The question of whether either man actually reached the pole is still a topic of acrimonious debate.[25]

Having participated in Peary's 1909 polar quest, Donald B. MacMillan organized his own northern venture, the Crocker Land Expedition, between 1912 and 1917. MacMillan's ambition was to search for Peary's alleged sighting of "Crocker Land" west of the northwest coast of Ellesmere Island. Although there is no land, Peary may have seen a shimmering mirage of one of the large ice islands that occasionally drift through this part of the Polar Basin.[26]

The Norwegian parliament did not pay great attention to Otto Sverdrup's arguments for Norwegian sovereignty over the High Arctic Islands. Had Norway not been under the control of the Swedish Crown at the time, the claim might have received more serious consideration. The Canadian government had to acknowledge that its own claim to the Arctic Islands rested rather tenuously on the Canadian "sector rule." The rule implied that all lands and oceans within specific longitudes, reaching all the way to the North Pole, lay within the jurisdiction of the nearest particular country within those longitudes. On the international scene, the sector rule was widely questioned. The Canadian government decided to do exactly what Sverdrup had suggested to the Norwegian government: send a small police force to the Arctic Islands.

In 1922, Captain Bernier was once again placed in command of his old ship, the *Arctic*. On August 21, supplies and equipment were landed for the first RCMP post, Craig Harbour, on the southeast coast of Ellesmere Island. In 1924, the *Arctic* entered Sverdrup's old Fram Harbour in Rice Strait and unloaded supplies for yet another RCMP post. Since Fram Harbour was not the intended location, only a tiny hut was left behind when the ship headed south. Visiting Inughuit hunters from Greenland must have been surprised to see the structure and the signboard, which read *Kane Basin RCMP Detachment*. The *Arctic* stopped on the southeast coast of Devon Island, where the Dundas Harbour RCMP post was established. In 1926, the *Beothic*, under the command of Captain E. Falk, returned to Fram Harbour and transferred the supplies across Buchanan Bay to Bache Peninsula. The inauguration of the Bache RCMP post took place on August 9, 1926. The Canadian flag was securely planted; sovereignty was no longer a matter of conjecture. It is ironic that Inughuit hunters and their families from Greenland were hired to assist the RCMP constables in upholding Canadian territorial claims. The Bache post became the starting point for many epic sled journeys conducted by the officers and their Inughuit assistants. In 1932, Corporal Stallworthy, Constable Hamilton, seven Inughuit, and 125 dogs headed westward to the west coast of Axel Heiberg Island in a futile effort to find a German scientist, H. E. Krueger, and his field party.[27]

The Bache post was closed in 1933, the year both Nansen and Sverdrup died and the year the Canadian Government paid 67,000 dollars to Sverdrup's family and the Norwegian Government.[28] Officially the payment was made in recognition of the tremendous scientific and geographical contributions made by Sverdrup and his men in the Canadian High Arctic.

Official photograph of the opening of the Bache Peninsula RCMP post on August 9, 1926. The photo was arranged by the late geologist and painter Maurice Haycock (7th from left) and "tripped" by the Greenlander Nookapeengwa (11th from left). Permission to use the photograph was kindly granted by Mrs. Haycock.

The Bache Peninsula region continued to be a favourite access point to the Canadian High Arctic for a variety of foreign expeditions, most of them based on the Greenland side of Smith Sound. Between 1934 and 1935, there was the Oxford University Ellesmere Land Expedition,[29] which spawned two additional expeditions, one by the geologist Robert Bentham (1936–38) and the second by the ornithologist D. Haig-Thomas (1937–38). During the 1937 Cambridge Expedition under J. M. Wordie,[30] T. C. Lethbridge carried out several cursory archaeological investigations, including a three-day visit to Sverdrup's "Eskimopolis site" on the Johan Peninsula coast.[31] Members of the Danish Thule and Ellesmere Land Expedition (1939–40) travelled through Flagler Bay and Sverdrup Pass en route to western Ellesmere Island and Axel Heiberg Island, but no new ground was covered. Upon their return to the Bache RCMP post, they found a message scratched on an old tin, informing them that "the store is closed." Germany had invaded Denmark, and Greenland was isolated.[32]

The Danish government's loss of administrative control of Greenland caused considerable concern in the American and Canadian capitals. Accurate weather forecasting in northern Europe greatly depended on knowledge of weather conditions in Greenland, a fact of equal interest to the German High Command and the Allies. Both the U.S. and the Canadian governments recognized the need to keep the Germans from occupying Greenland. In 1940, the Canadian government sent the RCMP vessel *St. Roch* on a historic voyage from Vancouver through the Northwest Passage to Halifax, under the command of Inspector Henry A. Larsen. Aside from strengthening sovereignty claims in the Arctic, the Canadian expedition had a considerably less publicized agenda: securing Greenland under Canadian government control. The plan was shelved when the Danish minister in Washington established the American–Danish Greenland Commission, essentially placing the administration (and protection) of Greenland under American control for the duration of the war. In 1943, Inspector Larsen received orders to take the *St. Roch* back through the Northwest Passage to Vancouver. The return voyage was successfully completed in 1944.[33]

Weather forecasting had also become a crucial component of Arctic aviation. Between 1947 and 1950, Canada and the United States jointly established a series of Arctic weather stations, including Alert and Eureka on Ellesmere Island and Resolute on Cornwallis Island. American and Canadian interests in the Far North strengthened considerably in the years leading up to the Korean war and well beyond. The "Pinetree Line," a series of radar stations along the 50th parallel, was a joint U.S./Canadian operation completed in the early 1950s. It was followed by the construction of additional warning systems, the Mid-Canada Line and the Distant Early Warning (DEW) Line. Foreign, especially American, interest in the Canadian Arctic was a matter of increasing concern in Ottawa. It was time, once again, to think of ways to substantiate Canada's sovereignty over the High Arctic. As before, the RCMP were called upon to fill that role, and so were the Inuit. This time they would not be imported from Greenland; they would be Canadian. Much has been said and written about the relocation of Inuit families to the far northern communities of Grise Fiord and Resolute Bay.[34] In August of 1953, the *C.D. Howe* transported a number of Inuit families from Port Harrison in Quebec and Pond Inlet on Baffin Island to the High Arctic. The initial plan was to establish three settlements, including one at Alexandra Fiord. Because of severe ice conditions in Smith Sound, the Alexandra Fiord settlement plans were cancelled. The Inuit families who were initially landed at the reactivated RCMP post at Craig Harbour on the southeast coast of Ellesmere Island were later moved to Grise Fiord. The remaining Inuit families were taken to the south coast of Cornwallis Island and unloaded on the beaches near the existing Resolute weather station and airstrip.

Instead of the planned Native settlement at Alexandra Fiord, the RCMP were instructed to establish a new station there, using whatever materials they could remove from the old Bache post. On August 18, 1953, the icebreaker *D'Iberville* anchored just east of Nares's old Alexandra Haven. Superintendent Larsen, Constables Sargent, Johnson, Jones, and Stiles, and Special Constable Ningoo stepped ashore, accompanied by civilian carpenter Richard Dorney, who would supervise the construction of the buildings. Eight days later, Larsen, Sargent, and Johnson departed for Craig Harbour. Two weeks later, Dorney was picked up by helicopter from the USS *Staten Island*, leaving Jones, Stiles, and Ningoo with family to occupy the station. The following summer the old buildings from the Bache post were dismantled and transported 25 kilometres south to join the three new buildings making up the Alexandra Fiord station. The post remained active for nine years.

Until the 1950s, scientific research in the High Arctic had proceeded on a very ad hoc basis and had usually been conducted by non-Canadians. Perhaps still concerned about its sovereignty claims, the Canadian government finally took charge of its own research agenda in the Far North. In 1953, G. Hattersley-Smith of the Defence Research Board of Canada, accompanied by R. G. Blackader of the Geological Survey of Canada, conducted glaciological and geological surveys along the north coast of Ellesmere Island. Additional surveys were carried out during the next couple of years.[35] In 1957, the Defence Research Board sponsored an extensive exploration of northern Ellesmere Island as part of Canada's contribution to the International Geophysical Year. Lake Hazen was chosen as the base for "Operation Hazen." Two years before, Ray Thorsteinsson and Yves Fortier of the Geological Survey of Canada had taken charge of "Operation Franklin," an impressive interdisciplinary effort to investigate and map vast regions of the High Arctic. The project also provided the participants with considerable expertise in handling the many complicated logistic requirements encountered in the remote and often severe environment. The idea of a multidisciplinary, government-supported, High Arctic research institution was borne. On April 5, 1958, the Canadian government created an organization which, many years later, became absolutely essential to our own research: the Polar Continental Shelf Project.[36]

For many years, High Arctic research was conducted almost exclusively by government researchers. The immense cost of providing flight hours and other support for work in the Far North was simply prohibitive for anyone else. Considerable credit must go to the second director of the PCSP, George Hobson, for expanding the role of the organization to include the support of university-based researchers, a practice being continued by the present director Bonni Hrycyk. During the past 20 years, numerous research teams have acquired a tremendous amount of knowledge about Canada's North. These activities, combined with the established communities of Grise Fiord and Resolute Bay, have provided Canada with the best possible evidence of Canadian sovereignty over the Arctic Islands.

In recent years, Canadian Arctic sovereignty claims have had to incorporate political realities never thought of earlier in the century. The map of the Northwest Territories is now divided into a number of geopolitical units such as Nunavut and the Inuvialuit, Gwich'in, Sahtu, Deh Cho, North Slave, and South Slave settlement areas. Archaeological research has played a significant role in the successful negotiation of Native land claims by providing the concrete evidence needed to show that indigenous populations were present in the Canadian Arctic at least 12,000 years ago, perhaps long before that. In the case of the Arctic Islands, indigenous occupation does not extend quite that far back in time, but still exceeds 4000 years. The process of settling Native land claims, granting compensation, and achieving self-government is ongoing , still far from completion. The issue of Native land claims goes directly to the heart of the relationship between people and their environment. By settling land claims, society acknowledges that indigenous peoples have certain legal rights to the land their forefathers occupied. As a concept, legal ownership of land had no meaning in the Arctic prior to Western contact. That is not to imply that Palaeo- and Neoeskimos never exerted any kind of control over particular hunting areas or that Indians and Inuit wandered into each others' territories with impunity. Tribal identity was not just a social arrangement of kinship ties and hunting partners; people also identified with the land and its resources. Modern assertions of territoriality and sovereignty, however, depend in the end on the ability of the claimants to defend their rights in a court of law.

14

Lessons from the Past

In the not too distant future much of the world's biological endowment may well be found in reserves, in islands of habitat surrounded by biologically depleted environments.

(George B. Schaller, 1988:98)

The Palaeo- and Neoeskimo families functioned as an integral part of their biosphere—one species among many. Aside from the infrequent appearances of long-distance trade items, such as iron and copper, their lives were totally dependent on what the immediate environment had to offer. Food, materials for shelter, clothing, transportation, tools, weapons, heat, and light had to be procured from the land and surrounding seas. The complete dependency and fragile nature of that relationship captures our imagination regardless of who we are, because, in essence, we all share the same genetic human heritage. Go back far enough in time and our ancestors were all hunters and gatherers. Perhaps it is that lingering awareness that makes us long for insights into the human capacity to respond to challenges under extreme conditions; to reach a greater understanding of the path we must take in our own struggle to survive.

We close in on the final years of the twentieth century with far more than a passing concern about the biosphere and our rapidly increasing role as a dominant and upsetting force in its evolution. Environmental pollution, extinction of fish stocks, destruction of rain forests, ozone depletion, the greenhouse effect, and associated global warming are topics much debated and publicized. Human ecologists, interested in the extent to which changing climatic and environmental conditions influenced past cultural developments, are keenly aware of those discussions. As we achieve greater awareness of our role as players in the game of global survival, the unquestioning enthusiasm for our technological ideology gradually diminishes. We are only beginning to understand some of the lessons our forefathers learned thousands of years ago, essentially because we have chosen to be ignorant of their wisdom. As a species we may be very powerful, but we are not omnipotent. The Palaeo- and Neoeskimos knew that their resources were limited; they were aware of the capriciousness of nature and their own place in the scheme of things. This is also the case for a large percentage of the present world's population. The difference today is that most of these people are governed by individuals or political parties mesmerized by the ideology of human invincibility. In the not-so-distant past, ecological wisdom came about as a matter of necessity, as indeed may soon be the case for us.

On these pages I have explored the human presence in one of the most severe regions in the world, where people persevered, even thrived at times, under the most rigorous conditions. Life was a precarious balancing act in which even minor changes challenged the human capacity to survive: a contest requiring not only reasonable harmony between the material, social, and spiritual worlds, but often a good deal of luck. It is the marginality of the High Arctic that makes its prehistory particularly fascinating. Cultural responses to changes in people's lives are more readily approached when alternatives are limited. As we have seen, the Arctic environment had little to offer as far as gathering was concerned; year-round or seasonal availability of game was the key to human survival.

Returning to the east coast of Ellesmere Island year after year, we began to understand the environmental and ecological dynamics that influenced the economic viability of areas such as the Bache Peninsula region. We noticed that the thickness of the sea ice was determined not only by temperatures during the winter, but also by the amount of snow blanketing the ice. The time of ice breakup was governed by many factors. The pattern of prevailing winds and spring storms influenced the expansion or contraction of the North Water polynya, which in turn controlled the sea ice conditions in adjacent bays and fiords. The presence or absence of sea ice provided greater or lesser access to various species of sea mammals, animals whose presence assured the well-being of the Native hunter and his family. Our limited insights would have added nothing to the Palaeo- or Neoeskimo hunter's awareness; he was well acquainted with the changeable nature of the Arctic environment and the ecological requirements of his prey. His greatest challenge involved decisions about where and when to seek out particular game, when to move from one area to another, and where to set up camp. The discovery of a location that regularly provided food for the entire group of extended families every spring and summer, regardless of shifting weather patterns, must have been magical. The Flagler Bay polynya was such a place, and its economic and social importance, especially during the late Dorset period, cannot be overestimated. The attraction of a polynya was perhaps even greater during more severe times, when late ice breakups and cool summers accentuated the uniqueness of the open water.

The Palaeoeskimos were technologically capable of hunting all land mammals and most sea mammals, the most notable exception being the large bowhead whales. Existence, however, depended not only on having the technology to procure game, but also on finding it and securing enough food to get through the lean times. Hunters and their families had to live a highly mobile existence dictated in large measure by the seasonal availability of their food resources. Such a seminomadic life required the means of transporting the group both summer and winter, the ability to construct different types of shelters to fit the seasons, and a relatively large region to exploit. We found that the east coast of Ellesmere Island was an integral part of the larger Smith Sound/Baffin Bay culture sphere. Even when the Bache Peninsula region had no permanent residents, hunters residing on the Greenland side of Smith Sound used the area as a seasonal hunting and staging ground for excursions into western Ellesmere Island and beyond. There can be little doubt that the Greenland side, between Etah and Cape York, provided a relatively greater abundance of food resources. These included migratory birds, such as dovekies and murres, which could be taken by the thousands at the bird cliffs. The annual expansion of the North Water brought narwhal, walrus, and bowhead whales into the bays and fiords of North Greenland long before the fast ice broke up along the east coast of Ellesmere Island. The ecological difference between the two sides of Baffin Bay and Smith Sound was probably accentuated greatly during periods of more severe conditions. At such times, I suspect, an even greater concentration of indigenous populations took place on the Greenland side. The Palaeoeskimos lived most of the year in small groups of one or two extended families. Occasionally they must have congregated in larger numbers to socialize and strengthen the cohesive spirit of a broader tribal identity. We have very little evidence of such annual assemblages until the time of the late Dorset people, who rekindled their community spirit in the economic safety of polynyas.

When reflecting on today's urban madness—energized by stressed commuters rushing madly between home and work, if they have either, desperately trying to keep in step with everything and everyone else—it is appealing to step back in time and imagine Palaeoeskimo families celebrating the long-anticipated bounty at the polynya. Not that their lives lacked trauma and suffering; nor that we necessarily wish to change places with them. What we appreciate, however, is the perception of a more defined existence, where each person had a designated cultural role: a place and time where an individual's obligations and responsibilities were clearly defined. The hunter and his family existed in a relationship of mutual dependency; children learned by watching, listening, and imitating the activities of their elders; the shaman did what he or she could to indulge the world of the spirits. Each person was important to the group, and each group was important to the tribe.

Although it is occasionally postulated that the precontact Inuit lived in a true egalitarian society, it is doubtful that such an entity ever existed. For one thing, theirs was a very male-dominated society, where power usually resided in the hands of the best provider. To be a great hunter was the pinnacle of success. The Palaeoeskimos had no way of supporting elite classes of priests and spiritual practitioners like those that developed in other parts of the world. There was no economic basis to sustain the development of a class system or social hierarchy, even in the spiritual realm. To dominate others, individuals or groups must attain some kind of power which usually translates into socioeconomic control. The prehistoric Arctic world provided few such avenues for individual domination, particularly during most of the Palaeoeskimo period. With greater technological efficiency, the Neoeskimos came closer to developing a social hierarchy based on an individual hunter's ability. In Alaska, the *umialiq*, the man who owned the large umiak used to hunt bowhead whales, was such a person—in some settlements, he still is. In the past he often supported more than one wife, lived in a bigger dwelling, kept larger dog teams, and enjoyed the respect of others. In a society where survival of the group depended on the success of the hunter, such a social arrangement was probably unavoidable. Another powerful person in the community was the shaman, whose ability to communicate successfully with the animal spirits was perceived to be another essential element of life. The shamans travelled to the moon or the bottom of the deepest ocean seeking contact with the mythological creators of the world and all its inhabitants. The ethnographic literature, however, leaves one with the impression that most shamans among the Inuit had to hunt for their own livelihood like everybody else.

When you live in a erratic, seemingly unmanageable environment, special attention has to be focused on the spiritual forces that control it. In times of great social stress, whether brought about by war or famine or by the ravages of incurable diseases, people's spiritual awareness is usually greatly heightened.

This is no different today than it was in the distant past. Were the impressive ceremonial gatherings of the late Dorset people in the spring and early summer related to a particularly stressful period in their lives? Was it a cult, led by one or more particularly impressive shamans?

The relatively small prehistoric population numbers in the Arctic do not necessarily reflect a greater awareness of the need to limit resource exploitation. The uncertain seasonal availability of most resources and limited technological abilities diminished the need for such concerns. We have seen how Palaeoeskimo technology remained relatively steady for thousands of years. Changes in the basic tool kit are measured in degrees: a slight narrowing or widening of microblades, shifting forms of the basic harpoon heads, the use of different lithic sources, and occasional changes in the style of seasonal dwellings. So why didn't the Palaeoeskimos develop more sophisticated ways of hunting, including the active pursuit of bowhead whales? Many elements are involved in the successful adaptation of new technologies. First, the innovative idea must be seen to have an obvious advantage. People are by nature a conservative lot; old harpoon head styles are not easily replaced. Second, the innovation must be timely. The history of inventions is replete with stories of great ideas advanced before their time and discarded. In several instances, we found lumps of coal on the floor of Thule culture house ruins on Skraeling Island.[1] No doubt the pieces had been found near coal seams on Bache Peninsula, and brought home as items of curiosity. If the lumps of coal had fallen by chance into the cooking hearths, the Thule Inuit would have discovered a new fuel source; but I doubt that it would have led to an industrial revolution on Ellesmere Island. Finally, there is the matter of transmitting new ideas to others, not an easy task for small isolated populations. In today's world—ruled by constant changes, forwarded instantly through evermore elaborate global communication systems—it is hard to conceive of a time (not all that long ago) when technological advancements were barely detectable for hundreds, even thousands of years. Yet, until a few hundred years ago, that was the "normal" state of affairs.

There is one lesson to which we need to pay particular attention: we must acknowledge the relationship between population numbers and environmental sustainability. No matter how technologically superior we believe ourselves to be, we cannot sustain unchecked population growth. In spite of our immensely more complex society and impressive state of technological mastery, the basic rules of sustainable life have not changed. What has changed is the scale of our ability to influence and alter the world we live in. Our world is glutted with examples of our technological innovations far outstripping our social ability to control them. Advanced hunting weaponry enabled Westerners to bring the bowhead whale close to extinction about a century ago, and the same fate continues to be shared by many other species. The edge of survival has become a sword much sharper, with a sweep much broader. It is a bizarre paradox that, on the one hand, accumulated and transmitted material knowledge is the basis for our current place in the hierarchy of life forms on Earth. Yet, in a very basic social sense, we have advanced hardly at all. Only the weapons have changed: the wooden club has become a nuclear bomb. We have treated our knowledge base quite selectively to suit our immediate ambitions, with little regard for wider implications. Unless we collectively wake up to reality and take evasive action, a lot more than the High Arctic will have to be abandoned.

The size of the Palaeo- and the Neoeskimo families and groups was largely controlled by economic circumstances. The impressive difference in size between many Thule culture winter settlements and most Palaeoeskimo sites reflects different capacities to hunt and store sufficient food for the winter. The fluctuating carrying capacity of the High Arctic ecosystem—not only from season to season, but from year to year—was an enormous challenge for human survival. Population increases were followed by decreases. I suspect that the two major periods of human migration into the Canadian Arctic and Greenland were kick-started by population pressures in the home territory. The initial migrations of both Palaeoeskimos and Neoeskimos took place during the latter stages of climatic warming episodes. In each case, an increase in the resource capacity of the western Arctic ecosystems had resulted in human population growth to the point where migration was an important option for survival, particularly when conditions gradually turned less favourable. It has been fashionable to scorn such unbridled environmental determinism or possibilism, much as it became popular to scoff at Malthusian population theory. Tribal numbers were controlled by high infant mortality, starvation, hunting accidents, and occasionally through infanticide and suicide. That was the hard reality of their lives. Population sizes fluctuated with the hunters' ability to obtain sufficient food, but rarely passed certain maximum or optimum numbers. Is there a globally sustainable limit to our numbers? During the past 80 years, the human population has increased from about 1.5 to 5 billion. How many more billions can the Earth sustain and, perhaps more importantly, under what conditions?

The birth of scientific principles and the acquisition of knowledge through the scientific process have been major forces in shaping the way in which we seek new insights. In some regions, human societies have reached a level of enormous technological complexity involving massive consumption of energy. The rest of the world is dragged along. The pace of change for humankind has accelerated to a frightening level, and so far we seem incapable of taking decisive action to put the brakes on. Can knowledge and wisdom not be made to serve more profound and fundamental interests? In a hopelessly materialistic society, is it not possible to strangle greed and the thirst for power? Why have millions of years of human evolution only succeeded in bringing us closer to wiping ourselves and most other species out? Perhaps in the human spirit there is a strain of madness. We may turn out to be the deadliest of mutations our battered planet has ever seen.

Such troublesome thoughts shatter the quiet, brilliant Arctic summer night, far removed from daily life as we are used to it. All along the shores of the world where stillness has an echo, there is evidence of past human life. For thousands of years people lived, loved, hunted, and died; yet all we see is the occasional cluster of house mounds, a few tent rings, hearths, boat stands, and meat caches. We feel that we can reach out and touch that life as we listen to the stories told by the silent voices of stone and bone. It is a small glimpse, to be sure: a few scenes from a larger picture we shall never see completely. The landscape lends its majestic splendour to our imagination, enabling us to fill in a background perhaps not too different from the one the people saw. It brings us closer to them, and makes us feel that surely there are lessons to be learned if only we pay attention to them. The human odyssey should be a quest for wisdom.

Notes

Chapter 1. Challenge of the Unknown

[1] For a discussion of climatic conditions during the Holocene see Bryson and Wendland, 1967; Dansgaard et al., 1969; Lamb, 1972, 1977; Nichols, 1968, 1975.

[2] An excellent introduction to anthropological archaeology is provided by Thomas, 1974 and 1989. See also Watson et al., 1971.

[3] For comprehensive discussions of radiocarbon dating in archaeology see Taylor, 1987, and Bowman, 1990.

[4] Explanation of various dating techniques and some of the difficulties encountered with their interpretation are provided by Thomas, 1974; McGhee and Tuck, 1976; Arundale, 1981.

[5] See Bowman, 1990, for a concise discussion of ^{14}C reservoir or source effects.

[6] Pavlish and Banning, 1980, and Bowman, 1990, describe the accelerator mass spectrometry (AMS) method of ^{14}C dating.

[7] Don Foote, 1967, used the systems approach in his area economic survey of the east coast of Baffin Island. Foote was one of several investigators responsible for stopping the planned use of nuclear explosions to construct a harbour on the shores of Bering Strait in the early 1960s (O'Neill, 1994).

[8] Steward, 1955, 1977.

[9] Thomas, 1989.

[10] Gould, 1978, and Kramer, 1979, provide collections of papers describing the theoretical underpinnings of ethnoarchaeology and the use of ethnoarchaeological approaches in different areas of the world.

Chapter 2. Window to the Past

[1] John Ross, 1819.

[2] For an account of William Baffin's remarkable 1616 voyage to the northern part of Baffin Bay see Markham, 1881.

[3] Although the Dutch and other nationalities had hunted bowhead whales along the west coast of Greenland long before John Ross's 1818 voyage, it was this event that expanded the slaughter of bowhead whales into Baffin Bay and Lancaster Sound. See Scoresby, 1820; Markham, 1875; Lubbock, 1937; Ross, 1985.

[4] An excellent series of articles dealing with evidence of Norse activities in North America has been published by the Viking Ship Museum in Roskilde, Denmark. See Clausen, 1993.

[5] Helge Ingstad's *Land Under the Pole Star* (1966) remains one of the best overall accounts of Norse Greenland.

[6] For theories and evidence relating to the earliest appearance of people in the North American Arctic and Subarctic see Larsen, 1968; Anderson, 1970, 1984, 1988; Dumond, 1977, 1984.

[7] Hopkins, 1979; Hoffecker et al., 1993.

[8] Gordon, 1975, 1976.

[9] Ackerman, 1984, provides an excellent summary of the prehistoric developments in the Bering Strait and Chukchi Sea regions.

Chapter 3. The Search

[1] Schledermann, 1981b; Zaslow, 1981.

[2] Taylor, J.G., 1968, 1984.
[3] Boas, 1901–1907.
[4] Schledermann, 1975b.
[5] Schledermann, 1978b.
[6] Dunbar, 1969.
[7] Kane, 1856.
[8] Hayes, 1867.
[9] Nares, 1876, 1878.
[10] Greely, 1886, 1888.
[11] Sverdrup, 1904.
[12] Schledermann, 1977b.
[13] Foster and Marino, 1986.
[14] Christie, 1967.
[15] Svoboda and Freedman, 1994.
[16] Stirling, 1980; Stirling and Cleator, 1981.
[17] Schledermann, 1980a.

Chapter 4. The True Pioneers

[1] Greely, 1886, 1888.
[2] For an account of Danmarks Expeditionen see Thomsen, 1917; Thostrup, 1917.
[3] Steensby, 1910, 1917.
[4] Knuth, 1952, 1967, 1984; McGhee, 1979.
[5] Louis Giddings was one of the pioneers of Alaskan archaeological and dendrochronological research. His excavations at Cape Denbigh, Cape Krusenstern and Onion Portage laid the foundation for much of our understanding about Alaskan prehistory. His book *Ancient Men of the Arctic* (1967) remains a classic in Arctic archaeological literature. See also Giddings, 1964; Dumond, 1977.
[6] Irving, 1957.
[7] Fitzhugh, 1976; Cox, 1978, 1988.
[8] The recognition by Diamond Jenness of an episode of Canadian Arctic prehistory older than the Thule culture was a masterful conjecture based on only a handful of stone artifacts. See Jenness, 1925.
[9] The illustrations and descriptions of seventeenth-century Lapland dwellings by Leems, 1767, have provided an important dimension to our appreciation of the interior social arrangements of central axis dwellings. The central placement of hearth and storage spaces flanked by sleeping and activity areas appears to be a universally adopted layout, undoubtedly maximizing available space.
[10] Nansen, 1897.
[11] Birket-Smith's, 1929, pioneering studies of the Caribou Eskimos were conducted during the Danish Fifth Thule Expedition from 1921 to 1924.

Chapter 5. Visitors from the Sunny Side

[1] Solberg, 1907.
[2] Meldgaard, 1952; Larsen and Meldgaard, 1958.
[3] Meldgaard, 1961.

[4] Meldgaard, 1991.
[5] A special issue of the Danish publication Grønland (Vol. 4-5-6-7, 1991) is devoted to the results of the excavation of the early Saqqaq settlement, Qeqertasussuk, in West Greenland. See Grønnow and Meldgaard, 1991a, 1991b.
[6] Møhl, 1986.
[7] Grønnow and Meldgaard, 1991a.
[8] Schledermann et al., 1990.
[9] Helmer, 1991.
[10] Grønnow and Meldgaard, 1991b; Meldgaard, 1991.
[11] Tuck, 1975, 1976.
[12] Mary-Rousselière, 1976.
[13] Helmer, 1986.

Chapter 6. The Arctic Renaissance

[1] For a comprehensive discussion of the Pre-Dorset/Dorset transition see Maxwell, 1985.
[2] Taylor, 1967; Arnold, 1980.
[3] Schledermann et al., 1990.
[4] Schledermann et al., 1991; Schledermann and McCullough, 1992a.
[5] Knuth, 1968.
[6] Nares, 1876.
[7] The first discovery of early Dorset sites in the High Arctic was made in 1977 during an archaeological site survey conducted for the Polar Gas Project. See Schledermann, 1978b.
[8] Taylor, 1968.
[9] Schledermann, 1978a; McCullough and Schledermann, 1989; Schledermann, 1990.
[10] Knuth, 1966/67.
[11] Nichols, 1975. Although cause-and-effect correlations between climatic and cultural episodes must be approached with caution, the northward movement of late Pre-Dorset does seem to coincide with a general climatic warming trend. In a similar vein, the end of the Saqqaq period in Greenland appears to have occurred at a time of very cold conditions between 500 and 100 B.C.

Chapter 7. Silent Shores

[1] Jones, 1968.
[2] The effects of changing climatic conditions on the distribution and availability of sea mammals leading to changes in human settlement patterns in the Arctic are discussed by Schledermann, 1976a, b; Schledermann, 1979a. See also Vibe, 1967.
[3] Harp, 1974/75, 1976; Thomson, 1981.

Chapter 8. The Shamans Gather

[1] Sverdrup, 1904.
[2] Schledermann, 1978a, 1990.
[3] Schledermann, 1981a.
[4] Schledermann, 1975a; Sutherland, 1987.
[5] Schledermann et al., 1990.

[6] Damkjar, 1987.
[7] Kane, 1856; Hayes, 1867.
[8] McCartney and Mack, 1973; Franklin et al., 1981.
[9] Damkjar, 1987.
[10] Hearth rows have also been found on Little Cornwallis Island (D. Hanna, Department of Archaeology, The University of Calgary, pers. comm. 1996).
[11] A relatively short hearth row with eight individual hearths was discovered by Schledermann and McCullough in 1992 on the Nûgdlît site in Northwest Greenland. The site is well known for its early Palaeoeskimo and Thule culture components. See Schledermann and McCullough, 1992b. Other hearth rows have recently been discovered near Littleton Island (T. Diklev, Qaanaaq, pers. comm. 1996).
[12] Taylor and Swinton, 1967; Jordan, 1979.
[13] Bryson and Wendland, 1967; Nichols, 1968.
[14] Harp, 1976; Plumet, 1982.
[15] D. Hanna, Department of Archaeology, The University of Calgary, pers. comm. 1996.

Chapter 9. The Arctic Whale Hunters

[1] Freuchen, 1935.
[2] Gilberg, 1976; Vaughan, 1991.
[3] Collins, 1935, 1937; McGhee, 1969/70; Ackerman, 1984; Anderson, 1984; Dumond, 1984.
[4] In many ways the Canadian Arctic Expedition of 1913–1918 was the scientific precursor to the Danish Fifth Thule Expedition (1921–24). See Jenness, 1922.
[5] Rasmussen, 1925 and 1927; Reports of the Danish Fifth Thule Expedition 1921-24 (12 volumes) under the leadership of Knud Rasmussen.
[6] Rasmussen, 1927.
[7] Mathiassen, 1927.
[8] Collins, 1952, 1955.
[9] Holtved, 1944, 1954. Moreau Maxwell, 1960, conducted the first systematic archaeological survey of northeastern Ellesmere Island and documented 33 sites, mostly relating to the Thule culture.
[10] Ingstad, 1966.
[11] Holtved, 1954; Schledermann and McCullough, 1980.
[12] Schledermann and McCullough, 1980; Arnold and Stimmel, 1983; McCullough, 1989.
[13] McCullough, 1989; Arnold and McCullough, 1990.
[14] Holtved, 1967.
[15] Ingstad, 1966.
[16] Schledermann, 1977a.
[17] Astrup, 1898.

Chapter 10. Vikings in the High Arctic

[1] Ingstad, 1969.
[2] Frydendal, 1993.
[3] Ingstad, 1966.
[4] Ingstad, 1966; Whitaker, 1985.

[5] Ingstad, 1966.

[6] Magnusson and Pálsson, 1965; McGhee, 1984a; Clausen, 1993.

[7] Gad, 1971; Wahlgren, 1986; Arneborg, 1993.

[8] Malmros, 1993.

[9] Sutherland, 1987.

[10] McCartney and Mack, 1973

[11] McGhee, 1984a, b; Sabo and Sabo, 1978; Schledermann, 1979b, 1980b, 1982, 1993.

[12] Knuth, 1952.

[13] Ingstad, 1966; Gad, 1971.

[14] Ingstad, 1966.

[15] Nares, 1876.

[16] Kane, 1856.

[17] Greely, 1886.

[18] RCMP, 1940.

[19] Ingstad, 1966, 1969.

Chapter 11. Death and Abandonment

[1] Frobisher, 1578; Asher, 1860; Hansen, 1966.

[2] Grove, 1988.

[3] Damas, 1969; Schledermann, 1976b.

[4] Schledermann, 1976a.

[5] Holm, 1914.

[6] Taylor, J.G., 1968, 1984.

[7] Schledermann, 1971.

[8] Schledermann, 1975b.

[9] Petersen, 1974.

[10] Ray, 1984; Spencer, 1959.

[11] McCullough, 1989.

[12] Sverdrup, 1904.

[13] Petersen, 1986; Fortescue, 1986.

[14] Holtved, 1954.

[15] Ross, 1819.

[16] Kane, 1856; Hayes, 1867. The population numbers cited by Kane and Hayes are perhaps on the low side, see Vaughan, 1991.

[17] Lubbock, 1937; Ross, 1985.

[18] Osborn, 1852:265–266.

[19] M'Clintock, 1859:124.

[20] Kane, 1854:133.

[21] Kane, 1856:108–109.

Chapter 12. Land of the Bears

[1] Petersen, 1860.

[2] Ulloriaq, 1976. Other accounts of the Baffinlanders' migration to Greenland can be found in Rasmussen, 1908; Petersen, 1962; Gilberg, 1974/75; Mary-Rousselière, 1991.

[3] M'Clintock, 1859.

4 Ulloriaq, 1976.

Chapter 13. A Question of Sovereignty

1 Note found on the wall of the Alexandra Fiord RCMP station, typed by Cst. R. M. Coombs on 3 September 1963.
2 Frobisher, 1578; Asher, 1860 (concerning Henry Hudson's voyages); Bugge, 1930 (account of John Davis's three voyages to Greenland); Gosch, 1897.
3 Ingstad, 1966.
4 Markham, 1881.
5 Ross, 1819.
6 Parry, 1821; Mirsky, 1970; Berton, 1988.
7 M'Clure, 1857.
8 Inglefield, 1853.
9 Reference to De Haven in Kane, 1854; Taylor, 1955.
10 Kane, 1856.
11 Rae, 1970.
12 M'Clintock, 1859.
13 Hall, 1864; Davis, 1876.
14 Tyson, 1874; Mowat, 1967.
15 Loomis, 1971.
16 Nares, 1876:66–67.
17 Nares, 1876:6.
18 Hendrik, 1878.
19 Greely, 1886; Brainard, 1929, 1940.
20 Schley, 1885; Powell, 1960.
21 Sverdrup, 1904.
22 Peary, 1907.
23 Low, 1904; Ross, 1976.
24 Bernier, 1909, 1939; Taylor, 1955.
25 Peary, 1907; Cook, 1911; Herbert, 1989.
26 MacMillan, 1918.
27 Robertson, 1934; Rivett-Carnac, 1973.
28 Fairley, 1959.
29 Humphreys et al., 1936; Stallworthy, 1936.
30 Wordie, 1938.
31 Lethbridge, 1939.
32 Vibe, 1948.
33 Larsen, 1947; Grant, 1993.
34 Marcus, 1992, 1995; Kenney, 1994; Tester and Kulchyski, 1994.
35 Hattersley-Smith, 1974.
36 Foster and Marino, 1986.

Chapter 14. Lessons from the Past

1 Kalkreuth et al., 1993.

References

ACKERMAN, R.E. 1984. Prehistory of the Asian Eskimo Zone. In: Damas, D., ed. Arctic. Handbook of North American Indians, Vol. 5. Washington: Smithsonian Institution. 106–118.

ANDERSON, D.D. 1970. Akmak: An early archeological assemblage from Onion Portage, Northwest Alaska. Acta Arctica Fasc. 16. Copenhagen: Ejnar Munksgaard. 80 p.

———. 1984. Prehistory of North Alaska. In: Damas, D., ed. Arctic. Handbook of North American Indians, Vol. 5. Washington: Smithsonian Institution. 80–93.

———. 1988. Onion Portage: The archaeology of a stratified site from the Kobuk River, Northwest Alaska. Anthropological Papers of the University of Alaska 22(1-2). 163 p.

ARNEBORG, J. 1993. Greenland, the starting-point for the voyages to North America. In: Clausen, B.L., ed. Viking voyages to North America. Roskilde, Denmark: The Viking Ship Museum. 13–21.

ARNOLD, C.D. 1980. A Paleoeskimo occupation on southern Banks Island, N.W.T. Arctic 33(3):400–426.

ARNOLD, C.D., and McCULLOUGH, K.M. 1990. Thule culture pioneers in the Canadian Arctic. In: Harington, C.R., ed. Canada's missing dimension: Science and History in the Canadian Arctic Islands, Vol. 2. Ottawa: Canadian Museum of Nature. 677–694.

ARNOLD, C.D., and STIMMEL, C. 1983. An analysis of Thule pottery. Canadian Journal of Archaeology 7(1):1–21.

ARUNDALE, W.H. 1981. Radiocarbon dating in Eastern Arctic archaeology: A flexible approach. American Antiquity 46:244–271.

ASHER, G.M. 1860. Henry Hudson the navigator: The original documents in which his career is recorded. London: Hakluyt Society. 292 p.

ASTRUP, E. 1898. With Peary near the Pole. London: C. Arthur Pearson. 362 p.

BERNIER, J.E. 1909. Report on the Dominion of Canada Government Expedition to Arctic Islands and Hudson Strait on board the D. G. S. *Arctic*, 1906-1907. Ottawa: Government Printing Bureau.

———. 1939. Master mariner and Arctic explorer: A narrative of 60 years at sea from the logs and yarns of Captain J.E. Bernier. Ottawa: Le Droit. 409 p.

BERTON, P. 1988. The Arctic grail: The quest for the Northwest Passage and the North Pole, 1818-1909. Toronto: McClelland and Stewart. 672 p.

BIRKET-SMITH, K. 1929. The Caribou Eskimos: Material and social life and their cultural position. I. Descriptive Part. Report of the Fifth Thule Expedition 1921–1924, Vol. 5. Copenhagen: Gyldendalske Boghandel, Nordisk Forlag. 306 p.

BOAS, F. 1901–1907. The Eskimo of Baffin Land and Hudson Bay. New York: Bulletin of the American Museum of Natural History 15(1&2).

BOWMAN, S. 1990. Radiocarbon dating. Berkeley and Los Angeles: University of California Press. 64 p.

BRAINARD, D.L. 1929. The outpost of the lost: An Arctic adventure. Indianapolis: The Bobbs-Merrill Company.

———. 1940. Six came back: The arctic adventure of David L. Brainard. New York: The Bobbs-Merrill Company.

BRYSON, R.A., and WENDLAND, W.M. 1967. Tentative climatic patterns from some late glacial and post-glacial episodes in central North America. In: Mayer-Oakes, W.J., ed. Life, land and water. Winnipeg: University of Manitoba Press. 271–298.

BUGGE, G.N. 1930. John Davis tre rejser til Grønland i årene 1585–87. Copenhagen: Det Grønlandske Selskabs Skrifter 7. 95 p.

CHRISTIE, R.L. 1967. Bache Peninsula, Ellesmere Island, Arctic Archipelago. Ottawa: Geological Survey of Canada Memoir 347. 63 p.

CLAUSEN, B.L., ed. 1993. Viking voyages to North America. Roskilde, Denmark: The Viking Ship Museum. 127 p.

COLLINS, H.B. 1935. Archaeology of the Bering Sea region. Smithsonian Annual Report for 1933. Washington, D.C.: Smithsonian Institution. 453–468.

———. 1937. Archaeology of St. Lawrence Island, Alaska. Smithsonian Miscellaneous Collections 96(1). 431 p.

———. 1952. Excavations at Resolute, Cornwallis Island, N.W.T. Annual Report of the National Museum of Canada for 1950–51, National Museum of Canada Bulletin 126:48–63.

———. 1955. Excavation of Thule and Dorset culture sites at Resolute, Cornwallis Island, N.W.T. Annual Report of the National Museum of Canada for 1953–54, Bulletin 136:22–35.

COOK, F.A. 1911. My attainment of the Pole. New York: Polar Publishing Co.

COX, S.L. 1978. Palaeo-Eskimo occupations of the north Labrador Coast. Arctic Anthropology 15(2):96–118.

———. 1988. Pre-Dorset occupations of Okak Bay, Labrador. The Northern Raven 7(3). 4 p.

DAMAS, D. 1969. Environment, history and Central Eskimo society. In: Damas, D., ed. Contributions to Anthropology: Ecological essays. National Museums of Canada Bulletin 230:40–64.

DAMKJAR, E. 1987. Late Dorset "longhouse" occupations of Creswell Bay, Somerset Island and their possible relationship to the Thule culture migration. Paper presented at the 20th Annual Meeting of the Canadian Archaeological Association, 22–26 April, Calgary, Alberta.

DANSGAARD, W., JOHNSON, S.J., MØLLER, J., and LANGWAY, C.C., Jr. 1969. One thousand centuries of climatic record from Cape Century on the Greenland Ice Sheet. Science 166(3903):377–381.

DAVIS, C.H. 1876. Narrative of the North Polar Expedition; U.S. Ship *Polaris*, Captain Charles Francis Hall commanding. Washington, D.C.: Government Printing Office.

DUMOND, D.E. 1977. The Eskimos and Aleuts. London: Thames and Hudson Ltd. 180 p.

⸻. 1984. Prehistory of the Bering Sea Region. In: Damas, D., ed. Arctic. Handbook of North American Indians, Vol. 5. Washington: Smithsonian Institution. 94–105.

DUNBAR, M. 1969. The geographical position of the North Water. Arctic 22(4):438–441.

FAIRLEY, T.C. 1959. Sverdrup's Arctic adventures. London: Longmans, Green and Co. Ltd. 305 p.

FITZHUGH, W. 1976. Paleoeskimo occupations of the Labrador Coast. In: Maxwell, M.S., ed. Eastern Arctic prehistory: Paleoeskimo problems. Memoirs of the Society for American Archaeology 31. 103–118.

FOOTE, D.C. 1967. The east coast of Baffin Island N.W.T.: An area economic survey, 1966. Ottawa: Report on file, Department of Indian and Northern Affairs.

FORTESCUE, M. 1986. What dialect distribution can tell us of dialect formation in Greenland. Arctic Anthropology 23(1&2):413–422.

FOSTER, M., and MARINO, C. 1986. The Polar Shelf: The saga of Canada's Arctic scientists. Toronto: NC Press Ltd. 128 p.

FRANKLIN, U.M., BADONE, E., GOTTHARDT, R., and YORGA, B. 1981. An examination of prehistoric copper technology and copper sources in western Arctic and Subarctic North America. National Museum of Man Mercury Series, Archaeological Survey of Canada Paper No. 101. 158 p.

FREUCHEN, P. 1935. Arctic adventure: My life in the frozen North. New York: Farrar & Rinehart. 467 p.

FROBISHER, M. 1578. A true discourse of the late voyages of discovery for the finding of a passage to Cathaya and India by the North West. Reprinted: The three voyages of Martin Frobisher...works issued by the Hakluyt Society, 1st series Vol. 38. London.

FRYDENDAHL, K. 1993. The summer climate in the North Atlantic about the year 1000. In: Clausen, B.L., ed. Viking voyages to North America. Roskilde, Denmark: The Viking Ship Museum. 90–94.

GAD, F. 1971. The history of Greenland I: Earliest times to 1700. Montreal: McGill-Queen's University Press. 350 p.

GIDDINGS, J.L. 1964. The archeology of Cape Denbigh. Providence, Rhode Island: Brown University Press. 331 p.

⸻. 1967. Ancient men of the Arctic. New York: Alfred A. Knopf. 391 p.

GILBERG, R. 1974/75. Changes in the life of the Polar Eskimos resulting from a Canadian immigration into the Thule District, North Greenland, in the 1860's. Folk 16-17:159–170.

————. 1976. Thule. Arctic 29(2):83–86.

GORDON, B.H.C. 1975. Of men and herds in Barrenland prehistory. National Museum of Man Mercury Series, Archaeological Survey of Canada Paper No. 28. 564 p.

————. 1976. Migod—8000 years of Barrenland prehistory. National Museum of Man Mercury Series, Archaeological Survey of Canada Paper No. 56. 310 p.

GOSCH, C.C.A. 1897. Danish Arctic expeditions, 1605 to 1620. 2 Vols. London: Hakluyt Society.

GOULD, R.A. 1978. Explorations in ethnoarchaeology. Albuquerque: University of New Mexico Press. 329 p.

GRANT, S.D. 1993. Why the *St. Roch*? Why the Northwest Passage? Why 1940? New answers to old questions. Arctic 46(1):82–87.

GREELY, A.W. 1886. Three years of Arctic service: An account of the Lady Franklin Bay Expedition of 1881–84, and the attainment of the farthest North. New York: Scribner.

————. 1888. Report on the proceedings of the United States Expedition to Lady Franklin Bay, Grinnell Land. 2 Vols. Washington, D.C.: Government Printing Office.

GRØNNOW, B., and MELDGAARD, M. 1991a. De første Vestgrønlændere. In: Qeqertasussuk: De første mennesker i Vestgrønland. Grønland 4-5-6-7:103–144.

GRØNNOW, B., and MELDGAARD, M. 1991b. Hvor blev de af? In: Qeqertasussuk; de første mennesker i Vestgrønland. Grønland 4-5-6-7:206–209.

GROVE, J.M. 1988. The little ice age. London: Methuen. 498 p.

HANSEN, T. 1966. Jens Munk. Copenhagen: Gyldendal.

HALL, C.F. 1864. Life with the Eskimaux. London: Sampson, Low, Marston and Searle.

HARP, E., Jr. 1974/75. A Late Dorset copper amulet from southeastern Hudson Bay. Folk 16-17:33–44.

————. 1976. Dorset settlement patterns in Newfoundland and southeastern Hudson Bay. In: Maxwell, M.S., ed. Eastern Arctic prehistory: Paleoeskimo problems. Memoirs of the Society for American Archaeology 31. 119–138.

HATTERSLEY-SMITH, G. 1974. North of latitude eighty: The Defence Research Board in Ellesmere Island. Ottawa: Defence Research Board. 121 p.

HAYES, I.I. 1867. The open polar sea: A narrative of a voyage of discovery towards the North Pole, in the schooner "United States." New York: Hurd and Houghton. 454 p.

HELMER, J.W. 1986. A face from the past: An early Pre-Dorset ivory maskette from Devon Island, N.W.T. Etudes/Inuit/Studies 10(1-2):179–202.

————. 1991. The palaeo-eskimo prehistory of the North Devon lowlands. Arctic 44(4):301–317.

HENDRIK, H. 1878. Memoirs of Hans Hendrik, the Arctic traveller serving under Kane, Hayes, Hall and Nares, 1853–1876. Translated by Henry Rink and edited by George Stephens. London: Trübner & Co. 100 p.

HERBERT, W. 1989. The noose of laurels: Robert E. Peary and the race for the North Pole. New York: Doubleday. 395 p.

HOFFECKER, J.F., POWERS, W.R., and GOEBEL, T. 1993. The colonization of Beringia and the peopling of the New World. Science 259:46–53.

HOLM, G. 1914. Ethnological sketch of the Angmagsalik Eskimo. Meddelelser om Grønland 39.

HOLTVED, E. 1944. Archaeological investigations in the Thule District. Meddelelser om Grønland 141(1 & 2).

———. 1954. Archaeological investigations in the Thule District, Nûgdlît and Comer's Midden. Meddelelser om Grønland 146(3). 135 p.

———. 1967. Contributions to Polar Eskimo ethnography. Copenhagen: Meddelelser om Grønland 182(2). 180 p.

HOPKINS, D.M. 1979. Landscape and climate of Beringia during Late Pleistocene and Holocene time. In: Laughlin, W.S., and Harper, A.B., eds. The first Americans: Origins, affinities, and adaptations. New York: Gustav Fisher. 15–41.

HUMPHREYS, N., SHACKLETON, E., and MOORE, A.W. 1936. Oxford University Ellesmere Land expedition. The Geographical Journal 87(5):385–443.

INGSTAD, H. 1966. Land under the Pole Star. New York: St. Martin's Press. 381 p.

———. 1969. Westward to Vinland: The discovery of Pre-Columbian Norse house-sites in North America. Toronto: The Macmillan Company of Canada. 250 p.

INGLEFIELD, E.A. 1853. A summer search for Sir John Franklin, with a peep into the polar basin. London: Thomas Harrison. 232 p.

IRVING, W.N. 1957. An archaeological survey of the Susitna Valley. Anthropological Papers of the University of Alaska 6:37–52.

JENNESS, D. 1922. The life of the Copper Eskimos. Report of the Canadian Arctic Expedition 1913–18, Vol. 12. 277 p.

———. 1925. A new Eskimo culture in Hudson Bay. Geographical Review 15:428–437.

JONES, G. 1968. A history of the Vikings. New York: Oxford University Press. 504 p.

JORDAN, R.H. 1979. Dorset art forms from Labrador. Folk 21-22:397–417.

KALKREUTH, W.D., McCULLOUGH, K.M., and RICHARDSON, R.J.H. 1993. Geological, archaeological, and historical occurrences of coal, east-central Ellesmere Island, Arctic Canada. Arctic and Alpine Research 25(4):277–307.

KANE, E.K. 1854. The U.S. Grinnell expedition in search of Sir. John Franklin: A personal narrative. New York: Harper and Brothers.

———. 1856. Arctic explorations: The second Grinnell expedition in search of Sir John Franklin, 1853, '54, '55. 2 Vols. London: Trübner and Co.

KENNEY, G. 1994. Arctic smoke & mirrors. Prescott, Ontario: Voyageur. 144 p.

KNUTH, E. 1952. An outline of the archaeology of Peary Land. Arctic 5(1):17–33.

———. 1966/67. The ruins of the Musk-Ox Way. Folk 8-9:191–219.

———. 1967. Archaeology of the Musk-Ox Way. Contributions du Centre d'Études Arctiques et Finno-Scandinaves, No. 5. Paris: École Pratique des Hautes Études. 78 p.

———. 1968. The Independence II bone artifacts and the Dorset evidence in North Greenland. Folk 10:61–80.

———. 1984. Reports from the Musk-ox Way. A compilation of previously published articles. Copenhagen: E. Knuth. 173 p.

KRAMER, C., ed. 1979. Ethnoarchaeology: Implications of ethnography for archaeology. New York: Columbia University Press. 292 p.

LAMB, H.H. 1972. Climate: Present, past and future. Vol. 1, Fundamentals and climate now. London: Methuen.

———. 1977. Climate: Present, past and future. Vol. 2, Climate history and the future. London: Methuen.

LARSEN, H. 1968. Trail Creek: Final report on the excavation of two caves on Seward Peninsula, Alaska. Acta Arctica Fasc. 15:7–79. Copenhagen: Ejnar Munksgaard.

LARSEN, H., and MELDGAARD, J. 1958. Paleo-Eskimo cultures in Disko Bugt, West Greenland. Meddelelser om Grønland 161(2). 75 p.

LARSEN, H.A. 1947. The conquest of the North West Passage: The Arctic voyages of the *St. Roch*, 1940-1944. Geographical Journal 110:1–16.

LEEMS, K. 1767. Beskrivelse over Finmarkens Lapper: Deres tungemaal, levemaade og forrige afgudsdyrkelse. Copenhagen: Kongel. Waeysenhuses Bogtrykkerie.

LETHBRIDGE, T.C. 1939. Archaeological data from the Canadian Arctic. Journal of the Royal Anthropological Institute of Great Britain and Ireland 69:187–233.

LOOMIS, C.C. 1971. Weird and tragic shores: The story of Charles Francis Hall, explorer. New York: Alfred Knopf. 367 p.

LOW, A.P. 1904. The government expedition to Hudson Bay and northward by the S. S. *Neptune*, 1903-1904. Ottawa: Geological and Natural History Survey of Canada, Annual Report, Vol. 16 (A):122–143.

LUBBOCK, B. 1937. The Arctic whalers: Glasgow: Brown, Son & Ferguson, Ltd., Nautical Publishers. 483 p.

MacMILLAN, D.B. 1918. Four years in the white north. New York: Harper.

MAGNUSSON, M., and PÁLSSON, H. 1965. The Vinland sagas: The Norse discovery of America. Baltimore: Penguin Books Ltd. 124 p.

MALMROS, C. 1993. Vedanatomisk undersøgelse af en nordbo-hovl af birk *Betula* fra Skraeling Island, arktisk Canada. Copenhagen: Nationalmuseets Naturvidenskabelige Undersøgelser 17.

MARCUS, A.R. 1992. Out in the cold: The legacy of Canada's Inuit relocation experiment in the High Arctic. Copenhagen: International Work Group for Indigenous Affairs.

————. 1995. Relocating Eden: The image and politics of Inuit exile in the Canadian Arctic. Hanover, New Hampshire: Dartmouth College. 272 p.

MARKHAM, A.H. 1875. A whaling cruise to Baffin's Bay and the Gulf of Boothia and an account of the rescue of the crew of the *Polaris*. London: Sampson, Low, Marston, Low and Searle. 319 p.

MARKHAM, C.R. 1881. The voyages of William Baffin, 1612-1622. London: Hakluyt Society.

MARY-ROUSSELIÈRE, G. 1976. The Paleoeskimo in northern Baffinland. In: Maxwell, M.S., ed. Eastern Arctic prehistory: Paleoeskimo problems. Memoirs of the Society for American Archaeology 31. 40–57.

————. 1991. Qitdlarssuaq: The story of a polar migration. Winnipeg: Wuerz Publishing Ltd. 196 p.

MATHIASSEN, T. 1927. Archaeology of the central Eskimo. Report of the Fifth Thule Expedition 1921–24, Vol. 4(1-2). Copenhagen: Gyldendalske Boghandel, Nordisk Forlag.

MAXWELL, M.S. 1960. An archaeological analysis of Eastern Grant Land, Ellesmere Island, Northwest Territories. National Museum of Canada Bulletin 170. 109 p.

————. 1985. Prehistory of the Eastern Arctic. Orlando: Academic Press, Inc. 327 p.

McCARTNEY, A.P., and MACK, D.J. 1973. Iron utilization by Thule Eskimos of Central Canada. American Antiquity 38(3):328–339.

M'CLINTOCK, F.L. 1859. The voyage of the *Fox* in the Arctic seas: A narrative of the discovery of the fate of Sir John Franklin and his companions. London: Murray.

M'CLURE, R.LeM. 1857. The discovery of the north-west passage by H.M.S. *Investigator*. London: Longmans, Brown, Green, Longmans & Roberts.

McCULLOUGH, K.M. 1989. The Ruin Islanders: Early Thule culture pioneers in the eastern High Arctic. Canadian Museum of Civilization Mercury Series, Archaeological Survey of Canada Paper 141. 347 p.

McCULLOUGH, K.M., and SCHLEDERMANN, P. 1989. The Ellesmere Island Research Project: Final report on the 1988 field season. Report on file, Archaeological Survey of Canada, Canadian Museum of Civilization, Hull, Quebec. 82 p.

McGHEE, R. 1969/70. Speculations on climatic change and Thule culture development. Folk 11/12:173–184.

————. 1979. The Palaeoeskimo occupations at Port Refuge, High Arctic Canada. National Museum of Man Mercury Series, Archaeological Survey of Canada Paper 92. 176 p.

————. 1984a. Contact between Native North Americans and the medieval Norse: A review of the evidence. American Antiquity 49(1):4–26.

————. 1984b. The Thule village at Brooman Point, High Arctic Canada. National Museum of Man Mercury Series, Archaeological Survey of Canada Paper 125. 158 p.

McGHEE, R., and TUCK, J. 1976. Un-dating the Arctic. In: Maxwell, M.S., ed. Eastern Arctic prehistory: Paleoeskimo problems. Memoirs of the Society for American Archaeology 31. 6–14.

MELDGAARD, J. 1952. A Palaeo-Eskimo culture in West Greenland. American Antiquity 17(3):222–230.

———. 1961. Sarqaq-folket ved Itivnera. Grønland 9:15–23.

———. 1991. Bopladsen Qajaa i Jakobshavn isfjord: En rapport om udgravninger 1871 og 1982. In: Qeqertasussuk, de første mennesker i Vestgrønland. Grønland 4-5-6-7:191–205.

MIRSKY, J. 1970. To the Arctic!: The story of northern exploration from earliest times to the present. Chicago: The University of Chicago Press. 334 p.

MØHL, J. 1986. Dog remains from a Paleoeskimo settlement in West Greenland. Arctic Anthropology 23(1-2):81–89.

MOSS, E.L. 1878. Shores of the polar sea: A narrative of the Arctic expedition of 1875–6. London: Marcus Ward & Co.

MOWAT, F. 1967. The polar passion: The quest for the North Pole. Toronto: McClelland and Stewart Ltd. 302 p.

NANSEN, F. 1897. Farthest north. London: Archibald Constable & Company.

NARES, G.S. 1876. The official report of the recent Arctic expedition. London: John Murray.

———. 1878. Narrative of a voyage to the Polar Sea during 1875–76 in H.M. Ships *Alert* and *Discovery*; with Notes on the Natural History. Fielden, W.H., naturalist to the expedition, ed. London: Low, Marston, Searle and Rivington.

NICHOLS, H. 1968. Pollen analysis, paleotemperatures, and the summer position of the Arctic front in the post-glacial history of Keewatin, Canada. Bulletin of the American Meteorological Society 49(4):387–388.

———. 1975. Palynological and paleoclimatic study of the Late Quaternary displacement of the forest-tundra ecotone in Keewatin and Mackenzie, N.W.T., Canada. Institute of Arctic and Alpine Research, Occasional Paper No. 15.

O'NEILL, D. 1994. The firecracker boys. New York: St. Martin's Griffin. 388 p.

OSBORN, S. 1852. Stray leaves from an Arctic journal; or, eighteen months in the polar regions, in search of Sir. John Franklin's expedition, in the years 1850-51. London: Longmans, Brown, Green & Longmans.

PARRY, W.E. 1821. Journal of a voyage for the discovery of a north-west passage from the Atlantic to the Pacific performed in the years 1819–20 in His Majesty's ships *Hecla* and *Griper*. London: John Murray.

PAVLISH, L.A., and BANNING, E.B. 1980. Revolutionary developments in carbon-14 dating. American Antiquity 45(2):290–297.

PEARY, R.E. 1907. Nearest the Pole. New York: Doubleday, Page & Co.

PETERSEN, C. 1860. Den sidste Franklin Expedition med "Fox", Capt. M'Clintock. Copenhagen: Fr. Waldikes Forlagsboghandel.

PETERSEN, R. 1962. The last Eskimo immigration into Greenland. Folk 4:95–110.
———. 1974. Some considerations concerning the Greenland longhouse. Folk 16/17:171–188.
———. 1986. Some features common to East and West Greenlandic in the light of dialect relationships and the latest migration theories. Arctic Anthropology 23(1&2):401–250.
PLUMET, P. 1982. Les maisons longues Dorsetiennes de l'Ungava. Geographie Physique et Quaternaire 36:253–289.
POWELL, T. 1960. The long rescue. New York: Doubleday and Company Inc. 303 p.
RAE, J. 1970. Narrative of an expedition to the shores of the Arctic sea in 1846 and 1847. Toronto: Canadiana House.
RASMUSSEN, K. 1908. The people of the polar North: A record. London: Kegan Paul, Trench, Trübner & Co. Ltd. 358 p.
———. 1925. The Danish ethnographic and geographic expedition to Arctic America: Preliminary report of the Fifth Thule expedition. The Geographical Review 15(4):521–592.
———. 1927. Across Arctic America: Narrative of the Fifth Thule Expedition. New York: G.P. Putnam's Sons. 388 p.
RAY, D.J. 1984. Bering Strait Eskimo. In: Damas, D. Arctic. Handbook of North American Indians, Vol. 5. Washington, D.C.: Smithsonian Institution. 285–302.
RCMP (ROYAL CANADIAN MOUNTED POLICE). 1940. Report of the Royal Canadian Mounted Police for the year ending March 31, 1940: Commissioner's Report, p. 119. Ottawa: Edmond Cloutier.
RIVETT-CARNAC, C. 1973. The establishment of the R.C.M.P. presence in the Northwest Territories and the Arctic. Canadian Geographical Journal 86(5):155–167.
ROBERTSON, D.S. 1934. To the Arctic with the mounties. Toronto: Macmillan.
ROSS, J. 1819. A voyage of discovery made under the orders of the Admiralty, in his Majesty's ships *Isabella* and *Alexander*, for the purpose of exploring Baffin's Bay, and inquiring into the probability of a North-West Passage. 2 Vols. London: Longman, Hurst, Rees, Orme and Brown.
ROSS, W.G. 1976. Canadian sovereignty in the Arctic: The *Neptune* expedition of 1903-04. Arctic 29(2):87–104.
———. 1985. Arctic whalers, icy seas: Narratives of the Davis Strait whale fishery. Toronto: Irwin Publishing. 263 p.
SABO, D., and SABO, G. 1978. A possible Thule carving of a Viking from Baffin Island, N.W.T. Canadian Journal of Archaeology 2:33–42.
SCHALLER, G.B. 1988. Stones of silence: Journeys in the Himalaya. Chicago: The University of Chicago Press. 292 p.
———. 1994. The last panda. Chicago: The University of Chicago Press. 299 p.

SCHLEDERMANN, P. 1971. The Thule Eskimo tradition in northern Labrador. M.A. Thesis, Memorial University of Newfoundland.

———. 1975a. A Late Dorset site on Axel Heiberg Island. Arctic 28(4):300.

———. 1975b. Thule Eskimo prehistory of Cumberland Sound, Baffin Island, Canada. National Museum of Man Mercury Series, Archaeological Survey of Canada Paper No. 38. 297 p.

———. 1976a. Thule culture communal houses in Labrador. Arctic 29(1):27–37.

———. 1976b. The effect of climatic/ecological changes on the style of Thule culture winter dwellings. Arctic and Alpine Research 8(1):37–47.

———. 1977a. Eskimo trappers on Ellesmere Island, N.W.T. The Western Canadian Journal of Anthropology 7(1):84–99.

———. 1977b. An archaeological survey of Bache Peninsula, Ellesmere Island. Arctic 30(4):243–245.

———. 1978a. Preliminary results of archaeological investigations in the Bache Peninsula Region, Ellesmere Island, N.W.T. Arctic 31(4):459–474.

———. 1978b. Distribution of archaeological sites in the vicinity of the proposed Polar Gas Pipeline and staging areas, N.W.T. Polar Gas Environmental Program Report. On file at the Arctic Institute of North America, The University of Calgary. 335 p.

———. 1979a. The "baleen period" of the arctic whale hunting tradition. In: McCartney A.P., ed. Thule Eskimo culture: An anthropological retrospective. National Museum of Man Mercury Series, Archaeological Survey of Canada Paper No. 88. 134–148.

———. 1979b. Norse artifacts on Ellesmere Island. Polar Record 19(122):493–511.

———. 1980a. Polynyas and prehistoric settlement patterns. Arctic 33(2):292–302.

———. 1980b. Notes on Norse finds from the east coast of Ellesmere Island, N.W.T. Arctic 33(3):454–463.

———. 1981a. Viking and Inuit finds in the High Arctic. National Geographic Magazine, May. 574–601.

———. 1981b. Inuit prehistory and archaeology. In: Zaslow, M., ed. A century of Canada's Arctic Islands: 1890–1980. Ottawa: The Royal Society of Canada. 245–256.

———. 1982. Nordbogenstande fra Arktisk Canada. Tidskriftet Grønland 5-6-7:218–225.

———. 1990. Crossroads to Greenland: 3000 years of prehistory in the eastern High Arctic. Komatik Series, No. 2. Calgary: Arctic Institute of North America. 364 p.

———. 1993. Norsemen in the High Arctic? In: Clausen, B.L., ed. Viking Voyages to North America. Roskilde, Denmark: The Viking Ship Museum. 54–66.

SCHLEDERMANN, P., and McCULLOUGH, K.M. 1980. Western elements in the early Thule culture of the eastern High Arctic. Arctic 33(4):833–841.

SCHLEDERMANN, P., and McCULLOUGH, K.M., 1992a. Buchanan Bay Archaeology Project: The 1991 field season. Report on file, Archaeological Survey of Canada, Canadian Museum of Civilization, Hull, Quebec. 27 p.

SCHLEDERMANN, P., and McCULLOUGH, K.M. 1992b. Crossroads Project 1992: Archaeological and ethnographic investigations in North Greenland. Ottawa: Report on file, Archaeological Survey of Canada, Canadian Museum of Civilization, Hull, Quebec. 15 p.

SCHLEDERMANN, P., McCULLOUGH, K.M., and DAMKJAR, E. 1990. The Goding Bay Archaeology Project: Report of the 1989 field season. Report on file, Archaeological Survey of Canada, Canadian Museum of Civilization, Hull, Quebec. 54 p.

SCHLEDERMANN, P., McCULLOUGH, K.M., and DAMKJAR. E. 1991. Ellesmere Island Archaeology Project: Report of the 1990 field season. Report on file, Archaeological Survey of Canada, Canadian Museum of Civilization, Hull, Quebec. 68 p.

SCHLEY, W.S. 1885. The rescue of Greely. New York: Scribner.

SCORESBY, W., Jr. 1820. An account of the Arctic regions with a history and description of the northern whale-fishery. 2 Vols. Edinburgh: Archibald Constable and Company.

SOLBERG, O. 1907. Beiträge zur vorgeschichte der Osteskimo. Videnskabs-Selskabets Skrifter II, Hist. og Filosofiske Klasse 2. Christiana (Oslo).

SPENCER, R.F. 1959. The North Alaskan Eskimo: A study in ecology and society. Washington: Bureau of American Ethnology Bulletin 171.

STALLWORTHY, H.W. 1936. An Arctic expedition. Royal Canadian Mounted Police Quarterly 3(3):149–172.

STEENSBY, H.P. 1910. Contributions to the ethnology and anthropogeography of the Polar Eskimos. Meddelelser om Grønland 34:255–405.

———. 1917. An anthropogeographical study of the origin of Eskimo culture. Meddelelser om Grønland 53:41–288.

STEWARD, J.H. 1955. Theory of cultural change: The methodology of multilinear evolution. Urbana: University of Illinois Press. 244 p.

———. 1977. Evolution and ecology: Essays on social transformation. Steward, J.C., and Murphy, R.F., eds. Urbana: University of Illinois Press. 406 p.

STIRLING, I. 1980. The biological importance of polynyas in the Canadian Arctic. Arctic 33(2):303–315.

STIRLING, I., and CLEATOR, H., eds. 1981. Polynyas in the Canadian Arctic. Canadian Wildlife Service Occasional Paper No. 45. 73 p.

SUTHERLAND, P.D. 1987. Umingmaknuna: Its people and prehistory. Inuktitut 66:47–54.

SVERDRUP, O. 1904. New Land: Four years in the Arctic regions. Translated by Ethel Harriet Hearn. London: Longmans, Green and Co.

SVOBODA, J., and FREEDMAN, B., eds. 1994. Ecology of a polar oasis: Alexandra Fiord, Ellesmere Island, Canada. Toronto: Captus Press Inc. 282 p.

TAYLOR, A. 1955. Geographical discovery and exploration in the Queen Elizabeth Islands. Ottawa: Department of Mines and Technical Surveys, Geographical Branch Memoir 3. 172 p.

TAYLOR, J.G. 1968. An analysis of the size of Eskimo settlements on the coast of Labrador during the early contact period. Ph.D. dissertation, University of Toronto.

———. 1984. Historical ethnography of the Labrador coast. In: Damas, D., ed. Arctic. Handbook of North American Indians, Vol. 5. Washington, D.C.: Smithsonian Institution. 508–521.

TAYLOR, R.E. 1987. Radiocarbon dating: An archaeological perspective. New York: Academic Press, Inc. 212 p.

TAYLOR, W.E., Jr. 1967. Summary of archaeological field work on Banks and Victoria Islands, Arctic Canada, 1965. Arctic Anthropology 4:221–243.

———. 1968. The Arnapik and Tyara Sites: An archaeological study of Dorset cultural origins. Memoirs of the Society for American Archaeology 22.

TAYLOR, W.E., Jr., and SWINTON, G. 1967. Prehistoric Dorset art. The Beaver 298:32–47.

TESTER, F.J., and KULCHYSKI, P. 1994. Tammarniit (Mistakes): Inuit relocation in the Eastern Arctic, 1939–63. Vancouver: UBC Press. 421 p.

THOMAS, D.H. 1974. Predicting the past: An introduction to anthropological archaeology. New York: Holt, Rinehart and Winston, Inc. 82 p.

———. 1989. Archaeology. 2nd ed. New York: Holt, Rinehart and Winston, Inc. 694 p.

THOMSEN, T. 1917. Implements and artefacts of the North-east Greenlanders: Finds from graves and settlements. Danmark-Ekspeditionen til Grønlands Nordøstkyst, 1906-1908. Meddelelser om Grønland 44(5). 357–496.

THOMSON, J.C. 1981. Preliminary archaeological findings from Shuldham Island, Labrador. In: Sproull Thomson, J., and Ransom, B., eds. Archaeology in Newfoundland and Labrador, 1980. Historic Resources Division, Government of Newfoundland and Labrador, Annual Report 1. 5–25.

THOSTRUP, C.B. 1917. Ethnographic description of the Eskimo settlements and stone remains in north-east Greenland. Danmark-ekspeditionen til Grønlands Nordøstkyst, 1906-1908. Meddelelser om Grønland 44(4). 177–355.

TUCK, J.A. 1975. Prehistory of Saglek Bay, Labrador: Archaic and Palaeo-Eskimo occupations. National Museum of Man Mercury Series, Archaeological Survey of Canada Paper No. 72. 727 p.

———. 1976. Paleoeskimo cultures of northern Labrador. In: Maxwell, M.S., ed. Eastern Arctic prehistory: Paleoeskimo problems. Memoirs of the Society for American Archaeology 31. 89–102.

TYSON, G.E. 1874. Letter from Capt. Tyson to the American Geographical Society. Geographical Magazine 1:125–127.

ULLORIAQ, I. 1976. Beretningen om Qillarsuaq og hans lange rejse fra Canada til Nordgrønland i 1860erne. Danish edition 1985. Translated by K. Olsen and edited by R. Gilberg. Det Grønlandske Selskabs Skrifter 27. Skjern, Denmark: Gullanders Bogtrykkeri. 204 p.

VAUGHAN, R. 1991. Northwest Greenland: A history. Orono, Maine: The University of Maine Press. 208 p.

VIBE, C. 1948. Langthen og nordpaa; skildring fra den Danske Thule og Ellesmereland ekspedition 1939–40. Copenhagen: Gyldendal.

———. 1967. Arctic animals in relation to climatic fluctuations. Meddelelser om Grønland 170(5). 227 p.

WAHLGREN, E. 1986. The Vikings and America. London: Thames and Hudson Ltd. 192 p.

WATSON, P.J., LeBLANC, S.A., and REDMAN, C.L. 1971. Explanation in archaeology: An explicitly scientific approach. New York: Columbia University Press. 191 p.

WHITAKER, I. 1985. The King's Mirror [Konung's Skuggsja] and northern research. Polar Record 22(141):615–627.

WORDIE, J.M. 1938. An expedition to North West Greenland and the Canadian Arctic in 1937. The Geographical Journal 92(5):385–421.

ZASLOW, M., ed. 1981. A century of Canada's Arctic Islands: 1890–1980. Ottawa: The Royal Society of Canada. 358 p.

Index